SCIENCE vs. RELIGION: THE 500-YEAR WAR

Finding God in the Heat of the Battle

by

David J. Turell, M.D.

PublishAmerica

Baltimore

First printing

ISBN: 1-4137-1381-5
PUBLISHED BY PUBLISHAMERICA, LLLP
www.publishamerica.com
Baltimore

Printed in the United States of America

Dedication

This book is dedicated first to the memory of Donna. She was taken much too early by an aggressive cancer, which she bravely fought, but remained very frightened and confused facing death. Although she asked questions of her religion and her rabbis, they could not help her. Nor could I, although I held the same beliefs I now hold, and tried to show her. I had not yet developed the background of material I now can present in this book.

The book is also equally dedicated to Susan who thinks so clearly. Our discussions have brought me to a more thorough understanding of my own philosophy. Organized religion and patterns of belief are too often developed from the conceits of humans, who presume to know *very exactly* God's intentions and *very exactly* the meanings of all the teachings in the Bible, and press others to accept their interpretations. True religion comes from within the individual, added by study from without. I am so thankful to Susan for her help.

And finally, it is dedicated to the memory of Mortimer J. Adler, whose book, *How to Think About God*, was so helpful to me in forming my thoughts.

Contents

Introduction   7

Chapter 1: Enemies or Helpmates?   13

Chapter 2: Our Designer Universe Fine-Tuned for Life   45

Chapter 3: Is Life a Glorious Accident? No Chance   70

Chapter 4: Is the Evolution of Humans a Glorious Accident?   88

Chapter 5: Our Hat Size is Too Big for Darwin   122

Chapter 6: Hallucination or Glimpse of the Afterlife?   143

Chapter 7: Belief in God Through Rational Philosophy   180

Chapter 8: Reflections on a Personal Theology   216

Index: 245

Introduction

In Western Civilization where monotheism predominates, everyone has to settle the issue of whether he believes God exists or not. Some find God rather easily as a gift of faith from their parents and their religion, never really questioning. Others, as part of a teenage rebellion, question everything their parents taught them, and settle the issue as part of personal growth into adulthood. Obviously some come to reaccept God, some become agnostics, and some atheists. What is contained here is a compendium of my search, my discoveries and my reasons for recognizing God as the source of all we behold. I faced the question not as a teenager but as an adult starting in college, and it has been a long journey for me. I knew I had to decide. I could not just leave it that I was an agnostic because I wasn't. With my medical training the science kept saying, "Everything can be explained; who needs God?" But the miracles I saw and experienced in my medical practice kept telling me there is a God. Without faith given to me, as I will explain, I had to be convinced, and I am convinced now that I have searched and studied. It might surprise you, but the search was primarily scientific and with logical deductive reasoning, not by delving into religious teachings as a sole approach—although philosophy and theology were part of the quest.

For over 500 years scientific discoveries have explained the seemingly unexplainable, and during the twentieth century at an ever faster and faster rate. Natural processes that seemed miraculous were explored and understood in ordinary terms, no longer requiring the supernatural explanations that religion had been providing. Scientists became convinced that given enough time and money they could discover how every natural process worked. They feel they don't need God to do this, and they have tried to convince the lay public of that expectation. This has set up an ongoing conflict between science and religion, a war of sorts, which I have discovered need not exist. The public, in general, has not accepted the assertion by science that God is not needed. Over 90 percent of us believe, while only 40 percent of all scientists express faith in God, falling to about 10 percent among leading scientists. In part, the conflict comes from the fact that science and religion have two different purposes: science studies the "how" while religion is concerned with the "why" of the universe and the life we experience. Studying both the "how" and the 'why" can bring them together, as I intend to show, but not by creating a religion out of science as some scientists have attempted. This is scientism: "formally defined [as] a psychological process of taking the currently accepted scientific theories about how the universe functions and subtly starting to regard them as if they were the absolute truth, beyond any further serious questioning. Thus the process of science becomes an "ism," becomes a dogmatic belief system, like many of our most dogmatic religions." (From the Forward by Charles T. Tart, Ph. D. for *Mindsight, Near-Death and Out-of-Body Experiences in the Blind*, Kenneth Ring & Sharon Cooper, 1999). Dogmatic approaches by both science and religion have kept them apart and as adversaries. The war between science and religion is a war that should never have occurred, but true to our human failings it did. The chapters that follow this Introduction contain the reasons why the war is a mistake.

I have written this book as a very personal account of my own search for God. Since I am attempting to present my reasoning for accepting God on scientific and logical grounds, it is important for the reader to understand my background and why I struggled. My personal history affects my reasoning and outlook, and my life should be understood by the reader to allow him to evaluate what I present. I was raised in a very secular family. My parents were first-generation native-born Americans, all my grandparents having come into this country from Eastern Europe.

My mother's family was absolutely secular. Their approach to religion was off-hand and as a subordinate part of their Jewish culture. They were American Jews, trying to assimilate. One aunt became Unitarian; another aunt who lived with me at the end of her life, dying of breast cancer in the brain, denied there was a God or an afterlife. My father's family were practicing Orthodox Jews, and he had been trained carefully in the religious practices. Upon marrying he had immediately accepted my mother's approach, but he never could get himself to eat pork or shellfish. My mother told me there was a God, and gave me a small child's book of Old Testament bible stories. She taught me right and wrong, as parents do, but I didn't hear much evidence that the rules came from God. From the time I was four years old until nine we lived in a predominantly Catholic neighborhood. Despite the fact I was sent to a synagogue Sunday school, and we all occasionally went to High Holy Day services, I had a two-foot tall imitation Christmas tree, was told about Santa Claus, and was given Christmas presents. My Catholic friends told me Santa didn't exist, and I had to insist, at about age seven, to my parents that we were supposed to celebrate Chanukah. Christmas disappeared.

My teenage years were no better: I celebrated a Bar Mitzvah by learning the Hebrew alphabet and rote-memorizing the Torah portions. I was bored by Sunday school and allowed to quit after the Bar Mitzvah was accomplished. At the Jewish Temple of my childhood faith in God was never an issue. God was simply assumed and faith not mentioned. Heaven was a concept not discussed. Arriving in college was another matter. I was suddenly exposed to all sorts of theological beliefs in dormitory discussions. I had no idea why I was the Jewish person I thought I was, other than I had been born into it. A letter to my Rabbi produced a list of books on Jewish history and theology, and having read them I concluded I liked being Jewish, but I was still no closer to God. The scientific training I received in college and medical school simply pushed me further into believing that science would eventually have all the answers about life and our Universe.

Out in a well-established medical practice I had time to begin reading outside the medical journals. My interests lead me to lay literature on astronomy, high-energy particle physics, quantum theory and the application of these subjects in the rapidly developing and exciting field of cosmology. I investigated books on the philosophy of cosmology. I also read several books on human evolution after seeing a cast of Lucy's footprints at Oldivai Gorge in Tanzania. I was, initially, a confirmed believer in the Darwin approach to evolution, as presented by the Neo-Darwin scientists: We had gradually evolved from one-celled animals, driven by survival of the fittest, with mutations appearing to adapt progressively complex animals to the threats of the environment. And further, I accepted the theory that the most primitive animals first appeared by happenstance with the proper cooperating molecules simply falling together by chance to start life.

All this time my consideration of God was still on the back burner. That is, until I recognized the amazing comparison between the Big Bang theory of the evolution of the Universe and the first few chapters of Genesis. How could the early writer/writers of Genesis have the intuition to describe the Big Bang before it was discovered? I was so taken with the parallelism I considered doing extensive research and writing a book comparing the two descriptions. But I didn't have to: Gerald Schroeder, Ph. D., a particle physicist and biblical scholar published *Genesis and the Big Bang* in 1990. I was vaguely aware of Schroeder's book from a review I had seen but I actually didn't discover Gerald Schroeder until 1998 when he was touring various American cities and appearing on talk radio to introduce his new book, *The Science of God*, and I attended a public lecture he held. That lecture and his two books convinced me the realizations I was developing on my own had a validity I could not deny.

Further, I recognized that the ability of our brain to create the development of the type of complex theoretical mathematics required to establish the physical laws of the universe, implied an amazing capacity of the mind, which was not required for humans to evolve in the Earth's environment. Where did that come from? It didn't seem to me that a hunter-gatherer in the Stone Age needed any of the capacities for higher math, aesthetics, creating art and music, or spirituality, for that matter. Our brain was the same then as it is now. Could it be that our enormous intellect really represents a challenge and an invitation to investigate and finally understand the underlying laws and the workings of Creation?

Concurrently, over a number of years I had heard from patients who described "near to death experiences" (NDE). These uniquely uniform descriptions, about a dozen of them, were especially impressive in presenting credible evidence for an after-life. These realizations coupled with the entire combination of events in my medical practice, and other considerations presented in the many books I have read, convinced me that God created the Universe, designed for life, and brought us forth on Earth. I have concluded that, very likely, the truth of the arrival of humans may involve a combination of creation and evolution, supporting the contention that God remains active as Creator, and not as an inactive originator who simply watches.

I have written this book for several groups of people. For those with a profound faith in God, it will be seen that science is not an enemy, but actually supports the Bible's writings in Genesis. For five hundred years science and religion have seemed to be foes, when in fact, science is unearthing facts that have brought considerations of God back into the books some of the scientists write. "The perception that religion requires faith alone is a misperception. Religion requires belief and belief is built on knowledge." (Schroeder, *The Science of God*). The faithful can turn to their Bible and read in Psalm 19:2-4: "The heavens declare the glory of God, and the firmament showeth His handiwork; Day unto day uttereth speech, And night unto night revealeth knowledge; There is no speech, there are no words, Neither is their voice heard." Why not turn to science to learn about that handiwork? As Elihu advised Job: "Harken unto this, O Job; Stand still, and consider the wondrous works of God. Dost thou know how God enjoineth them, and causeth the lightening of His cloud to shine? Dost thou know the balancings of the clouds, the wondrous works of Him who is perfect in knowledge?" (Job 37:14-16). Why not learn how the universe works and understand some of God's knowledge? The knowledge science provides does not replace theology but actually supports it.

Unfortunately, the American Public remains blissfully unaware of scientific findings that would actually enhance their faith, if they knew of them. For example, only 42 percent of college graduates, questioned by the Gallop Poll in 1993, knew that the dinosaurs died out over 50 million years ago. Sixty-five percent of non-college graduates had no idea when they died (*Surveying the Religious Landscape, Trends in U.S. Beliefs*, George Gallop, Jr. & D. Michael Lindsay, 1999). By briefly presenting a simplified scientific story of the creation and development of the universe as we now see it, and also by giving information on the origin of life and the process of evolution, I may be able to convince the reader that understanding these areas of science is worthwhile, and can enhance faith. Perhaps I can improve the general level of scientific education.

This book is also for the Creationists, some of whom deny scientific facts, as though they are the enemy, when such facts are widely accepted by both atheistic and believing scientists. I will show that a belief in a theistic Creation and in the process of Evolution can be combined. Of course, this book is also for folks like myself, searching, perhaps struggling, along the path to God. In this latter group will be independent thinkers, some of whom are within organized religion and some of whom, like myself, are disenchanted with the rigidity of doctrine in organized religion, and seek their own way. Nowhere in the Bible is there a commandment to establish organized religion, only a suggestion to pray in fellowship. Not that I am advocating that the reader should consider leaving his religion, only that he allow and follow a flexibility of thought, finding ways to become most comfortable with a system of beliefs. I am still Jewish and expanding what I believe. This book will provide a body of information with which to work, and the books quoted will offer readers an expanded bibliography to aid in their search for scientific facts and religious truth that makes them most comfortable. At the end of the book, although I present reflections on the personal theology I have developed, there is no intent to proselytize or to convince the reader that what I believe is the *only* truth. I have no right to try to do that. "If there is such a thing as objective truth, some of us are dead right and others dead wrong. Tolerance is necessary not because everybody is equally right, but because we have no way of proving once and for all which of us is right." (Kitty Ferguson, *The Fire in the Equations; Science, Religion and the Search for God*, 1994).

And finally, this book is an appeal to atheists and agnostics to reconsider their positions, presenting, as it does, a number of arguments for the existence of God. This book does not attempt a proof of God. By definition that is impossible. God, by "the criteria of science and reason is an unknowable concept. We cannot prove or disprove God's existence through empirical evidence or deductive proof." (*How We Believe*, Michael Shermer, 1999). The book does attempt to persuade "that God exists either beyond a reasonable doubt or by a preponderance of reasons in favor of that conclusion over reasons against it." (*How to Think About God*, Mortimer J. Adler, 1980). I have used Adler's book as a guide.

This book presents both sides of many issues. The reader must have an opportunity to make up his own mind, not driven in one direction by carefully selected and slanted material. I intend to use Occam's Razor (William of Occam, 1285?-1349?, English philosopher and theologian) in my deductive reasoning as taught in medical school: one should not assume the existence of more items than are logically necessary to reach a logical conclusion, or as actually taught to me, if you find a logical deduction using only the known facts, you will be right about 90 per cent of the time. Further, for simplicity I use male gender, unless a female pronoun is required. God is obviously genderless; however, in my usage He will be masculine. Further, as you have already seen in this Introduction, I place the references to quotes and sources right in the text. I think this is an easier way of providing the reader with references than hunting in the back of the book for a specific note.

Chapter 1: Enemies or Helpmates?

Currently many proponents of science and religion are doing battle. On one side are the extreme pronouncements of atheistic scientists that everything discovered about the universe can be explained without resorting to a concept of God. On the other side is the extreme insistence by Creationists that God took a literal "six" of our days to create the cosmos, resting on the seventh. This chapter describes that conflict and by presenting some of the extreme pronouncements demonstrates that the opponents can't possibly hear each other, when it is clear to me that both areas of our knowledge have much to offer each other. There have been suggestions that science and theology should be kept completely separate. I disagree. What is reasonable is to study a middle ground suggesting that scientific discoveries actually support religious belief.

The battle between science and religion started about 500 years ago when scientists began to explain our universe and their findings did not fit the authorized version presented by the Catholic Church. Although the Bible does not describe any such arrangement as the Earth set centrally located in the Universe, the early Catholic Church insisted it had to be so. This anthropocentric mistake comes from a presumption by theologians that if the Bible said God created us, we must be most important to the Universe, and therefore central in location with everything revolving around us. This is a prime example of mistaken theology and philosophy, springing from the self-centered thoughts of human beings, attempting to read the true intentions of God. It took a courageous beginning by Nicolaus Copernicus (1473-1543) who first described the Earth revolving around the sun near the center of the Universe, to set in motion a scientific revolution that overturned the Church's doctrines. "Courageous" because the Church's power could be life threatening. Johannes Kepler (1571-1630) advanced the new science by developing laws of planetary motion and immensely irritated the Church by describing elliptical orbits, when proper theology demanded perfect circles. Simultaneously Galileo (1564-1642) developed the telescope enlarging the science of astronomy with his discoveries, as one example, the four largest moons of Jupiter, and perhaps is most famous as a symbol of the battle against Church authority. His condemnation by the philosophers and theologians of the Catholic Church was not reversed until 1992. That it took so many years is symbolic of the antagonism between established religion and science.

It also took centuries of scientific discoveries to place our Earth out on the second spiral arm of a small galaxy in a small local group of galaxies, in a corner of the vastness of our Universe, not the center. The strength of religious beliefs is such that even a free thinker like Copernicus placed the sun near the center of the Universe as he presented his theory. He had no reason to question the religious beliefs he had been raised with, that human beings were central to the universe.

Along with these "heretical" attacks on the church-prescribed anatomy of the universe, Leonardo da Vinci (1452-1519) was wondering why fossils from the sea were being found in the Alps. The final blow was Darwin's *Origin of Species*(1859), which had the audacity to suggest that humans had evolved from ape-like forms. The continuing battle between science and religion was joined. Up to that point the Western world was quite content with the Genesis version of Creation. "Aided by a media that loves to reduce complex issues to the simplicity of a Super Bowl,…science is generally depicted as dispassionate, rational, and non-believing. Religious people are generally represented in the media as conservative, backwards, trailer-park dwellers. Fundamentalists and 'creationists' are usually featured only when attempting to get public schools to teach the Genesis version of the Creation alongside biology and evolutionary theory…" (*Don't Know Much About The Bible*, Kenneth C. Davis, 1998). This division between scientists and Creationists can be changed by starting a dialogue between the two groups. Of course that involves opening up minds to accept discussion and listening to opposing views. Not a likely prospect, viewing the current standoff, and how minds are so tightly closed on both sides.

The strength of fundamental religious beliefs was brought home to me by a patient of mine, a wonderful woman who was the wife of a minister. She actively worked with congregants, advising and counseling, a marvelous help to her husband. She and I got into a discussion and I described to her some of the wonders of the universe. She absolutely refused to accept what I was outlining. It was not in the Bible and she simply could not accept the facts I told her. If it wasn't described in the Bible, it didn't exist.

In some minds lies the concept that as science advances knowledge to explain what is seemingly miraculous, religion and God retreat. It is referred to as the "God of the Gaps" (*Skeptics and True Believers*, Chet Raymo, 1998). God remains only where science has not entered or has not explained. That is true only if the idea is accepted that science can explain everything and it is only a matter of time until every secret is revealed. Even many scientists won't buy that approach. But many of them do think that by reducing whatever it is they are studying to each component part, they will eventually reach a satisfactory understanding of the whole subject. (This is referred to as Reductionism). William Dembski disagrees: "To suppose that all the gaps in extraordinary explanations must be fillable by natural causes cannot be justified...Not all gaps are created equal. To assume that they are is to presuppose the very thing that is in question, namely naturalism," by which he means the ability of science eventually to explain everything. Some gaps may require God (*Intelligent Design, The Bridge Between Science and Theology*, 1999). Godel's Theorem (1931) is proof that not everything can be explained: he conclusively demonstrated "that mathematical statements existed for which *no* systematic procedure could determine whether they are either true or false" (*The Mind of God*, Paul Davies, 1992). This, of course, applies in the field of theoretical mathematics, which is the basis of some parts of science, especially particle physics, quantum theory, and much of cosmology. Reducing everything to its parts (Reductionism), itself has a problem: there is no question that when all the parts are acting as a whole something transcendent may appear. Neuro-anatomists can describe parts of the brain, microbiologists can pick apart chemical processes in cell function, but none of them can tell us where the mind or consciousness, or sense of "self" comes from.

And yet many scientists feel that everything can be explained satisfactorily if given enough time and the explanation of enough parts. Since God is needed only to fill the gaps, there is no need for God, or there will be no need in time. Chet Raymo, raised as a Roman Catholic, is one of those scientists. He is a professor of physics and astronomy at Stonehill College in Massachusetts, and writes a weekly science column for the Boston Globe. He counsels his readers to apply the aesthetic emotions of religion in a worship of science: "If we can surrender the ancient dream of immortality, then we can begin building a new theology, ecumenical, ecological, non-idolatrous. It will emphasize our relatedness and our interrelatedness, our stewardship rather than our dominion. It will define our value by our participation in a cosmic unfolding; we are flickers of a universal flame—galaxies, stars, planets, life, mind—a seething cauldron of creation. Natural and supernatural, immanent and transcendent, body and spirit will fuse in one God, revealed in his (sic) creation. On this speck of cosmic dust, planet Earth, the universe has become conscious of itself. The creation acknowledges the Creator. Our lives are sacramental. We experience the creation in its most fully known dimension. We celebrate. We worship." And his God is the god of science in which he rejoices. We can explain it all and revel in our knowledge. There will be no mysteries! At least there is some spirituality in his viewpoint.

Michael Shermer expresses a very similar viewpoint in his book, *How We Believe. The Search for God in an Age of Science* (1999). Shermer is the publisher of Skeptic magazine, the director of the Skeptics Society, and teaches the history of science, technology and evolutionary thought at Occidental College in Los Angeles. He is a kindred spirit with Chet Raymo (whom he quotes), as portions of his explanation of why he abandoned Christianity show: "I found meaning in the apparently meaningless universe presented by science. Without God, I am bluntly told, what's the point? If this is all there is, there is no use. To the contrary. For me quite the opposite is true. The conjuncture of losing my religion, finding science, and discovering glorious contingency [a theory of Stephen Jay Gould, describing each accidental step of evolution depending on previous ones, Chapter 4] was remarkably empowering and liberating. It gave me a sense of joy and freedom. Freedom to think for myself. Freedom to take responsibility for my own destinies. With the knowledge that this may be all there is, and that I can trigger my own cascading changes, I was free to live my life to the fullest. The universe takes on a whole new meaning when you know that your place in it was not foreordained, that it was not designed for us---indeed, that it was not designed at all. If we are nothing more than star stuff and biomass, how special life becomes. If the tape were played again and again without the appearance of our species, how extraordinary becomes our existence, and correspondingly, how cherished. You do not need a spiritual power to experience the spiritual. You do not need to be mystical to appreciate the mystery. Standing beneath a canopy of galaxies, atop a pillar of reworked stone, or inside a transept of holy light, my unencumbered soul was free to love without constraint, free to use my senses to enjoy all the pleasures and endure all the pains that come with such freedom. I was enfranchised for life, emancipated from the bonds of restricting tradition, and unyoked from the rules written for another time in another place for another people. I was now free to try to live up to that exalted moniker—*Homo sapiens*—wise man."

Funny, but I feel all of his exaltation and freedom in life, knowing all the science he knows, while accepting God. I don't feel constrained at all.

Unlike Shermer, Paul Davies in his book, *The Mind of God*, describes scientists, devoid of any sense of joy or elation from their discoveries, who feel " that science has robbed the universe of all mystery and purpose, and that the elaborate arrangement of the physical world is either a mindless accident or an inevitable consequence of mechanistic laws. 'The more the universe seems comprehensible, the more it also seems pointless,' believes physicist Steven Weinberg. The biologist Jacques Monod echoes this dismal sentiment: 'The ancient covenant is in pieces: man at last knows that he is alone in the unfeeling immensity of the universe, out of which he has emerged only by chance. Neither his destiny nor his duty have been written down'." With sentiments such as these, no wonder profoundly religious people are suspicious of science. On the other hand the 'fine tuning' found in the Big Bang research has lead Nobel Laureate Leon Lederman to note in his book *The God Particle*, (1993) in a section at the very end of the book entitled 'Obligatory God Ending' that a number of physicists "yearn to 'know the mind of God'", he not being one of them. Paul Davies is one of them and his book is so named. Gerald Schroeder, already mentioned in the Introduction, firmly believes in God, and another outstanding example of the effect the discoveries are having is the phenomenon of the life of John Polkinghorne, who was a theoretical physicist at the University of Cambridge with Stephen Hawking (the discoverer of Black Holes). In his fifties he left and became an Anglican clergyman and theologian. He has published a series of books, very recently, *Belief in God in an Age of Science* (1998). Two other scientists in *The Conscious Universe* (1990) and in *The Non-Local Universe*(1999) ask for an end to the conflict between religion and science. Robert Nadeau, a historian of science and Menas Kafatos, a physicist, are both professors at George Mason University. In their conclusion from the latter book: "Applying metaphysics where there is no metaphysics, or attempting to rewrite or rework scientific truths and/or facts in the effort to prove metaphysical assumptions, merely displays a profound misunderstanding of science and an apparent unwillingness to recognize its successes. Yet it is also true that the study of science can indirectly reinforce belief in the profoundly religious truths while not claiming to legislate the ultimate character of these truths...Science in no way argues against the existence of God, or Being, and can profoundly augment the sense of the cosmos as a significant whole", by which they mean conscious living beings and the material universe are really one and the same. "Let us, therefore, put an end to the absurd two-culture war and get on with the business of coordinating human knowledge in the interests of human survival in a new age of enlightenment that could be far more humane and much more enlightened than any that has gone before".

Paul Davies, who is a professor of theoretical physics, comments in the same vein. "Many people see religion on the defensive against the onslaught of scientific progress. They think of science as undermining or displacing religion. As scientists unlock more and more secrets of nature, so they reveal a universe of stunning beauty and ingenuity, a grand cosmic scheme truly worthy of our awe and celebration. Science alone cannot adequately cater for (sic) our spiritual needs, but any religion that refuses to embrace scientific discovery is unlikely to survive the 22ⁿᵈ century." (www.metanexus.net, Metaviews 039.2000.04.14).

The increasing speculation among cosmologists about God and religion has created some very odd suggestions, typified by Tipler's "Omega Point", described in his book, *The Physics of Immortality* (1994). Frank J. Tipler is a Professor of Mathematical Physics at Tulane University. He claims to have found mathematics to prove that in the "ultimate future", "(but also in the present and past) there must exist a Person Who is omnipotent, omniscient, omnipresent, Who is simultaneously both transcendent to yet immanent in the physical universe of space, time and matter…The physics shows the Person to have a 'pointlike' structure, so I will call Him/Her the *Omega Point.*" He then caps these assertions with two other assertions: "Remarkably, the argument boils down to a proof that we will be granted eternal life because it is probable that the Omega Point loves us!" and, "the Omega Point can be a solid foundation of support for all of the great human religions." The afterlife will be created by a giant computerization of the universe, each of our personalities and souls will be simulated, and we will never know the difference in the system he proposes! The dust cover of the book is more outrageous: "With the publication of THE PHYSICS OF IMMORTALITY, science has found God." Polkinghorne "condemned it as replacing ultimate fellowship with God by something comparable to a giant self-conscious encyclopedia." (John Leslie in *Modern Cosmology and Philosophy*, 1998).

We humans have always had a deep yearning to approach and have a relationship with the spiritual. "The predisposition to religious belief is the most complex and powerful force in the human mind and in all probability an ineradicable part of human nature." (*On Human Nature*, Edward O. Wilson, 1978). Tipler's overly strained application of his mathematics is certainly an example of Wilson's observation as is Raymo's spiritualization of pure science, quoted above. The original revolutionaries, Copericus, Kepler, Galileo, and subsequently Newton and Darwin, were not attacking religion; they each had a profound faith in their Creator and were simply trying to explain what they found in the world around them. They were attacking the teachings of religion, invented by humans who obviously did not have all the answers, but who presumed to speak for religion as though infallible. For example, the current misconception of Darwin attacking God's creation is wrong. Darwin accepted original creation: "There is a grandeur in this view of life, with its several powers, having been originally breathed by the Creator into a few forms or into one; and that, whilst this planet has gone on cycling on according to the fixed law of gravity, from so simple a beginning endless forms most beautiful and most wonderful have been, and are being, evolved." (*Origin of Species*, sixth edition, 1872). Later in his life Darwin did confess in private writings to giving consideration to agnosticism. Isaac Newton believed in his God as the Creator. According to Wilson, since the time of the Neanderthals, who appear to have practiced rudimentary religion, "mankind has produced on the order of 100 thousand religions….religion is one of the major categories of behavior undeniably unique to the human species." It is not surprising that the 'early' scientists maintained a belief in a Deity as they explored His Works.

Atheism and agnosticism are more recent attributes of research cosmologists and evolutionary scientists, seduced by the extraordinary explanatory power of their science. The tide may not be turning back among the cosmologists, but there is a marked drift to wonder and speculate about the source and meaning of the fine-tuning and design they find in the mechanics of the universe (see Chapter 2). And the most important point: the presence of many atheists and agnostics among these scientists, does not detract or negate their findings that should be so compelling to those of faith. Pope John Paul II on many occasions has stated science and theology should support each other: "Science can purify religion from error and superstition, and religion can purify science from idolatry and absolutes." (*Skeptics and True Believers*). He has also given support to Darwinian evolution: "If the human body has its origin in living material which pre-exists it, the spiritual soul is immediately created by God." (*Don't Know Much About The Bible*). The Pope at a conference on "Physics, Philosophy and Theology: A Common

Quest for Understanding" (1988) encouraged continuing research to unify the four fundamental forces in nature (*The Mind of God*).

Non-scientists, regular folks, both of faith and those who are not, should not hide from the discoveries in cosmology over the last 50 years. "To invoke God as a blanket explanation of the unexplained is to make God the friend of ignorance. If God is to be found, it must surely be through what we discover about the world, not what we fail to discover." (Paul Davies, quoted by Raymo). People, like my patient who did not wish to listen to a description of the revealed wonders of the universe because it offended her rigid belief in the Bible, need to overcome this prejudice against science and come to see what science has provided for them that supports their beliefs. I am not attacking belief in the history and messages in the Bible. Our knowledge of God comes from the Bible, but it will always be incomplete. God is shrouded in mystery, and is only partially knowable. Humans can only guess at His intentions and reasons. Organized religion is made up of human beings who are sincere in their beliefs and faith, but those beliefs may only be a guess at the truth. Think about it, everyone thinks their religious beliefs are the 'right' ones. Wars and conflicts are commonplace in our history due to religious differences. The Crusades in Palestine were against 'heathens', people in fact, who followed the Muslim religion, in their Koran accepted the Old and New Testaments, and considered Jesus a prophet! Protestants and Catholics divide Ireland in a fight that has gone on since Elizabeth I invited Protestants to live in Ireland four centuries ago. And for seven centuries the Balkans have seen almost continuous fighting among Roman Catholics, Eastern Orthodox Catholics, and Muslims. Religious beliefs are so strong they make us warlike, and so strong as to close our minds around our beliefs like a vise.

We act as if we have all the answers. But do we have all the answers? What if I can ask questions that have no answer? Why did God first reveal Himself personally to the ancient Hebrews? Why was monotheism only confined to the Western world before missionaries spread the knowledge? Are the Eastern religions wrong to believe in their planes of existence, their interpretation of a universe containing a highest Divine Reality as their equivalent of our God. They believe their religions are the correct ones. And don't they have a right to that belief? No one has the *right* set of answers. We in the West have a personal God, and are supplied rules of life through biblical teachings. They in the East use contemplation and meditation to seek the Ultimate Truth of the universe. In the West we have remarkably divergent opinions about which of our religious teachings are correct. We each believe those ideas that bring us the most comfort, usually the ideas from the religion we are born into, not the ones that are universally most correct, because no one knows surely and absolutely which are the most correct ideas, or the most correct religious practices (Ravi Ravindra, Professor and Chairman of Comparative Religion at Dalhousie University, Halifax, Nova Scotia. Meta-List.org, Metaviews 073, 2000). I am not attacking anyone's faith, only suggesting that minds are allowed to become open to accept scientific material that may well be surprisingly supportive of religious concepts already existing within a person's view of religious truth.

Gerald Schroeder in both his books has conclusively shown that interpretations of the original five books of Moses (the Torah), the first five books of the Old Testament, read in the original ancient Hebrew, literally have predicted much of the Big Bang theory of cosmology and our fossil ancestors. "No incentive existed to prompt commentators one and two thousand years ago to speculate about prehuman hominids." (*The Science of God*). To find God in the sciences of cosmology and evolution is to see these Biblical predictions based on interpretations from the Talmud (about 500), and by Rashi (1050), Maimonides (1190), and Nahmanides (1260). "Conflicts between science and religion result from a misinterpretation of the Bible". (Maimonides in *Genesis and the Big Bang*). It is vitally important to go back to these original documents, and to the commentaries by scholars who were intimate in their knowledge of ancient Hebrew. It is only here that the deeper meanings and interpretations can be found. Of special importance is the biblical commentator Onkelos (about 150 A.D.) who translated the original Hebrew text of the Torah into Aramaic, the common language of the Middle East for several centuries before and after the start of the current calendar. "Aramaic, a Semitic language, is sufficiently similar to Hebrew to allow it to serve as a linguistic cross-reference. By translating the Hebrew into Aramaic, Onkelos provided definitions to words, the meanings of which had become obscure. This source is still in such standard use that it is referred to as 'the translation'." (*Genesis and the Big Bang*). The original Five Books can still be read in the original script. The scribes who copied the Torah through over three thousand years made extremely rare mistakes. The Torah of the ancients and the Torah in a modern synagogue are exactly the same. The Dead Sea Scroll of the complete Book of Isaiah is an exact duplicate of the Book of Isaiah in modern Torahs, and is on exhibit in a special museum in Jerusalem. Hershel Shanks in *The Mystery and Meaning of the Dead Sea Scrolls*, 1998, describes these scrolls, a "thousand years older than the oldest extant Hebrew Bible" as indicating, "that, all in all, modern copies are amazingly accurate."

The King James Version of the Bible is so far removed from the original sources that it is useless for studies similar to those conducted by Schroeder. The original Torah in Hebrew was translated into the common language Aramaic during Jesus' time. The Vulgate bible, in Latin appeared in 405, the Old Testament translated from original Hebrew and the New Testament from Aramaic. William Tyndale, an English priest, working in Germany (the Catholic Church in England did not want an English version as a way of remaining the supreme authority on biblical interpretation), created the first English Bible in 1526, and was killed for his trouble (Davis, *Don't Know Much About the Bible*). His translation was the basis for the King James Version of 1611, which covered the first 12 books of the Old Testament. It was created over a seven-year period by a group of scholars translating existing manuscripts, at a time when critical studies as to authenticity and accuracy of translations had not yet been developed. There were no commentaries. As a result when such scholarship in translation appeared, there was much criticism and a number of revisions were created into the 20th Century (V.V. Raman, www.metanexus.net, 1/17/02). The King James Version and other English Bibles are not adequate or useful, in any sense of the words, to compare to the scientific theories of the creation of the universe or the appearance of life. Unless a version is obtained that uses the ancient Hebrew texts with the appropriate commentaries as shown in Schroeder's books. As I have learned, translations of the New Testament, closer to the original writings, also offer debatable portions. It is reported the Vulgate Bible used the Greek translation of Joshua (a Hebrew name), which became Jesus (Davis, *Don't Know Much About the Bible*). Another example from my student days at Bates College: many of the professors were Doctors of Divinity given Bates' background as a Northern Baptist Seminary until the 1850's. In a bible class that was required, the professor offered the opinion that the following famous verse, Matthew 19:24 was a mistranslation: Jesus said "Again I tell you, it is easier for a camel to go through the eye of a needle than for a rich man to enter the kingdom of God." He pointed out that if one letter were different in the word for "camel" in the original language, it became "thread", and he was of the opinion this was a better approach to the text. Is the meaning of the Bible in the eye of the beholder or the eye of the needle? The lay reader needs expert commentaries and the commentaries will disagree with one another. One last example from the Old Testament: the sixth commandment is really "you shall not murder", not "thou shall not kill". (*The New Oxford Annotated Bible*). The difference has enormous ethical import: *murder* is a criminal act, but society has the ethical right to *kill* a criminal for the good of societal needs. The King James Version may be familiar, and comfortable, but not very helpful when the issue is comparing science to religious teachings to support belief.

If science is to be used as one of the bedrocks of religion, how trustworthy are the facts it presents? Just as religion is a distillation of ideas from many theologians and philosophers who critically debate and criticize each other, the Scientific Method is just as rigorous. First a hypothesis is developed to provide a connecting idea between some possibly-related facts. Experimentation is performed to test this new thought. The results are published in a reputable, peer-reviewed journal for review by other scientists. Other groups repeat the experiments. If two or more repetitions confirm the findings, the hypothesis becomes a theory. A group of theories may become a law by the same process. Along the way letters-to-the-editor will provide discussion and comment, as will presentations at scientific conventions. The final outcomes are the result of a consensus of opinions. And these opinions will have intellectual and emotional overlays, based on preconceived ideas and other agendas; scientists are after all as human as the rest of us. It is the overall consensus that protects the results from error.

My wish is that scientists studying evolution and the so-called "creationists" could work together with the same give-and-take used in the scientific method. Unfortunately the two groups are adversarial: on the creationist side, protecting what the latter view as their inviolate Biblical beliefs, while the scientists push their knowledge forward and ignore the objections on the side of creation. As Wilson observes: "The mind cannot comprehend the meaning of the collision between irresistible scientific materialism and immovable religious faith." To make my position clear, my thinking falls in the middle, between both sides. I believe the scientific findings that describe the workings of the universe. I believe evolution happened, but I disagree with the scientific conclusion that all of this is the result of chance occurrences. I believe that science and religion can be reconciled and the processes of evolution and creation are both operative. Currently there is a literary war being waged by defenders on both sides. As you might imagine the writers are talking right past each other, not listening to the other side at all. To demonstrate the battle we must now present material from both sides.

To acquaint myself with creationist literature, I have reviewed recent material, a creationist monograph, which presents some of the "new scientific discoveries that support creation," *Creation versus Evolution; New Scientific Discoveries*, by Ralph O. Muncaster, 1997. Further, I have carefully read a 344-page book, *Darwin's Leap of Faith*, by Ankerberg and Weldon, 1998. Commenting first on Muncaster, I can accept a large portion of his argument. But what disturbs me are the mis-statements. In a box labeled Hoaxes and Mistakes, describing fossils found during "the intensive search for 'missing links' [are] a number of mistakes and even fraud" offered as follows: 1) "Java Man—the discoverer later rejected it stating that a human and ape were found in proximity." This may have happened during early scientific discussions, but anthropologists now place Java man in an evolutionary group called Homo erectus (See Johanson & Shreve below). 2) "Peking Man—Tools and human bones were found near the apes whose brains they were eating (monkey brains are still eaten in China)." This *was* an early objection of Louis Leaky, the famous anthropologist, but Peking Man is considered authentic by current anthropologists and is also in the Homo erectus group (pg. 67, *Lucy's Child, The Discovery of a Human Ancestor*, Donald Johanson & James Shreeve, 1989). 3) "Lucy–Reclassified as an extinct ape." Not true. She is classified as Australopithecus afarensis, not an ape but an early ground-dwelling Hominid (Johanson & Shreeve). On the other hand, in the same box in the monograph two statements are absolutely on the mark: Piltdown Man was a hoax and Ramapithecus, thought at first to be an early human, was reclassified as an ancestor of the Orangutan.

Another set of statements concerning Neanderthals I found as untrue, are: "It was once thought that the Neanderthal was a man. But recent genetic DNA research indicates the chromosomes DO NOT match those of humans. They DO match those of bi-pedal primates (apes)." The truth is human DNA differs from chimpanzee DNA by roughly two per cent. Chimps are in the ape family. If we use Muncaster's reasoning, what does that make us? And: "There is NO evidence that Neanderthal practiced any form of worship or religion." If that is the case, then why did the Neanderthals have bone alters and practice burial of the dead? Wilson reports: "at Shanidar, Iraq, sixty thousand years ago, Neanderthal people decorated a grave with seven species of flowers having medicinal and economic value, perhaps to honor a shaman." Is this an invention of Wilson's, a scientific lie? I interpret these "problem" declarations presented by Muncaster as representing the Creationists' difficulty in accepting human evolution from lower forms. Is it moral in the defense of religious belief to create an appearance of apparent intellectual dishonesty?

However, there is much of his presentation I agree with. The cosmologic scientific facts he uses are correct in his argument that the Big Bang does imply a Creator. (See Chapter 7). His material on the improbable likelihood of DNA forming by chance fits the scientific facts, and has been supported by some scientists (Schroeder and Polkinghorne among others). The reasoning is the following: since the Big Bang there has not been enough time to have evolution, controlled totally by chance, to have developed life and allowed us to appear (see Chapter 2). In these ideas, in my opinion, he is on solid ground *in part* because his facts are correct. In a scientific debate all facts must be employed, not just the ones that fit preconceived beliefs, even religious beliefs. For an honest debate between science and the Creationists, a debate which is badly needed for progress to occur, the Creationists should heed the words of Pope John Paul II quoted above and now repeated: "Science can purify religion from error and superstition, and religion can purify science from idolatry and false absolutes."

Before discussing *Darwin's Leap of Faith*, I must first present "Old Earth Creationism" and "Young Earth Creationism" for the readers who do not know these terms. Muncaster who appears to be an Old Age Creationist himself, does not take sides in his definitions, and states either concept is correct, and depends upon the individual's beliefs. He feels both are consistent with the Bible, stating that the Hebrew word "yom" can be translated as 'day' or 'era'; therefore, creation took six days or six eras. The "Old Earth View recognizes scientific evidence that the earth is billions of years old." The "Young Earth View uses semantic arguments to conclude the *Bible* clearly indicates *6 literal* 24-hour days." The Young Earth Creationists by working totally from Genesis must make an effort to refute a much larger amount of scientific assertions than the Old Earth Creationists, who accept much of the time frame of the Big Bang theory, including the age of the earth. Obviously, both groups attempt to refute evolution in the material they present.

Ankerberg and Weldon have written *Darwin's Leap of Faith* from the Young Earth perspective. As a result I found a much larger amount of scientific material that I would consider misstated, or described in a false way. I could spend several pages of this chapter listing such statements and offering different facts to dispute their points, but my comments about Muncaster's incorrect statements in his monograph suffice to illustrate the character of misstatements that tend to be presented.

The authors insist that only their interpretation of the bible is correct, without exception. Since these authors defend Genesis in its literal meaning, they defend the story of Noah, and declare there was a worldwide flood. In fact, to fight the theory of evolution, they need the flood to cover the entire earth. They use it to claim that the geologic layering of the earth was affected by the flood; so much so, that the layers can be interpreted to mean the earth is only "10,000 to 20,000 years [old]" (pg. 296). Further, since the aging of layers is a scientifically coordinated effort using radioisotope dating, geologic layer dating, and using fossils, by claiming the flood messes up the dating, it puts those pesky fossils in their place as not being evidence for evolution. "There are significant scientific evidences for a global flood. And most cultures *around the world* have written traditions of a universal flood. How does such a cultural consensus arise if there has only been a local flood to destroy the inhabitants of Mesopotamia? Why do people in India, China, and all around the globe have universal flood traditions? The logical answer is because the whole world was flooded, just as geological evidence indicates. (If 70 percent of the earth is currently under water, the idea that it was once 100 percent covered with water should not be considered impossible.)" It is the statement in parentheses that is a logical "howler" for those of us who are not so literal in interpretation of the Bible. Superficially that statement sounds logical as they try to pass it off. But just stop and think about the implications of how much water is involved. Before they made these assertions about a worldwide flood, they had quoted from Genesis 7:19-20: "They rose greatly on the earth, and *all* the high mountains under the heavens were covered. The waters rose and covered the mountains to *a depth of more than twenty feet.*" (My italics). Now let's consider the elevation of the highest mountain, Mt. Everest, slightly above 29,000 feet! That is 5.5 miles above sea level, and conservatively granting that the continents average 5,000 feet above sea level, during the biblical flood 30 percent of the earth had to be 4.5 miles under water and the oceans (70 percent) added 5.5 miles of water depth. Granting an average ocean depth of 5,000 feet (one mile), simple calculation tells us that the flood, to have occurred, had to add to the existing volume of water in the oceans an additional 8.1 times that volume. (An additional 5.5 times over the oceans, added to 3/7 of 4.5 times over land or 2.6 times.) Even if "all the springs of the great deep burst forth" and "the floodgates of the heavens were opened," as they quote from Genesis 7:11-12, such an additional volume of water requires a miracle from God to create that volume of water. They do not claim a miracle, nor does the Bible. Further, the added weight of the excess water would have forced the earth to change its orbit unless God held it in place by another miracle, again for which there is no evidence.

I have always assumed a local flood, a possibility they deny. In fact, recent studies by archeologists and oceanographers strongly support the occurrence of massive floods in the region of the Black Sea about 7,000 years ago. Near Sinop, a city on the north coast of Turkey, there is evidence of a pre-flood shoreline 500 feet under water and a rectangular site with stone blocks, wood and probably ceramics. Chemical analysis of "core samples" yielded evidence consistent with interpreting that people once occupied the site. There was further evidence that the inundation was rapid, wide in scope and probably killed many people (From a paper in the *American Journal of Archeology*, reported October 1, 2001 in the *N.Y. Times*, by John Noble Wilford). The Black Sea is only 500 miles from Palestine and Mount Ararat is in Eastern Turkey. Earlier in the year, marine geologists had suggested that an overflowing Mediterranean Sea had flooded the Black Sea about 7,600 years ago (J.N. Wilford, *N.Y. Times*, 1/9/01). Scientific theories about the source of the flood (or floods) point to the end of the last ice age 10-11,000 years ago, with melting of the glaciers occurring over several thousand years. It is thought that the retreating glaciers may have created "ice dams" which when they broke released huge seas of melt water resulting in floods over hundreds of square miles ("Did Noah's Flood Really Happen", Gregg Easterbrook, www.beliefnet.com, October 2001). This research illustrates that science can explain the origin of historical accounts in the Bible. As Easterbrook comments: "a deluge of the scope and depth documented by the new study may well have seemed to its survivors in the ancient Middle East as though the waters had covered the whole of the Earth. At the time the Noachian passages were composed, no one knew other continents even existed." If the glacial melt theory is correct, and it is in dispute from another research team, (*Houston Chronicle*, "Scientists doubt latest version of Noah epic," Robert Cooke, *Newsday*, 1/15/03) this would account for the widespread stories of ancient massive floods throughout the Northern Hemisphere, as pointed out by Ankerberg and Weldon.

But how about the Ark itself? There have been reports of an object under the glaciers on Mount Ararat resembling a boat, but thought by some to be rock formations. As described in Genesis 6:15, the instructions of 300 cubits long, 50 cubits wide and 30 cubits high translate into a boat 450 feet long, 75 feet wide and 45 feet high. (A cubit is 18 inches.) A giant boat for those days, but was it big enough to carry "every living substance which was upon the face of the ground," (Genesis 7:23) and enough provisions for 150 days afloat? We now know there are currently five million species on Earth, as undoubtedly there were in the time of the floods. And how did Noah manage to get llamas from South America and kangaroos from Australia to the Middle East, as well as other exotic animals from all over the Earth? Genesis does not specifically mention plant life, but by implication all plant species had to be on board also, in order to survive 150 days under water. Therefore, I doubt the Ark as described in Genesis really existed, but our ancestors were survivors and I won't be surprised if remains of an ark-like boat turn up one day, having been built to help animals and people survive in those local floods.

As literalists, Ankerberg and Weldon appear to accept the rainbow God used as a sign of his covenant with Noah as a very 'first' appearance of a rainbow. Since the rainbow appears around the world to everyone, they claim this proves a worldwide flood. My bible, taken from the Masoretic text, the first Hebrew text with vowels, written after 500 A.D. by Jewish scholars from the original text, makes no mention that it is a 'first rainbow', only that it is a sign of the covenant with Noah (Genesis 9:8-17). God spoke with Noah and used the rainbow as a continuous sign for the future. The rainbow is due to prismatic action by raindrops breaking up the spectrum of light, as every school child knows. This is an underlying physical law of a physical property of matter.

Let me raise another scientific objection to their insistence on six literal days for creation, and an earth that is only 10-20,000 years old. When night fell on the sixth day and Adam looked up, what did he see in the darkened sky? Perhaps the moon if it were out, but according to modern science, no stars and no Milky Way!! The nearest star is four light years away. Our Milky Way is 100,000 light-years across. According to the New Earth Creationists' theology our current sky should show only a very few scattered stars, considering the speed of light and remembering that a light-year is the distance that photons of light travel in one year. George Sim Johnston points out this obvious problem in *Did Darwin Get It Right? Catholics and the Theory of Evolution*", 1998. Catholics accept the fact that "Genesis was written in the archaic, pre-scientific idiom of the ancient Palestinians", and is not accepted literally. Kenneth R. Miller, a professor of biology at Brown University who believes in God, also uses starlight to be highly critical of

Creationists in his book, *Finding Darwin's God, A Scientist's Search For Common Ground Between God and Evolution* (1999). The Creationists claim that Adam did see stars. He notes that to solve the problem some Creationists claim that the speed of light was "*much* faster in the past, and that accounts for the light from distant galaxies that is now reaching us from billions of light-years away". Other Creationists declare: "the photons of light energy were created at the same instant as the stars from which they were apparently derived, so that an observer on earth would have been able to see the most distant stars within his vision at that instant of creation." (Miller quoting J.C. Whitcomb & H.M. Morris, *Genesis Flood*", pp.343-344, 1961).

Ankerberg and Weldon, the authors of *Darwin's Leap of Faith*, like Whitcomb and Morris, must believe God created the universe, but not all at once, adding new laws of nature now and then. From my study of science, I believe God created the universe and its controlling natural laws all at once, and, in light of that, I have a right to my interpretation of my Bible. Their inventive explanations illustrate the power of their faith, which overrides any intellectual curiosity they both must have to investigate alternate interpretations, considering their multiple doctorate and masters degrees. They know what they know on faith and have no need to go further. If they are satisfied with that, so be it. I know I cannot change them, nor should I try. Miller characterizes their Creation Science as "nonsense", a sign of the war between scientists and religion. I don't think such an inflammatory statement helps to bring people together.

We can all disagree about the Bible and our interpretation of its stories. It is obvious that I prefer a mixture of faith and scientific explanation. Just as I have a right to my approach, they have a right to theirs, which is to state that only the literal interpretation of the Bible is correct. I am not disturbed by my disagreement with them, but their book makes it clear that, if they knew my interpretation, they would be tremendously disturbed with me. What upsets me much more, however, is their contention over and over throughout the book that there is a conspiracy among scientists to "protect" the concept of evolution. I found at least eleven quotations in the book impugning the intellectual honesty of scientists in general, claiming scientists distort, ignore and invent facts or theories. On the contrary, the scientific method does pit scientists against each other, struggling to find physical truths, theories and laws to explain the true workings of the universe. In my view they are only trying to explain God's handiwork. These scientists are intellectually honest and 40 percent of them believe in God. Of course, there is the occasional dishonest scientist who fakes results but with every experiment required to be published for peer review, and to be successfully repeated by another independent laboratory for positive verification, he will be found out. There is no massive collusion or conspiracy in the scientific community to protect evolution. But this is what the authors say: "Because God has created us as rational creatures, it may even be argued that sin against reason is a sin against God. Scientists should *know* better. And, generally, in their rational moments they do. They know the universe didn't arise from literally nothing. They suppress the truth when they try to make it seem as if it did. *That* is the sin. Most scientists, it seems, prefer to disguise their belief in magic by making the idea of chance origins appear scientific and rational. Why? Because they do not like the consequences of having to seriously consider the implications of a Creator God." And the following assertion: "Most Americans have bought into scientific myth-making, the garnering of scientific data in such a manner as to make evolution *seem* possible." The scientists are deemed sinners by these authors; those scientists (who don't know they are sinners) are proud of their methods and believe they are being intellectually honest in performing their research. To my mind it is just as much a sin upon the part of the authors to vilify scientists the way they have, because of a disagreement in belief. My God did not intend to be defended by accusations of willful dishonesty directed toward people who sincerely feel they are being honest.

Miller has a rebuttal. The Creationists "version of God is one who intentionally plants misleading clues beneath our feet and in the heavens themselves. Their version of God is one who filled the universe with so much bogus evidence that the tools of science can give us nothing more than a phony version of reality. In other words, their God has negated science by rigging the universe with fiction and deception. To embrace that God, we must reject science and worship deception itself."

Gerald Schroeder is an example of a sincerely honest and very religious scientist, who as a biblical scholar and a physicist, in his book, *Genesis and the Big Bang*, refutes the Creationists contention (without mentioning them) that the Noachian Flood upsets the scientific record for the age of the Earth in terms of the study of archeology and paleontology. Schroeder uses the ages of Adam and his descendents stated in Genesis to calculate the time at which Tuval-Cain lived. Tuval-Cain is identified in the Bible as the person who first forged brass tools. By Schroeder's Biblical estimate, he lived approximately 4,400 years ago. Amazingly, the earliest brass tools housed in the Israel

Museum are aged scientifically as being 4,400 years old! Tuval-Cain lived during Noah's life, prior to the Flood. "The matching of the biblical and archeological dates for the inception of the Bronze Age is doubly instructive because it occurred in the post-Adam, but pre-Flood, period. While helping to confirm the biblical calendar, it also dispels the reasoning that the Flood altered the fossil record. If the Flood had caused the claimed changes, then all pre-Flood events would be in error. The biblical date ascribed to the early Bronze Age, which occurred in that block of time *following Adam but preceding the Flood*, eminently matches the archeologically established date for this same event. Both the archeological record and the biblical record are valid." I wonder how Creationists would answer this observation.

Not surprisingly, in the battle of words and ideas between these two antagonistic groups, scientists also have been less than honest in many areas, attempting to defeat religion by any means possible. It was scientists in the late 19th century who created the myth that Christopher Columbus and all his contemporaries thought the earth was flat. "Their purpose was to fell religion in its war with science. What better strategy than to attribute clearly wrong-headed ideas to a wrong-headed enemy? The beauty of the flat-earth myth was its preposterousness." The ancient Greeks knew the earth was round and in the third century B.C. Eratosthenes had accurately calculated its circumference. Medieval scholars such as the Venerable Bede, Roger Bacon and Thomas Aquinas "accepted and deepened [this] classical knowledge with their own analyses and calculations". Two books created the myth: the first by a physician John William Draper, *History of the Conflict Between Religion and Science*, 1874; the second, by Andrew Dickson White, a scientist who became the first president of Cornell University, *History of the Warfare of Science* With Theology in Christendom", 1896. (*Wall Street Journal*, "Columbus's Circle", by Julia Vitullo-Martin, 10/9/99). The lack of intellectual honesty on both sides, generated by an intense emotionalism that always accompanies intra-religious and anti-religious debate, is truly astounding. As Adler observed in *How to Think About God* atheists are passionately anti-religious and will always raise serious philosophic questions attacking belief in God. No one is willing to accept the philosophy of 'live and let live'.

Currently in the battle, on the side of evolutionary science is the recent book, *The Tower of Babel* (1999), by Robert T. Pennock. He is an assistant professor of philosophy, specializing in the philosophy of science, at the University of Texas at Austin. I fully support him in defending scientific findings as acceptable facts upon which to base one's thinking. Unfortunately the many valid points he makes are drowned in a deluge of specific refutations he makes of creationist statements in their literature. They won't be listening to him or in responding will be on the attack, and the more casual reader will find trouble wading through all of it. In fairness, Pennock has given his book a specific purpose: he intended the book to be a "field guide to help science teachers understand who is attacking them and why." He also makes the book a wake-up call to the fact that creationists are in full battle dress to bring creation science into the classrooms of the country and limit or drive out the teaching of evolution and Big Bang cosmology. On August 11, 1999 the Kansas Board of Education severely limited the teaching of evolution, and removed all questions about evolution from required tests. With an "unmistakable reference to creationist science they wrote that 'no evidence contradicting a current scientific theory shall be censored'." (*Houston Chronicle, Washington Post* article anticipating their action, 8/9/99). On August 13, 1999 a *Wall Street Journal* editorial interpreted the Board's action: "This is what we think is the message these Kansans are sending to the world: 'About 35 years ago, you folks banned our religion from the public schools. So we've just voted to drop your religion from the public schools. Now maybe you'd like to sit down and negotiate a deal'." Prior to that in 1995 Alabama mandated that all biology books have a sticker describing evolution as a controversial theory; life's origins should be considered a theory not a fact. In 1996, the legislature in Tennessee considered and almost passed a bill requiring that evolution be taught as a theory, not fact. In 1997 the Texas Board of Education turned down, by a narrow majority, a proposal to remove all consideration of evolution from the biology texts. (*Chronicle/Wash. Post*). Pennock's fears that creationists will drive valid science out of the classrooms are obviously well founded, but I don't think his book contains the ways to solve the conflict, since he is also in full battle dress. (My own discussion of solutions is in Chapter 8.)

Because of his objectives, I feel his book has some serious weaknesses, beyond the obvious lack of possible solutions. While his declaration that he is a Quaker seems to sound somewhat condescending and self-serving, I believe he sincerely does "not mean to attack the sincerity or intentions of creationist believers...[and]...none of what I write should be taken as an attack upon religion in general or Christianity in particular...[and also]...I strongly believe in the freedom of religious belief (or unbelief)." An obvious weakness is that he must maintain a general appearance of unity among evolutionists; you cannot fight any enemy and appear to have conflict in your own ranks. Evolutionary Paleontologist Conway Morris's entire first chapter in *The Crucible of Creation* (1998) explores the lack of consensus. Pennock does devote a few pages in his Chapter 2 to differing Darwinian theses, but does not impress the reader with the marked degree of intellectual conflict, making an offhand comment that "disputes can get pretty exciting and even contentious." Michael Behe (*Darwin's Black Box*, 1996), whose book pokes huge holes in Darwin's theory notes the tendency to be protective of Darwinism: "Unfortunately, too often criticisms have been dismissed by the scientific community for fear of giving ammunition to creationists. It is ironic that in the name of protecting science, trenchant scientific criticism of natural selection has been brushed aside." Behe, a professor of biochemistry at Lehigh University does not consider himself a creationist. "I have no reason to doubt that the universe is billions of years old. I find the idea of common descent (that all organisms share a common ancestor) fairly convincing, and have no particular reason to doubt it." As I have previously indicated, those are my feelings exactly. Yet Pennock tries to pin a creationist label on Behe, in defense of Pennock's beliefs in Darwinism.

Why do scientists defend the Darwin theory so strongly? Because the major body of scientists really thinks it is the only theory with which they have to work, despite the contentious disagreements in their literature. It appears that human psychology prefers pat explanations rather than endure uncertainty when faced with a confused situation. And amazingly this applies just as much to scientists, from whom one would expect a marked degree of pride in logic. "Normal science often suppresses fundamental novelties because they are necessarily subversive of its basic commitments". Scientists tend to be so wedded to paradigms that much of laboratory experimentation "seems to be an attempt to force nature into the preformed and relatively inflexible box that the paradigm supplies". "In science... novelty emerges only with difficulty, manifested by resistance, against a background provided by expectation". Eventually awareness appears of the paradigm's inability to fully explain the phenomenon in question (*The Structure of Scientific Revolutions*, Thomas Kuhn, 1962). That 'awareness' has not yet occurred in the scientific community.

At the university level objective research adverse to the Darwin theory is hampered by two factors. The first is the tenure system, which is built upon the premise that life-long tenure without fear of being fired allows free reign of thought. Young teachers are fearful of bucking the existing paradigm while struggling to achieve tenure. Obviously, after reaching the tenure goal, their research can take whatever tack they wish. The second problem is closely related to the first. Grant money for research is also tied to the paradigm and is hard to obtain if the research proposal is out of line with current thinking.

Scientists are correct in being wary of creationists. The creationist literature, as I have shown, certainly 'doctors' scientific facts to fit their need to protect their beliefs. That is intellectually dishonest, if a debate is to be conducted on rational grounds. Pennock also 'doctors' reality, by not mentioning respected scientists who have raised very critical objections to the tenets of Darwinism, after critically studying an overall synthesis of scientific evolutionary findings and pointing out major flaws. Among many I will mention, here are some objecting scientists covered throughout this book: Gerald Schroeder, a particle physicist, *The Science of God* (1997) and *Genesis and the Big Bang*(1990); David Foster, a scientific consultant, *The Philosophic Scientists* (1985); Robert Shapiro, a professor of chemistry at New York University, *Origins: A Skeptic's Guide to the Origin of Life* (1986); and John Polkinghorne, a theoretical cosmologist who worked with Stephen Hawking, and now is an Anglican theologian, *Belief in God in an Age of Science*(1998).

Pennock makes it a special point to 'trash' the mathematical theories of a famous astronomer, Sir Fred Hoyle, who concluded that complex animals could not arise by chance (see Chapter 3); and he mentions Stuart Kauffman in passing, not describing in any detail Kauffman's strong objections to the current theories of the origin of life (Chapter 3). I recognize that some of these author/scientists invoke God in their discussions, but they do not put God into the scientific studies. Behe is quite clear on this point, although he is convinced that intelligent design lies behind the origin of life and the progress of evolution. There is nothing wrong with conducting scientific experiments without God in one's scientific work, and reaching conclusions as a theist in one's private life. Pennock is absolutely correct to defend "the *methodological* materialism of science, which says that science cannot use supernatural cause to explain the natural world. To explain by natural cause does not make a field antireligious; as Pennock wryly notes, science is no more atheistic than plumbing. 'To say nothing of God is not to say that God is nothing'." (Review of *Tower of Babel, Scientific American*, Eugenie C. Scott, August 1999). However, once a scientist does his experimentation, and reports his results, he is free to accept God in his private thoughts.

Once a scientist has reviewed the world scientific literature, he has the right to conclude that intelligent design needs to be invoked as an explanation privately in his own thoughts but he may also do it publicly. Del Ratzsch, an academic philosopher of science, concludes that investigation of supernatural design should be included in scientific research when it appears warranted (*Nature, Design and Science: The Nature of Design in Natural Science*, 2001). Michael Behe has done just that, and Pennock has declared literary war against him. A brief review of the battle between them is important, because it illustrates two professors, one of the philosophy of science and the other of microbiology, forcefully disagreeing in a proper debate of very different ideas. Generally this type of battle is confined to the pages of arcane scientific journals, and is not seen by the general public.

Darwin's Theory of Evolution is quite simple in its proposal: Species adapt very slowly to the changing demands of nature. He had seen these adaptations during his studies, especially in the Galapagos Islands. He assumed that these gradual changes would eventually lead to entirely new species. "I do believe that natural selection will generally act very slowly, only at long intervals of time. As natural selection acts solely by accumulating slight, successive, favourable variations, it can produce no great or sudden modifications, it can act only by short and slow steps." (Darwin quoted in, *Evolution: A Theory in Crisis*, Michael Denton, 1985). He knew that huge gaps were present in the fossil records of his day, and that no gradualism was present in those records, but he assumed those gaps would subsequently be filled in by future findings. To date those gaps have never been filled, and are a source of great debate and controversy among Darwinian scientists, and of course, a great source of ammunition for those who disagree with Darwinism, the Creationists. It also provides much critical material for those scientists who accept evolution, but feel Darwinism, with its gradualism and reliance on chance is very incomplete. Darwin did not know how inheritance worked. He did not know that "successive variations" were due to chance mutations. The Austrian monk Gregor Mendel's studies on plant genetics, started in 1856, and published in 1867, was not discovered in its obscure journal and did not appear in general knowledge for almost four decades (around 1900) after Darwin offered his theory in *Origin of Species*, first published in 1859. "Some intermediate forms, such as whales and snakes with legs, have been discovered … The slow changes that Darwin's theory of gradualism seems to require are not generally observed. One species may appear to be descended from another, but the fossil record generally does not show how one evolved into another."(*The Evolutionists; the struggle for Darwin's soul*, Richard Morris, 2001). This must be further emphasized: "Darwin was acutely aware that the edifice he had constructed was entirely theoretical. His claim was, not that natural selection had actually been seen to create new species, but that in theory it *could* (sic) create them." (*Did Darwin Get It Right; Catholics and the Theory of Evolution*, George Sim Johnston, 1998).

In his book Behe uses the concept of "irreducible complexity" to make his point that the organization of life, represented by the plants and animals scientists study, is so complex, it could not have arrived by Darwinian gradual evolution, but requires "intelligent design." Behe defines irreducible complexity as "a single system composed of several well-matched, interacting parts that contribute to the basic function, wherein the removal of any one of the parts causes the system to effectively cease functioning." Behe's quote continues with this modifier: "an irreducibly complex system cannot be produced directly (that is, by continuously improving the initial function, which continues to work by the same mechanism) by slight successive modifications of a precursor system, because any precursor to an irreducibly complex system that is missing a part is by definition nonfunctional. An irreducibly complex system, if there is such a thing, would be a powerful challenge to Darwinian evolution." Pennock recognizes the dangers to the theory of evolution in this definition by quoting from Darwin: "If it could be demonstrated that any such complex organ existed, which could not possibly have been formed by numerous, successive, slight modifications, my theory would absolutely break down." Pennock and Behe both agree that irreducibly complex systems, if present, form a powerful argument against gradual Darwinism. Agreement between the authors ceases at this point. Pennock states: "Behe needs to be able to show that there are indeed irreducibly complex systems and that they are unreachable by Darwinian means."

Behe uses a number of very complex biologic systems to make his point. I'll review just one, the process of blood clotting, but suggest that the reader dig into Behe's book to appreciate the full import of his argument. Blood clotting is obviously vital to life and had to develop in the very beginning of the history of animals. Any wound must form a barrier to losing too much blood or the animal dies. Further, the barrier or clot must remain confined to the area of the wound. Uncontrolled clotting throughout the entire circulatory system obviously results in death also. When I was in medical school the clotting mechanism we learned covered nine or ten steps, but that was over 40 years ago. My count from Behe's up-to-date diagram suggests 17 steps currently, and that does not include the platelets and tissue factors that initiate the process. The mechanism is called a 'cascade', moving from one chemical reaction to another, converting inactive forms of chemicals to active forms, in interlocking steps, with feedback mechanisms that literally study each step and make sure each step be conducted properly. The word 'cascade' originally referred to a series of individual rapids on a river. To run a cascade without flipping the raft, the paddlers have to set up the raft to enter the first rapid in such a way that after the run through that rapid they are in proper position to enter the second rapid, run it properly, enter the third rapid in the right position, and so forth until the end of the cascade. The feedback mechanism in this analogy comes from the planning at the riverbank before the run and using one's memory to reconstruct the plan while traversing the cascade. Clotting is way more complex than my river analogy. To be certain the reader fully appreciates how complex consider the following description: a wound occurs with bleeding. Tissue chemicals A and B are released, stimulating little particles in the blood called platelets to act. They start chemical C in action which produces D. When enough D is present, chemical E appears, stops more D from appearing, and starts the production of F. When enough F is produced, G appears to stop F and start H. Up to this point I have described two feedback steps (in science they are called 'loops') in a group of 17, each step self-controlled. I don't think I need to carry this description further just envision 15 more steps like these. This is the system in humans and any other organisms where the blood is pumped through the body under pressure. We are at 17 of these clotting steps currently, and I anticipate the story is not yet over with several more steps to be found in future research. In simpler animals where the circulatory fluid is not under high pressure, clotting systems are much shorter in length, since the loss of fluid is much easier to stop under low pressure.

Pennock attempts to undo Behe the only way he can, by claiming that the mechanisms described by Behe are not irreducibly complex: he states that Behe has not demonstrated that all of the "components [of a system] are required for the function."... "The very complexity of these systems makes it extremely difficult to tell whether they are indeed irreducibly complex, and the data Behe gives are insufficient to support his claim for in no case have all the components of these systems been identified and studied....In a complex interacting causal system even if we know that knocking out any single factor results in the loss of a given function we cannot say that knocking out two, for instance, might not restore it by some other means." This, to my medical mind, is pure unadulterated poppycock. Blood clotting requires each and every part of the process to conduct itself properly and without danger to the animal and despite the fact not everything is known completely about the process, I can categorically make that statement. By definition blood clotting is irreducibly complex. Pennock forges on: "Behe tells us that he cannot imagine any way around the apparent irreducibility in his examples but even just upon reviewing his book other biologists have been able to suggest some specific biochemical pathways that *might* work." (My italics.) Might!! As effectively? If a hematologist specializing in blood clotting made such a statement at a medical meeting he would be laughed out of the hall.

Pennock quotes "Biologist Allen Orr" to support his point: "An irreducibly complex system can be built gradually by adding parts that, while initially just advantageous, become—because of later changes—essential. The logic is simple. Some part (A) initially does some job (and not very well, perhaps). Another part (B) later gets added on because it helps A. This new part isn't essential, it merely improves things. But later on A (or something else) may change in such a way that B now becomes indispensable. This process continues as further parts get folded into the system. And at the end of the day, many parts may be required." This is a typical Darwinian assumption, but it does not get around the objection that every part of such a system is necessary from the beginning. Experimenting with possibly 'advantageous' changes cannot result in the precise clotting that is needed in animals with a pumping heart. It would simply result in dead animals.

Kenneth Miller (*Finding Darwin's God*) attacks Behe's concept of irreducible complexity, and he also uses blood clotting as an example. Both men are scientists, Miller a professor of cell biology, Behe a professor of biochemistry. Both believe in God, and both believe that evolution occurred. There the similarity stops. Miller describes clotting in the lobster, a simple two-step system, using a different set of proteins than in human clotting. Miller then proceeds to attack Behe: "The construction of a two-component clotting system nicely demonstrates something else as well. It dashes any claim that there is only one, irreducibly complex, mechanism to clot blood." Miller misses Behe's point. Behe thinks all blood clotting mechanisms found in animals are irreducibly complex, and cannot have happened by chance. Miller, on the other hand, thinks that evolution can work out these advances by the Darwinian method of chance mutation and natural selection. After all, there is a pattern of development of body styles that shows animals developing from simple structures to very complex ones.

Miller feels the biochemistry must have done the same. It can create, and must have created the simple and the most intricate of blood clotting mechanisms. He does admit, "Can we know for sure that this is how blood clotting, or any other biochemical system, evolved? The strict answer, of course, is that we cannot". Miller covers the evolution of biochemicals in his Chapter 5. Certainly if body styles follow a pattern of evolutionary development, then biochemicals should be expected to do the same, if the Darwin Theory is to be totally consistent. This concept is disputed by Michael Denton (*Evolution: A Theory In Crisis*, 1985) using studies of a very common biochemical, hemoglobin, the red-colored carrier of oxygen in the blood. The method he describes involves obtaining the sequences of amino acids in hemoglobin, and comparing those sequences in different "related animals" in the evolutionary scheme, determined by body type. "Thousands of different sequences have been compared in hundreds of different species. From comparing the protein's amino acid sequences ...it is impossible to arrange them in any sort of evolutionary series."

The dispute between Miller and Behe comes from their individual theology. Miller describes his belief that God set the whole mechanism running at Creation, and evolution thereafter takes care of itself and can use chance, as in Darwinism. Behe feels "intelligent design" is involved, and doesn't differentiate between a Creator/Creation that had the future planned, or that steps in from time to time to make adjustments. In the abstract both theologies sound reasonable. In evolution, pre-planned or with adjustments added, all animals have had to have the ability to stop a leak, or die. Whether it is an early, simple animal form, which has a low pressure circulation of fluid (not blood) moving around in a continuous space between tissues and organs, or a highly developed animal with a pumping heart driving blood at high pressure through arteries and veins, the problem for the clotting system is the same. Stop the leak locally, quickly and effectively. Don't clot the whole animal. This requires a precise regulation of the clotting mechanism: it demands layer upon layer of steps, with careful feedback required at each step, to be sure that just enough of each part is produced in the right amount and in the right order.

Darwin's Theory of Evolution does not provide a way of achieving this degree of complexity. As evolution is theorized to have happened, the process "works" by starting with random mutations, a series of passive events, which change the plant or animal only slightly and then "natural selection", the demands of nature, steps in to decide what change is good and what is bad. Darwin's theory assumes cumulative complexity, one little step at a time growing into an extremely complex system, as contrasted to 'irreducible complexity', a system which has to be tested by nature in its whole finished form, as anything less is unworkable. Behe makes a very effective point. How did evolution create blood clotting, which requires so many interdependent steps to work properly, by gradually adding a step here and a step there through chance mutations at random, while at the same time blood and hemoglobin were being invented by evolution? Primitive blood and primitive clotting had to develop simultaneously and then evolve into more complex blood with more complex clotting. That seems highly improbable through the process of chance mutations, especially because of the requirement of precise regulation of the steps. And when the issue of a pumping heart with a high blood pressure is thrown into the mix, how did evolution manage the arrival of the pumping heart and complex blood clotting at the same time? Perhaps God built chance into the process, but that does not seem logical to me.

Michael Shermer, the skeptical author mentioned earlier in this chapter, also quotes from Pennock's book to attack Behe's definition of irreducible complexity: "Philosopher Robert Pennock has pointed out that [the] last phase [of the definition] employs a classic fallacy of bait-and-switch logic— reasoning from something that is true "by definition" to something that is proved through empirical evidence." (*How We Believe*). This is nit-picking semantics. Behe may not have expressed his definition to fit the niceties of the logic of philosophers, but when one looks at some of his examples from the biochemistry of various animal processes, they are irreducibly complex, considering the evidence of how precisely controlled they are to produce the effect desired. Further, there does not appear to be a way that these processes could develop stepwise because the steps are so interdependent. Neither Pennock nor Shermer are scientists, but they illustrate that the findings of science are in dispute not only among scientists and but also among those who try to interpret scientific findings. (See Chapter 4, where the same point is made, comparing the theories of Gould and Morris, two world-renowned evolutionary scientists.)

Before proceeding, this is a good point to stop and review the lineup of the various combatants in this war, as it is possibly getting confusing. There are several groups of scientists. First are those scientists who defend Darwin against all possible alterations of the original proposal of accidental mutations and very gradual change from one species to the next. A second group of scientists, having noted that evolution seems to move forward by fits and starts, argue within Darwinism that there is an alternative. They propose that evolution pauses without change for long periods and then suddenly jumps forward (punctuated equilibrium, discussed in Chapter 4). A third group of scientists, looking at the precise design of this universe and the extraordinary development of humans and especially our intellect and consciousness, discuss deeper meanings and even the actions of God. Individuals in this latter group feel that something is lacking in the Darwin theory and indirectly infer God (Davies) or directly invoke God, Polkinghorne and Schroeder as examples.

Other rivals to the Darwin scientists are those scientists and philosophers who also feel that Darwin's theory is incomplete and lacks a very important element. They point to the unexplained appearance of life and the complexity of living organisms, and offer the proposition that an input of extra information is required for life to appear and evolution to have occurred, information that could not have been developed by chance through the accidental mechanism described by Darwinism. These proponents of "intelligent design" are represented in this chapter by Dembski and Behe. The intelligent design group is attacked by evolutionists, who strongly defending Darwin, consider them 'creationists' in disguise, sort of sneaking in the back door. In a sense the Darwin defenders are correct. 'Intelligent design' implies a supernatural source for the information required, raising the issue of God, the Creator. However, the intelligent design group believes evolution occurred. They especially accept the scientific findings of geology and cosmology. They do not form a part of the final group of protagonists, the young earth and old earth creationists who believe God created all the plant and animal species, evolution not required, and thereby attack and deny much of the scientific findings most of the world accepts. This summary should provide a good outline of the various groups in the fight.

Emotion creates so many different groups, and this is why: In any debate no one should presume to tell you what to think. That person is a fool to try. And a greater fool is the recipient who accepts another's conclusions without applying his own input. How to think, how to reach valid conclusions, that is, valid for one's self requires thinking, judgments, logic and canceling out emotion. And it is that last item, emotion, which is so difficult to remove when dealing with religion, religious beliefs, and with beliefs about God.

Religion, with its instinctual appeal to the spiritual, is primarily thought and belief at an intense emotional level, and this tends to override logical thought, especially in sacred philosophy when there is a competition of ideas.

Science, on the other hand, has also assumed the emotional trappings of a religion. Many scientists are so consumed with the principle of Reductionism, because it has worked so well, they seem to have an unreasoned optimism that given enough experimental time, almost anything can be explained, again beyond the bounds of reason. The reason scientists are so wed to the principle of Reductionism is their belief in the philosophy of Materialism. The basic belief of "so-called 'scientific materialism' is that nothing exists except matter, and that everything in the world must therefore be the result of the strict mathematical laws of physics and blind chance." (Modern Physics and Ancient Faith, Stephen M. Barr, 2003). Remember that matter is made up of enormous amounts of energy, as in Einstein's famous $E=mc^2$ formula and shown in atomic bomb explosions. In the scientists' minds this means everything in the universe is covered by this philosophic belief system. They feel they can explain everything going backward or forward in time by learning and applying the laws of physics, and allowing for blind chance to play a role.

What is closer to the truth is the fact that scientific findings, which contain the hope to find an explanation of everything, actually support many of the Creationist beliefs. It is the scientists, blinded by their innate optimism, (really an emotion) who fail to recognize the futility of their quest to explain everything and thereby remove any need for God. The "God of the Gaps" may in fact be the God of Reality. There are aspects of reality that appear to require God, as this book will show. But science has become another form of religion to many scientists. That there is a high prevalence of atheism among scientists is well known. From 1913 to 1998 surveys have shown that a steady 40 percent believe in God. In 1913, 50 percent believed in some form of afterlife, and that is now reduced to 40 percent. However, those figures are for all scientists. When the survey is confined to members of the National Academy of Sciences, our leading research scientists, over 90 percent are atheists or agnostics. To explain the 40 percent overall 'believer' total, "evidence suggests that there is more personal religion among physicians, engineers and members of other technological occupations that involve applied science."(Scientists and Religion in America, Larson & Witham, Scientific American, September 1999). As a physician who dealt for 40 years with the magical properties of the human body, I can readily understand the religious attitude of medical doctors. To see a baby born is to see a miracle, and miracles fall in the realm of religion. Atheists and atheistic scientists would have us believe that inanimate molecules somehow or other banded together and figured out how to create life totally by accident! As Chapter 3 will show, mathematically there is no chance.

Over the next century I anticipate that many researchers in evolution and cosmology, in their personal lives will again recognize a need for God and accept intelligent design. The design of life is so surprisingly complex and convoluted there is the likelihood that everything about life cannot be explained, even eventually, by scientists picking it apart bit by bit. Reductionism, which has worked so well so far will die hard, but it will die. Many scientists do not currently anticipate this outcome, but from the small number of scientists now criticizing the dogma of Darwin, I expect to see a larger and larger group appear as the complexity of the evidence grows. Science and Religion will grow to work together. How might this happen? Pauline Rudd, Ph. D., a Research Fellow in the Glycobiology Institute of the University of Oxford provides an answer that should appeal to all of us who profess to be religious: "So how, at a professional level, are scientists and theologians to address the problem of communicating directly with each other on a day by day basis? If we are afraid of unresolvable conflict we can avoid the risk by trying to compartmentalise our personal scientific and spiritual lives so that they never meet. At the next level up, the scientific and religious communities can do the same thing. That way everyone is safe in their own world, we ring fence our disciplines with unintelligible jargon and no one gets hurt, but is this really the way things should be? What of our common search to understand God and His relationship with Man today? I believe we are being challenged as never before to develop and expand our religious doctrines to accommodate the rapidly growing database of human knowledge and understanding. If the existing religions are going to be sufficient for our needs in the next millennium, I suggest that one of the major tasks for all who profess a religious commitment will be to reflect on the current knowledge emerging from their particular discipline [in the sciences] and to relate this to the innermost needs of the human spirit.

For science and religion are just two of the starting points from which we can begin to describe different facets of the world and of ourselves – and both involve penetrating the darkness of unknowing, pushing back barriers of ignorance and dispelling misinformation to enlighten our understanding of the Universe and our place within it. And once we allow light from each to enlighten the other our interpretation of earlier insights will inevitably be changed, transfigured by the blaze from our new vision." (Dr. Pauline Rudd, University Research Lecturer and Senior Research Fellow University of Oxford, website Meta-List.org, Metaviews 076, 2000). But until that vision of the future happens, religious people should freely employ the findings of science without prejudice, not dissuaded by the atheism of the discoverers, as suggested by Pope John Paul II. We will now look at the scientific facts that simply shout that God must exist.

Chapter 2: Our Designer Universe Fine-Tuned for Life

Since I cannot anticipate the degree of knowledge each reader has about the sciences of astronomy and cosmology, I must now give a description of the workings of the universe we have appeared in. This will not be a complicated analysis, because I am not an expert in either discipline, but I have been an avid reader of the books they have produced for the lay person. This description must be understood first in order for the reader to follow my reasoning for presenting this chapter with the title it has. Although the physical laws that underlie the mechanics of the universe are not fully understood, an amazingly accurate set of theories has been discovered in the 20th Century, has been confirmed by experimentation, and is called The Standard Model, in cosmology the basic Big Bang Theory, and in quantum mechanics, the theories of the four forces (*The Whole Shebang*, Timothy Ferris, 1997).

According to the Model, the universe began approximately 15 billion years ago in a massive explosion from a singularity, a mathematical concept of a point of infinite curvature of space with infinite density, infinite temperature, and infinite pressure, where the equations of general relativity break down. Both space and time were created at this instant. Let me repeat that: both space *and* time were created. The cosmologists claim they can take their theories back to an instant equal to 10^{-43} of the first second of time, the point at which the equations break down. That is a fraction of a second with a one placed over 10 followed by 42 zeros! The early universe then "inflated" at a rate of 10^{50} (10 followed by 49 zeros) faster than the current expansion rate, resuming the present rate at a time indicated by the fraction 10^{-30} of the first second. The universe has continued expanding at this slower rate ever since. All of that activity in such minute fractions of the first second is estimated from formulas developed by theoretical mathematicians based on astronomical observations and the characteristics of high-energy particles (*Coming of Age in the Milky Way*, Timothy Ferris, 1988). I promise not to use much of the complicated stuff. I presented it to show you just how small and how large are some of the measurements the scientists swear by.

And swear by it they do. In the preface to his book, *The Inflationary Universe*, Alan H. Guth (1997), a theoretical particle physicist who is a professor at the Massachusetts Institute of Technology, describes the standard big bang theory in glowing terms: "The traditional big bang theory has become widely accepted because, as far as we can tell, it gives an accurate picture of how our universe has evolved. The description has been tested, either directly or indirectly, for times as early as one second after the beginning up to the present... Despite its name, the big bang theory is not really a theory of a bang at all. It is really only a theory of the *aftermath* of a bang. The equations of the theory describe how the primeval fireball expanded and cooled and congealed to form galaxies, stars, and planets, all of which is a tremendous accomplishment. But the standard big bang theory says nothing about what banged, why it banged, or what happened before it banged". Deeper in the book he adds: "At this time there is no reliable experiment that is inconsistent with the standard model." The standard model comes from a theoretical mathematical melding together of astronomical observation, starting scientifically in ancient Egypt, Einstein's concepts of relativity, and the very recent discoveries of particle physics during the 20th Century. Physicists conduct experiments which blast matter apart at very high energies, in the so-called atom smashers, really particle accelerators of various designs, thereby revealing the properties of the underlying components that are blasted apart.

The first moments of the big bang created a very high temperature energy soup, called plasma, with high-energy particles that coalesced into the atomic particles that most of us learned in school, the protons, positrons and electrons. The universe came equipped with four forces or "interactions": gravity which acts as an attraction between all bodies in space; electromagnetism which has to do with the attraction and repulsion of charged particles; the strong force which holds nuclei of atoms together; and the weak force which allows the decay of particles from some atoms (as in radiation from uranium). These forces control all the interactions occurring between particles, creating what we call matter from energy. Matter and energy are two forms of the same thing, various particles of energy. "The strong force must be balanced with the weak force to a degree of one part in 10^{60}. If the strong force were any weaker, atomic nuclei could not hold together and only hydrogen would exist. If the strong force were only slightly stronger, hydrogen would be an unusual element, the sun would not exist, water would not exist and the heavier elements necessary for life would not be available. If gravity's force were changed by only one part in 10^{40}, stars like our sun would not exist but only stars either too hot or cold to support life." (*A Case Against Accident and Self-Organization*, Dean L. Overman, 1997).

At first, tiny particles of matter and anti-matter were created, (protons and antiprotons) both of which theoretically should have been formed in equal amounts and destroyed or annihilated each other. Due to a radiation decay of a certain energy particle some of the matter particles survived the annihilation process, resulting in a slight majority of matter particles created. It is from those particles (protons) and other particles that all the elements appeared, creating all the matter of the universe. "In the balance between the electromagnetic force and the force of gravity, the number of electrons must be meticulously balanced to an accuracy of one part in 10^{37} with the number of protons. Without such a precise balance stars and planets would not have formed (Overman). Science can explain *how* this happened but not *why*. The scientists have no explanation why that particular particle decay decided to occur or why everything was arranged with such precision. Scientists simply shrug it off: as Alan Guth commented within his discussion of this type of process: "nature actually behaves in this peculiar way."

By three minutes and 40 seconds after the Big Bang the elementary particles had joined forming a universe mixed with just three elements, 23 percent helium and 75 percent hydrogen nuclei, and a tiny amount of lithium, about one part in a billion, accounting for 98 percent of all the matter in the universe (Guth & Ferris). At this point the universe was a mass of boiling plasma made up of the elements just listed, with some areas slightly more dense, from which stars then formed about one-half billion to one billion years after the Big Bang (Associated Press & CNN.com, reports on NASA press conference, 1/8/02). Because the space created in the expansion was not entirely smooth, in those regions the then existing elements were clumped together, creating mass and attendant gravity, gathering in more and more material until the intense gravitational pressure fused the original elements; the fusion reactions ignited the stars to give off light and heat. The stars then clumped together into galaxies. The elements (all heavier) other than helium, hydrogen and lithium were manufactured under tremendous gravitational pressure and heat within the heavier stars, creating all the other natural 89 elements, many of which are necessary for life, as we know it. The heavier elements spread throughout the universe when many of those stars exploded. The exploding stars are called supernovas and are a mixed blessing: With the explosions the 89 elements spread all over the universe; but the explosions released enormous amounts of extremely dangerous radiation, and if a star blew apart near the earth, all life could be wiped out.

Galaxies formed around very active centers and rotate around those centers, with a black hole as the "engine" of each one. The centers are the birthplace of new stars, the explosion of stars, and are an environment of intense radiation. Everything in the universe is in motion, the underlying reason for "relativity" as I will explain later; the galaxies are slowly spinning around their centers as they move through space. They are either elliptical in shape and appear as a clump of stars, or spiral with arms like a pinwheel. Our sun is out on the second spiral arm of our home galaxy (the Milky Way we see in the night sky), far away from all the dangerous activity near the center. Our galaxy is composed of hundreds of billions of stars. It is 100,000 light years across. Distance in the immensity of the universe is measured in light years; obviously the distance traveled by light in one year, at 186,000 miles a second, is 5,878,000,000,000 miles. The nearest galaxy to us is Andromeda, 2 million light years distant, and much larger than we are. That means the closest galaxy, besides our own, that we can study, is offering us information that is obviously two million years old. The nearest star to us in our galaxy offers information four years old! We are part of a small galaxy group, about 20. That is just as well. Galaxies can pass through each other creating tremendous interactions that could easily disrupt life on Earth if it happened here. The Milky Way and Andromeda are approaching each other, but not to worry. They will meet in two billion years!

Galaxies are grouped through space, in large and small groupings. There is a "great wall" of galaxies in one region and other walls in other areas. Generally they are placed as if on the surface of bubbles in space. Astronomers are currently mapping the universe sector by sector to understand the overall large structure and to survey the billions of galaxies out there. Considering the number of galaxies observed so far by the Hubble telescope, and the number of stars in the average galaxy, the number of stars in the universe is almost too numerous to comprehend. As the universe continues to expand new galaxies are formed, adding to the number of stars. Until the past decade the expansion rate of the universe was thought to be slowing slightly, due to the attraction of gravity between clumps of matter, both matter emitting light and matter that emitted no light, or "dark matter".

One theory, previously entertained, was that if there was enough matter present in the universe, expansion would eventually stop due to the pull of gravity by the matter the universe would then contract into a Big Crunch, a singularity like the one that gave us the Big Bang. The calculations about Big Bang/Big Crunch involved apparent mass and gravity, and since the current studies are based on mass we can see, mass that puts out light, the hunt was on to find dark matter, plenty of which exists. But was it enough to create the Crunch? The guess was probably not, but not to worry either way: if a big crunch were to happen the estimate is about 100 billion years in the future; and closer to home we can look forward to a much 'earlier' event: when our sun dies in five billion years, it will expand destroying the solar system, or our galaxy meeting Andromeda in two billion years may do the job. And we think the current two millennia in our calendar represent a long time.

The Big Crunch theory appeared to die in 1998. Two independent studies appeared which described the expansion of the universe as speeding up due to a theorized mysterious force (called quintessence) counteracting the effects of gravity. (*The Runaway Universe*, Donald W. Goldsmith, 2000). The cosmologists used exploding stars, supernovas, in distant galaxies to measure distances and the speed of expansion. Supernovas put out consistent amounts of light; since the dimmer they appear, the further away they are, distances could be fairly accurately estimated. The two studies verified each other closely, which rapidly led cosmologists to accept the results (Harvard-Smithsonian Center for Astrophysics press release No. 01-13, 12/10/01). The acceleration appears to have begun in the past five or six billion years, as if the expansion of space from the time of the Big Bang created a new force, referred to as "dark energy", since it cannot be seen. This dark energy is thought to account for about two-thirds of the mass of the universe ("The Universe Might Last Forever, Astronomers Say, but Life Might Not", *N.Y. Times*, Dennis Overbye, 1/1/02). Dark matter appears to make up 30 percent of the universe, which means somewhat less than five percent represents all visible or ordinary matter, including all living matter (*Washington Post* online, 4/30/01). Other scientific papers since 1998 have continued to confirm that the universe will continue to expand by demonstrating that the geometry of space is "flat", an underlying requirement for continuing expansion (*Nature* 404, 955-959, 27 April 2000), and for the appearance of life (*Faster Than The Speed Of Light*, Joao Magueijo, 2003). Further, there is not enough dark matter to provide the gravity to counteract the expansion (spacedaily.com, reporting on a paper by Drs. Heavens and Verde of Rutgers and Princeton, 12/17/01).

Now that I have described our enormous home, which is 12 to 15 billion years old, as estimated by the standard model of the big bang theory, let us look at the evidence the scientists have produced to validate the theory and its estimate of the age of the universe. In 1948 George Gamow and colleagues predicted the big bang would leave behind, even this many years later, some residual radiation; and he estimated the temperature of that radiation to be about five degrees Kelvin. Kelvin degrees are centigrade degrees above absolute zero; absolute zero, the lowest temperature which can be reached, is minus 273 degrees centigrade or 460 degrees Fahrenheit below the freezing point of water (32 degrees). At the Bell Laboratories in 1965, Penzias and Wilson, working to develop a radio telescope, stumbled into a background sizzle they did not expect. Its temperature was three to three and a half degrees. Working with other scientists, they soon realized they had found Gamow's predicted radiation, and won a Noble Prize for their serendipity. To further nail down this confirmatory finding of the big bang theory, in 1989 the Cosmic Background Explorer satellite (COBE) was launched by NASA. The results in 1992 were spectacular: the temperature was 2.726 degrees, the plot of the wavelength of the cosmic microwave background fit the predicted curve almost exactly, and the structure of the background radiation fit, again almost exactly, the predicted slight irregularities in space that allowed matter to clump and form stars (*The Whole Shebang*, Timothy Ferris, 1997). And finally, the data fit the predictions of Guth's inflation theory. "The agreement was gorgeous! To a theoretical physicist, there is no greater joy than to see this curious activity we call calculation—the depositing of ink on paper, followed by throwing away the paper and depositing new ink on more paper—can actually tell us something about reality!" is Guth's enthusiastic comment.

COBE was the first study of its kind and upon further study it was recognized that the results were very close to predictions but not close enough to fully validate the Big Bang Theory. It was followed by a series of other studies, which have refined and further confirmed the observations each using slightly different techniques, and reported between 2000 and 2001. "The agreement among various groups and approaches 'is both stunning and humbling,' [commented] astrophysicist Michael Turner of the University of Chicago," after reviewing the results. He had predicted the results using a different method several years before. Paul Richards of the University of California was a leader of one study (MAXIMA) and characterized his results by stating, "This study provides strong confirmation that, overall, we're using the right model to describe the universe." (*Washington Post* online, by Kathy Sawyer, 4/30/01, covering the American Physical Society meeting, 3/30/01, where MAXIMA, BOOMERANG, and DASI results were reported and discussed). A fourth study was from Carnegie Mellon University (see their press release 5/24/01 and *Science* issue of the same date). Their team was able to demonstrate the "acoustic oscillations" found in the cosmic microwave background also appear in the distribution of matter in the universe. "Not only do these results provide support for the Hot Big Bang Inflationary Model, but they also show we understand the physics of the early universe. The physics can take us forward in time, or backward in time," commented the lead author, Christopher Miller. In 2002 the Cosmic Background Imager (CBI) added even further proof by providing a very refined picture of the acoustic oscillations, which fits the predicted acoustical pattern predicted by the inflationary theory. These sound waves date from 300,000 years after the Big Bang, representing ripples in the then boiling plasma, and although not boiling now can still be measured in the cold universe. Guth's comment on this study mirrored his earlier ones: " 'The CBI data allows us to have a completely new test' of cosmologic models—and the models are passing the test." (*Science Magazine*, Vol. 296, No. 5573, pp. 1588-89, 5/31/02).

In December 2002 further confirmation of Big Bang Theory model came from ongoing studies of the cosmic microwave background (CMB) with DASI (Degree Angular Scale Interferometer), a radio telescope array at the South Pole. The cosmologic mathematical models predict that light waves coming from the CMB should be polarized, that is, organized in one direction, just like polarized sun glasses. This is exactly what the DASI study found: "A measurement of the polarization is a critical test of the theory…The polarization is detected with high confidence, and its level and spatial distribution are in excellent agreement with the predictions of the standard theory." (*Nature* 420, 772-787 (2002), 19/26 December 2002, and also *Nature* 420, 763-771 (2002), 19/26 December 2002, articles by Erik Leitch, John Kovac et al). Leitch proudly noted: "If the light hadn't been polarized, that would mean that we would have to throw out our whole model of how we understand the physics of the early universe." In February 2003 NASA announced the results of further more refined studies of the CMB by WMAP (Wilkinson Microwave Anisotrophy Probe) in an orbit, perpendicular to the earth's orbit, one million miles away from earth toward the sun. Its findings set the age of the universe at approximately 13.7 billion years, plus or minus 200 million years; it showed further evidence that the universe is "flat" and will expand forever. Once again the observations "all fit," and "have really tightened the results," according to the researchers ("Cosmos brought into focus," Eric Berger, *Houston Chronicle*, 2/12/03). The CMB studies are not complete, are therefore ongoing and are anticipated to continue to confirm the mathematical predictions.

The reader might conclude that such enthusiastic statements from leaders of the studies are self-serving scientific spin. Not so. The results were predicted years ago from mathematical computations and are truly an astounding demonstration of the powers of the human mind in exploring the mechanics of the universe. *Scientific American* (Vol. 265:2, August 2001) excitedly commented on the importance of the studies under a headline: "The Peak of Success. The big bang theory clicks together better than ever." And offered the following: the Big Bang theory is supported by four pillars: 1) the cosmic microwave background radiation (now proven); 2) the abundance of lighter elements from which the heavier elements were made in the early very hot universe (now proven by particle physicists); 3) the outward velocity of distant galaxies, shown to be increasing (now proven); and 4) the large-scale structure of the universe shows the microwave background fluctuations are present in the arrangement of the galaxies (now proven by the Carnegie Mellon study).

The amazing success of all the scientific work in this field during this century is due to Reductionism, breaking up mechanisms into component parts, and understanding each part. The scientific study of the Big Bang is by no means complete. How gravity works is understood, but not why or how it exists (Schroeder, *The Science of God*). The predicted particle, the graviton that transmits the force of gravity has not been found. Much of Quantum Theory is poorly understood. For example, a quantum (definition: a particular bundle of energy) acts as either a particle or an energy wave, depending on the method of measurement, but never both at the same time. This means that an experimenting scientist actually affects the way a quantum acts, depending upon the experimental method he uses!! Although the current mathematical formulas accurately predict the outcome of quantum experiments, it is because the math computes an average of the actions of many quanta. One quantum, the predicted Higgs boson and the force fields it controls has not yet been found, because the "atom smashers", to use an old term, are not yet powerful enough in the energy produced to break the Higgs out of the matter smashed.

A major problem is that the mathematics of Einstein's special and general theories of relativity beautifully describe the large-scale characteristics of the universe but are totally inconsistent with the mathematics of quantum theory, which accurately describe the very tiny bits of energy called quanta. Hopefully in the future, a description of a quantum gravity theory, probably utilizing a developing mathematical concept of as yet undemonstrated particles called "super strings", and combined with the Higgs particle characteristics which are yet to be analyzed, will help complete the mathematics of a "Grand Unified Theory", a mathematical construct that would fully explain the total workings of the Big Bang (*The Elegant Universe*, Brian Greene, 1999).

Another very complex mathematical approach to a Grand Unified Theory has been recently developed and combines theories of relativity and quantum theory into "loop quantum gravity" (LQG). This theory proposes that the reality of our universe "is built of loops that interact and combine to form spin networks." It appears to predict that spin network "architecture gives rise to space and matter." ("Throwing Einstein for a Loop"), Amanda Gefter, *Scientific American*, Vol.: 287, No. 6, December 2002; also discussed in *Science & Spirit*, Vol.:13 Issue 6, November December 2002 describing the work of Fotini Markopoulou-Kalamara, Ph. D.) Either theory (string or LQG) may eventually turn out to be the best explanation of the workings of the Big Bang, but these formulas won't explain the *why* of the Big Bang.

Why did it happen? Why are we here? In most instances a 'whole' provides more than the sum of its parts, and what Reductionism supplies is an explanation of how the big bang worked, but not why. The design is described, but what is not explained is why that design especially allowed for us? We are here because the design of the universe led to our appearance. What follows is a list of some of the design requirements to set up the universe we observe; some of the manufacturing tolerances required by the observed physics of the standard model of the big bang theory. Then we will look at the fine-tuning that allowed for the development of life.

"How Special was the Big Bang" is the title of a section in Roger Penrose's book, *The Emperor's New Mind* (1989). He is a professor of Mathematics at Oxford, and is considered one of the world's greatest theoretical mathematicians. He considers how precise the initial conditions forming the big bang had to be to create our universe, this universe, the one we observe and study. As an important aside, what this implies is that an enormous number of other universes could have appeared from different initial conditions, and in the minds of some scientists might have appeared and exist *somewhere*. For this particular universe to exist the initial conditions had to be precise to one part in $10^{(10)^{123}}$! If you tried to count out this number, you could not in your lifetime, or the lifetime of the universe, which is 10^{18} old, measured in seconds! In 1979 "Penrose calculated that the probability of [this] universe occurring by chance was one in 10^{300}." (Overman). In this latter computation the initial conditions at the Big Bang are not included or assumed, thereby tremendously increasing the odds.

It is when the various conditions are studied individually that the reasons for the enormity of Penrose's calculation become apparent. The initial energy had to be accurate within one part in 10^{120}. The expansion rate had to be within one part in 10^{55} to overcome the intense gravity, or the universe would have immediately collapsed (*Universes*, John Leslie, 1989). On the other hand, once the "inflation" period within the first second had occurred, the continuing expansion rate had to be tuned to within one part in 10^{14} to allow the formation of stars (Guth), that is, a "flat" universe, the only kind that allows life to appear (Majueijo). In Einstein's equations of General Relativity there is a function called the 'Cosmologic Constant' representing a counteracting force to gravity, adjusted to zero by one part in 10^{120}. There had to be the conservation of one proton in ten billion during the annihilation process with anti-protons to allow matter to appear in the universe, as previously described. And since all matter particles at this level decay, and gradually disappear, it is vital to our existence (no pun intended) that the half-life of the proton is 10^{32} years long. Matter won't disappear any time soon. This list is much larger, but I'll stop here. I previously promised as few big numbers as possible and here I am breaking my word, but the point has to be made. The entire process is extremely delicate in all of its intricate interactions.

The adjustments among the four forces that control the processes are just as spectacular. If either the nuclear weak force (working within atoms) or gravity varied in either of their strengths by as little as one part in 10^{100}, the universe could not have continued expanding. Electromagnetism, which allows molecules to form, "should have overwhelmed gravity when the universe was about a second old", but this effect was stopped by the "precisely equal charges" between protons and electrons in the universe, allowing gravity to create the universe with the current distribution of matter at the necessary rate of expansion (David Levy, *Parade Magazine*, 6/21/98).

If the nuclear strong force (acting on the nucleus of the atom) were two percent stronger, no atoms would have formed. If it were one percent weaker carbon would not have formed. Our sun could not have formed if either gravity or electromagnetism varied from their strength by one part in 10^{40}. (Leslie) So as not to pound the subject of fine-tuning to death, I'll simply state there are over 20 major parameters (physical characteristics) that made our universe in the form it has, which is a form that allows life. George Sim Johnston (*Did Darwin Get it Right?*, 1998) refers to fine-tuning as "the specificity of the formation of the universe", and asks his readers to imagine "a wall with thousands of dials; each must be at exactly the right setting— within a tolerance of millionths—in order for carbon-based life to eventually appear in a suburb of the Milky Way." A bit of an overstatement, but adding up major and minor components, roughly 100 different fine-tuned characteristics is closer to the true total to create a universe that allowed a planet like the earth to appear, and then permitted life to begin. (William Dembski, *Intelligent Design*, 1999).

Some of the other fine-tuning factors included in that total of about 100 are as follows: we are here precisely because our sun is the kind of star it is. Stars come in many varieties and sizes, burn for longer or shorter periods, and there are unstable ones which can explode. Ours is medium-sized; it is stable, should burn about ten billion years, and is currently five billion years old. It has burned long enough to allow conditions that permit life to appear on earth. If the sun were larger it would have burned faster and could have been finishing its life by now, and we might never have arrived. The sun sits in a perfect spot for us, in a quiet position not too close to other stars, half way out the disc of our galaxy on the second spiral arm, away from the hostile center of the galaxy, where new stars are formed, stars explode and radiation is rampant. Half the stars in our galaxy are in pairs or trios, not a healthy climate for planets. The Earth's orbit, whose distance from the sun dictates the degree of heat we receive, is out of place when compared to the other planets. Each planet is approximately twice the distance from the sun than the next closer planet: "in millions of kilometers, the distances from the sun are Mercury 58, Venus 110, Earth 150, Mars 230, asteroids 440, Jupiter 780, Saturn 1430 and Uranus 2880." (Schroeder, *The Science of God)*. Earth should be where Mars is, and we sure would be a cold place. The Earth's orbit is almost circular, varying by only three percent. "Were it as elliptical as the orbit of Mars, we would alternate between baking when closer to the Sun and freezing when distant". (Schroeder).

Not only is the amount of heat received from the Sun remarkably constant year 'round, "the temperature of the Earth's surface has remained remarkably constant over [its history], a fact [based on] the presence of liquid water" for most of that history and attested to by the presence of water-based life on Earth for over three and a half billion years of its four and a half billion year existence (Davies, *The Cosmic Blueprint*, 1988). The heat from the sun has increased about 30 percent since the Earth was formed, but the carbon dioxide in the atmosphere, which has always provided a necessary greenhouse effect to hold heat on Earth's surface, declined as living plants appeared, using the carbon dioxide to manufacture themselves; the decline in carbon dioxide, allowed more heat to escape, "matching rather precisely the increasing output of heat from the Sun."

Another important mechanism for controlling carbon dioxide levels is the so-called "carbon dioxide-rock cycle," which works in the following way. The earth is specially constructed of a hot liquid core of molten iron and nickel, kept hot by radioactive decay of uranium and other radioactive metals. The thin low-density outer crust of the earth floats and moves over the core as a series of plates. These plates rub against each other, and actually dive under each other, creating earthquakes and volcanic activity. Warming of atmospheric temperature increases the weathering of rocks such as granite, made of calcium silicate. The calcium of this chemical combines with carbon dioxide to form limestone, which is carried into the oceans by rain. The removal of carbon dioxide from the atmosphere by weathering tends to lower the earth's temperature. The limestone is deposited on the ocean floor and eventually is carried deep under a continental plate, where it is decomposed by heat and carbon dioxide is released by volcanic activity into the atmosphere, thereby raising the earth's temperature (*Rare Earth*, Ward and Brownlee, 2000).

The carbon dioxide-rock cycle acts as a global thermostat as do plants (the first life here), which breath in carbon dioxide and breath out oxygen; the early plant life provided the oxygen animals breathe and in the upper atmosphere created ozone which protects the Earth from ultra-violet rays. With this protection, living forms could leave the oceans and start to live on land (Davies). The Earth is also very fortunate in all the water it has. The first life forms could develop safely deep in the oceans, protected from ultra-violet rays. Part of this water came trapped in the material that coalesced to form the Earth. There is much frozen water in space: the comets we see, Hale-Bopp for example, are large dirty snowballs and recent research shows that small comets hitting the upper atmosphere act to replenish the oceans. The Earth's average temperature maintains most of the water in liquid form, and during the earth's history the temperature never got hot enough to evaporate water off into space. That is what must have happened on Mars, which has small ice caps, but has evidence on its surface of great water flows in the past.

Another protection, that most people are unaware of, is the magnetic field around the Earth, which deflects the sun's lethal radiation. The field comes from movements of the molten iron-nickel core of the Earth. The earth has to have enough radioactive elements to supply the heat to keep that core molten and moving, the movement actually being convection currents due to heat differentials. Since those heavier radioactive elements formed late after the birth of the universe, a living planet like ours requires a sun of about the age it is, and also of high metal content, similar to the metal content in the earth. Stars with high metal content are the only ones that have been discovered to have planets orbiting around them (*Rare Earth*). The magnetic field has another beneficial effect: it helps, along with gravity, to hold the atmosphere around the Earth. The sun's radiation is "ionizing", that is, it puts electrical charges on the various gas particles, including water vapor, high in the atmosphere. Electrical charges are themselves magnetic, and it is their attraction to the magnetic field, which holds them close to us. These and other conditions sustaining and protecting life were described in an article by Guillermo Gonzalez, a research astronomer at the University of Washington, (*Wall Street Journal*, 7/16/97): "the presence of a large moon to stabilize a planet's axial tilt and slow down its rotation rate; the absence of novae and supernovae [exploding stars]; and the presence of a "gas giant"—a Jupiter-like planet— (using its enormous gravity) to regulate the influx of comets." Jupiter has kept asteroids, comets and meteorites from striking the earth as often as might have happened. Gonzalez comments that he "could list well over two dozen other astronomical constraints" [to sustain life] and points out: "there exists only a small 'window of opportunity'—both in space and time—for life to form in the Milky Way."

By now you are realizing how very special our planet is. In fact that very 'specialness' has lead two scientists to write the book, *Rare Earth, Why Complex Life Is Uncommon in the Universe*. The authors are Peter D. Ward, Professor of Geologic Sciences, and Donald Brownlee, Professor of Astronomy, both at the University of Washington in Seattle. They contend the many characteristics of the earth that allow life, are so precise and so carefully organized, that a planet like the earth must be extremely rare in the universe, if another one like it even exists at all!! "If some god-like being could be given the opportunity to plan a sequence of events with the express goal of duplicating our 'Garden of Eden', that power would face a formidable task. With the best intentions, but limited by natural laws and materials, it is unlikely that Earth could ever be truly replicated". "The physical events that led to the formation and evolution of the physical Earth required an intricate set of nearly irreproducible circumstances." As true scientists, not wishing to mention God, they consider the construction of the "core, mantle and crust, could have come about only through the *fortuitous* assemblage of the correct elemental building blocks". (My italics). And they used the word fortuitous in another quote: "The existence of larger and more complex life occurred only late in Earth history, ...and the evolution and survival of this more fragile variant of terrestrial life seem to require a highly fortuitous set of circumstances that could not been expected to exist commonly on other planets".

Obviously, for life to appear at all it must appear on planets circling (orbiting) stars. In recent years over 100 planets have been discovered orbiting stars other than our sun. To offer the best odds for life to start, it appears our universe was fine-tuned from the beginning to start planet formation very shortly after the Big Bang. In fact, an ancient planet has been discovered that apparently formed about one billion years after the Big Bang, that is, 12.7 billion years ago. ("Methuselah of planets found," *Washington Post*, Kathy Sawyer, 7/11/03; *Science,* Vol. 301, Number 5630, 11 July 2003, 193-196). With over 100 billion galaxies in the universe and roughly 100 billion stars in each galaxy the number of planets in the universe must be truly enormous.

Life can appear only in very special circumstances, and only in environments that are very protected. Some of these protections of life were described by David Levy, the discoverer of 21 comets, including his most famous one, Shoemaker-Levy, which the world watched hitting Jupiter in July 1994 through Hubble Telescope photos (*Parade Magazine*, 6/21/98). He points out that ice floats. We all know that, but what may not be understood is that most substances contract as they get colder. If that happened with water, the ice would sink to the bottom and eventually as that process repeated itself, entire bodies of water would freeze solid, possibly destroying life. When water freezes it expands, and by floating on the surface protects living forms in the liquid water underneath. Levy also notes the sky is dark at night. Your probable response is, of course, we are turned away from the sun. But there is another major reason: there are so many stars in the universe; their light should make the night sky very bright. (This is called Olber's Paradox, posed by an astronomer in Germany almost two centuries ago.) One reason the stars don't light up the sky is the expansion of the universe; with all parts retreating from each other after the big bang, the light hasn't had time to get here. The other reason is the dilution of matter in the universe related to the initial inflationary phase in the first second after the big bang. The stars are too diluted now to give such a concentrated effect. If all that light were to get here we would be bathed in so much radiation life would be destroyed. In a static everlasting universe we would have been bathed in light and radiation, and we would not be here. The inflationary period was an extremely important adjustment in the big bang allowing our existence.

We are here, and we are made primarily of four major elements: carbon, hydrogen, oxygen and nitrogen, the major components of proteins, the building blocks of our organs. These four are the most flexible for the creation of life (Levy). Other combinations of elements, for example based on silicon, are predicted as being less adaptable for life. "Carbon is the fourth most abundant element in the universe and the most abundant element that is solid at temperatures when water is liquid." (Schroeder, *Science of God*). In the 1960's astronomer Fred Hoyle predicted the process by which carbon is manufactured inside stars. He considered it a "lucky fluke, a rather tricky process involving the simultaneous encounter of three high speed helium nuclei, which then stick together" forming carbon. This can occur only at "certain well-defined energies…the sort of energies that helium nuclei have inside large stars". (Davies, *The Mind of God*). These reactions must occur within a tiny portion of time: 10^{-16} of a second. (Schroeder). Now just think of the amazingly complex minute adjustments necessary to create carbon in this universe, upon which our life is based. Fine-tuning is the perfect term to describe it. Remember that all the elements heavier than hydrogen, helium and lithium were spread throughout the universe by supernova explosions, which also spewed out extremely dangerous radiation if any life was close enough to be affected.

By this time you have realized that the universe is an extremely hostile place, and we live in a very protected cocoon, a very tiny region compared to the size of the whole structure. The temperature in space is close to absolute zero. The astronaut's space suits are heated, oxygen supplied, properly pressurized and shielded from radiation. Hopefully meteorites can be avoided by their space vehicles. Watch for 'shooting stars' at night to realize how common they are. We have romanticized the dinosaurs in recent years. They dominated life on Earth for 150 million years, and became extinct within a few months after an asteroid about 6 miles across blasted into the Gulf of Mexico. That was 65 million years ago. Squirrel-sized mammals survived and we are here. Good luck or good planning? (Schroeder). We are in a very protected area of the universe, but we have the intelligence the dinosaurs did not have, to recognize the dangers to the Earth. Astronomers are currently mapping the asteroids looking for ones that might cross the path of our orbit. Perhaps we will be able to launch missiles with atomic warheads to knock an asteroid into a safer direction away from the Earth. (The effect of asteroid collisions on evolution is discussed at length in Chapter 4.)

We have an intelligence no other living beings before us have had. We are aware of our surroundings far more deeply than any other living being. The family dog is aware of his family and his environment. He is alert to danger, but he is not aware that he is aware. He does not have consciousness. Only human beings do. He does not question why he is alive or why he is aware. Only we do. We live in a universe that has a design capable of creating beings with consciousness. We are here and we can study our universe. The study of the universe, the science of cosmology and particle physics, has uncovered a very precise design that has lead to human beings. We are conscious human beings capable of unearthing how we arrived. In John Polkinghorne's view (remember he is the theoretical physicist turned Anglican theologian) "the evolution of conscious life seems the most significant thing that has happened in cosmic history and we are right to be intrigued by the fact that so special a universe is required for its possibility". (*Beyond Science: The Wider Human Context*, 1996).

Paul Davies, the theoretical physicist, agrees with Polkinghorne. He describes his very similar view of the universe we have discovered: "Traditionally, scientists [have] assumed that the origin of life was a chemical fluke of stupendous improbability, a quirk of fate unique in the entire cosmos. If so, then we are alone in an otherwise sterile universe, and the existence of life on earth, in all its exuberant glory is just a meaningless accident. On the other hand a growing number of scientists suspect that life is written into the fundamental laws of the universe, so that it is almost bound to arise wherever earthlike conditions prevail. If they are right—if life is part of the basic fabric of reality—then we human beings are living representations of a breathtakingly ingenious cosmic scheme, a set of laws that is able to coax life from non-life and mind from unthinking matter. How…impressive is such a magnificent set of physical principles…In my view, the discovery that life and mind have emerged as part of the natural outworking of the laws of the universe will be strong evidence for a deeper purpose in physical existence." (www.metanexus.net, metaviews 039.2000.04.14.)

Was this universe designed to create us, as Polkinghorne and Davies suggest, or is it an improbable accident? To remind you, Alan Guth in the preface to his book *The Inflationary Universe*, carefully instructed the reader that all the theories of the Big Bang referred to the *aftermath* of the bang, not why the bang itself appeared. And yet, like most scientists, he avoids the issue that is the subject of this book: where did the Big Bang, itself, come from? *Who* or what created the Big Bang? Guth begs the question. He concluded his first chapter, "The Ultimate Free Lunch" by stating: "Conceivably, *everything* can be created from nothing. And 'everything' might include a lot more than we can see. In the context of inflationary cosmology, it is fair to say that the universe is the ultimate free lunch." A free lunch? Perhaps, but only *after* the big bang! Guth thinks it is an accident of nature. Or was there Divine creation? To allow for his 'ultimate free lunch,' Guth makes the assumption that 'nothing' is composed of a froth of quantum particles which can pop into and out of existence. I take issue with Guth's logic. The issue revolves around the definition of 'nothing.' Cosmologists have found that the 'vacuum' of space in our universe is really filled with the quantum froth (*The Elegant Universe*). However, that is *our* space in *our* universe. No one can ever know what happened *before* the Big Bang. He is making assumptions from his knowledge of the space he knows *after* the Big Bang.

Let me further explain my disagreement with Guth. Surveys show that about 40 percent of scientists believe in God, and by implication assume there was a creation. Among the 60 percent of those who do not, and who want to avoid the necessity for a 'creator', are theoretical mathematicians struggling to come up with some explanation for the Big Bang itself. They are trying to theoretically travel mathematically before or behind the bang, or to "smear it out" by appealing to quantum mechanics, which is still pretty mysterious. "'Quantum uncertainty' allows the small but finite possibility of something coming into being from nothing via what is known as a quantum fluctuation. [These] fluctuations are phenomena that relate to the laws of nature within our universe." (Guth). Our universe did not begin to form as space and time until after the Big Bang. Quanta are bundles of energy that appeared out of the Big Bang. To guess that the Big Bang came out of 'quantum fluctuations' presumes quanta were present before the Big Bang; what created them?

Brian Greene, Ph.D. a full professor in physics and mathematics at Columbia University, in his book, *The Elegant Universe* (1999), describes mathematical studies in 'superstring theory', which is an attempt to pull together quantum theory and Einstein's theory of relativity. The new theory involves ten or eleven dimensions, not just the current four, and describes vibrating strings and stretched out flattened strings called membranes (or 'branes' for short), as the forms underlying all of the reality we know. None of these mathematics computations has been experimentally proven, but their "beauty and elegance", as the mathematicians put it, suggest they contain elements of the truth. The theory is also partially an attempt to understand what happened before the Big bang. Greene admits we may never know. "No one has any insight on the question of how things actually did begin. In fact, our ignorance persists on an even higher plane: We don't know whether the question of determining the initial conditions [before the Big Bang] is one that is even sensible to ask, or whether it is a question that lies forever beyond the grasp of any theory." It is really very difficult for scientists to escape a creator. We only understand quantum theory as part of the laws of nature of our universe as Guth tells us. Therefore, it appears the clearest conclusion, based on the mathematics of the Big Bang, is that quantum phenomena began to exist only when space-time started, following the Big Bang!

However, scientists continually try to avoid finding a true beginning to the universe with its implication of creation or a creator. Andrei Linde, Ph. D., a leading cosmologist from Stanford University, has argued that Guth's inflation theory could allow an infinite past "and therefore the universe did not have an unexplained and uncaused beginning in the big bang theory." Stephen Hawking has invoked imaginary time to create a concept that did not require a beginning and proposed that space had no boundaries ("Cosmologists catch glimpse of the beginning," Mike Martin, *Research News & Opportunities in Science and Theology*, Vol. 3, No. 5, January 2003; also, *Science* Vol. 295, pg. 1476, 22 February 2002). Alan Guth and his associates (Alexander Valenkin and Arvind Borde) may have put an end to the theoretical physicists' quest to avoid a beginning for the universe in a paper presented in 2002. In further study of inflation theory and quantum gravity they have demonstrated that "inflation can't provide much insight into the moments leading up to the big bang at the leading edge of space and time. They found that space may have a distinct boundary and time may point in only one direction—the future, toward 'everything that will ever be'." The boundary is at the Big Bang, and the authors refer to it as a "past boundary" which they admit is just a "fancy name for beginning." It is their answer to Hawking's 'no boundary' proposal, which suggests that it is possible to study the period before the Big Bang. Their mathematics demonstrate that "something initial had to set everything into motion. That 'something'—the process of creation—remains a mystery." (Martin) (Their paper was presented at the symposium to honor Stephen Hawking's 60th birthday, "The Future of Theoretical Physics and Cosmology Symposium," Centre for Mathematical Sciences, Cambridge, England, January 2002; publication of the proceedings, August 2003; see also, www.arXiv:gr-qc/0110012 v2, 14 January 2003, "Inflationary spacetimes are not past-complete," Borde, Guth & Vilenkin.) Scientists are left with the prospect of facing their ultimate challenge: Guth et al have shown there is not a blockage to investigating what might have occurred before the Big Bang. The math establishes that there is no 'before' before the Big Bang. There is nothing. How was the universe possibly created from nothing? That the Guth presentation is solid is confirmed by Andrei Linde (a participant in the symposium) who has stated their proof is correct. "[Their] boundary represents the absolute origin of space, time, and matter," commented James Moreland, teaching the philosophy of science at Talbot School of Theology, La Mirada, California. (Quoted by Mike Martin).

In fairness to Guth, his work on a 'boundary' before the Big Bang seems to have changed his thinking to some degree. Instead of considering a 'quantum fluctuation', he now hopes to study "a transition from [a] state of 'absolute nothingness' to a small universe. I think that's a problem that we're hoping to be able to solve sometime." (*Research News & Opportunities in Science and Theology,* July/August 2003, Conversations section, pg. 5). Does he really think he can find what lies behind and beyond the boundary? An exotic science still sought after by the theoretical physicists or God? "There's certainly something there we don't understand. But for me, calling it God doesn't help, because I don't really know what the word 'God' means." Logic tells me I have to choose God.

Before the reader jumps to the conclusion I have absolutely demonstrated scientific proof of creation, and therefore a Creator, I must caution that I haven't. Atheistic scientists are not willing to accept something from nothing when it implies a Creator. The reader may not remember that on page 49 I stated that the Big Crunch theory 'appeared' to have died in 1998. Only *appeared* to die. Attempts to 'find' a cyclic universe with no beginning and no end continue. In May 2002 another form of the Big Bang/Big Crunch cycle theory appeared based on superstring/membrane mathematical research. In the model presented, "the visible universe exists within a three-dimensional membrane that can be simplistically imagined as a stretchy rubber sheet. Another 'brane', separated from ours by a microscopic distance, contains a 'dark matter' universe. The bang that creates the matter and radiation in each new cycle comes from the periodic collision of these two branes. Serial universes are created and then disperse into space, one after another, with each cycle lasting trillions of years." (washingtonpost.com, "New Theory of Universe Goes Beyond the Bang," Susan Okie, 5/13/02; *Science*, Vol. 296, Issue 5572, 1436-39, "A Cyclic Model of the Universe," Steinhardt & Turok, 5/24/02). Remember that this proposal is based solely on superstring theory, which currently is unproven, but the claim that it appears to fit with the current theories of inflationary cosmology is disagreed with by Guth et al, based on mathematics presented at the Hawking symposium.

The scientists and the natural philosophers have another suggestion to avoid a Creator. John Leslie, the Professor of Philosophy at the University of Guelph, Canada, author of, *Universes*, concludes his entire book of philosophic discussion of scientific cosmologic findings with this final sentence: "Much evidence suggests… *that God is real and/or there exist vastly many, very varied universes.*" Stated simply, the alternative for positing God is to assume that there are an enormous variety of universes with an enormous variety of characteristics, and only this particular universe has the natural design and laws to permit our appearance. What looks like purposeful design by a Designer is just the luck of the draw! We are here because Nature shuffled the cards long enough to come up with the right combination, lucky us! My own reaction is this presents a total violation of Occam's Razor, my cardinal rule in logical thinking. Dragging in a whole flock of universes we cannot observe or prove just complicates and confuses the issue. In proper logical reasoning we must limit ourselves to only those facts we can know, and we only can know *this* universe. Allowing anything we can imagine or think of creates only confusion, and destroys logical thinking. I can imagine a herd of pink elephants running across the Serengeti in Tanzania, but I know I also have to imagine the huge spray-painting machine they ran through, to have any sense of reality about the scene.

Brian Greene agrees, "It will be extremely hard if not impossible, for us ever to know if the multiverse [multiple universe] picture is true. Even if there are other universes, we can imagine that we will never come into contact with any of them." (*The Elegant Universe*). Therefore, how can we prove they exist? Despite that obvious comment, scientists who persist in proposing multiple universes try different mathematical concepts. One approach uses our universe's black holes, through which there may be an entry to other universes; our universe may have come from a black hole in another universe (For a full discussion of this theory see *The Life of the Cosmos*, Lee Smolin, 1997). Since multiple universes pop up through the black holes of other universes, according to this theory, one can imagine a whole huge cluster of universes like the huge pile of bubbles in a bubble bath. As with many scientific attempts at explaining the origin of our universe, this one also does away with a start or a 'creation', as the process is presumed to have gone on forever. It also means that any or all of these multiple universes have the same or similar physical laws, having been 'born' from each other, and therefore many of them will be capable of allowing the development of life.

The theoretical mathematical concept of black holes has been accepted by science; each is an area of such density and gravity that all nearby matter is sucked in—nothing can leave, and even light is pulled in. Theoretical mathematicians can point to many mathematical predictions of astronomical objects that were later proven by direct observation to actually exist. To prove this multiple-universe proposal of theirs requires not just the theoretical math, but also a valid observation of a black hole, which on the face of it is impossible. The fact that a black hole has such intense gravity that even light cannot leave, means we cannot ever see one, nor prove that there is another universe on its other side. In fact, astronomical observations have provided inferential proof of the existence of black holes. The evidence is very strong and has been accepted by science as definite proof they exist. We can prove the existence of something we cannot see (a black hole) by the effects of its gravity; we cannot get to its other side.

Andrei Linde has another proposal for multiple universes based upon his theory of "Chaotic Inflation," in which he theorizes that the inflationary period after the Big Bang had many regions of differing rates of inflation. This created an enormous number of 'inflationary domains,' each one becoming a baby universe, each of which have different laws, permitting one or more to allow life. He calls this a 'multiverse structure', and states that it removes the "need anymore to assume that some supernatural cause created our universe with the properties specifically fine-tuned to make our existence possible." The reason he proposes this version of our universe is that it attempts to answer questions he raises while avoiding the 'supernatural'. "If our universe did not exist sometimes in the distant past, in which sense could one speak about the existence of the laws of Nature which govern the universe? We know, for example, that the laws of our biological evolution are written in our genetic code...We need to know what emerged first at the moment of the universe formation: the universe or the law describing the universe. It is equally hard to understand how any law could exist prior to the universe formation, or how the universe could exist without a law. One may assume that there is only one possible law, and it exists in some unspecified way even prior to the emergence of the universe...A better possibility would be to consider all logically possible combinations of universes. Given the choice among different universes in this multiverse structure, we can proceed by eliminating the universes where life would be impossible. This simple step is sufficient for understanding [the] many features of our universe that would otherwise seem miraculous." Linde also admits that "inhabitants [of each universe] will never know anything about the existence of other 'universes' with different properties.". ("Inflation, Quantum Cosmology and the Anthropic Principle," Andrei Linde, a chapter in *Science and Ultimate Reality: From Quantum to Cosmos* (2003); www.arXiv:hep-th/0211048 v2, 8 Nov. 2002). This convoluted version of the universe is his failed attempt to avoid considering creation by God: he really has no answer to what created the Big Bang.

Scientists who raise the issue of multiple universes are "guilty of what they accuse religious people of doing: taking refuge in the unobservable." ("Designed for Living", by George Sim Johnston, in *Wall Street Journal*, 10/15/99). "Smolin's theory is typical of the wildly speculative character of much of modern cosmology and the lengths to which many scientists will go to construct naturalistic explanations. It involves a commitment to *metaphysical naturalism*, that what is studied by the human and nonhuman sciences is all that there is," God obviously excluded("Is Intelligent Design Science?" Bruce Gordon, in *Signs of Intelligence*, 2001). So in a sense the argument is back to pink elephants.

What pops out of the exotic mathematics used by the theoretical physicists are pink-elephant-like entities: "mirror worlds, alternate universes, new families of particles, new forces, multiple hidden dimensions of space." Originally this math accurately predicted, for example, Einstein's curved space-time and the weirdness of quantum physics, all totally different than the reality we experience, but subsequently proven by experimentation. Now, as examples in this chapter show, "theoretical physics has become a refined form of creative play, in which testing out wacky ideas mathematically continually outruns experiment. Sometimes it outruns experiment so far the ideas are barely testable even in principle, but that doesn't stop it being enormous fun for those intellectually equipped to play the game." ("Strange Matters: Mathematics and the Playful Side of Physics," Jon Turney, *N.Y. Times*, 9/29/02). Theoretical cosmologist, Joao Magueijo, has a totally irreverent view of these mathematical attempts. "Although no one has the faintest idea of how to test these theories with current technology, everyone is quick to claim that he alone holds the holy grail and that the others are all charlatans. The two leading quantum gravity cults [string theory and loop quantum gravity]…don't connect with experiment or observations at all, [and] they have become fashion accessories at best, at worst a source of feudal warfare." (*Faster Than The Speed of Light, 2003*). If the mathematics is not capable of being proved by real experiments, then the exotic predictions are simply flights of fancy. They cannot be used to avoid a consideration that God exists and created the universe. I follow Mortimer J. Adler's approach in *How to Think About God* (1980) that rational philosophical inquiry cannot *prove* God exists, but can *persuade* that God exists from "a preponderance of reasons in favor of that conclusion over reasons against it," and "only beyond reasonable doubt." My reasoning tells me the cosmologic evidence, developed in the past 50 years, requires a Creator, our God. The progressive discoveries have demonstrated an absolute beginning for the universe and its end in infinite expansion. Other evidence in the following chapters adds to the 'preponderance of reasons.'

Before leaving this Chapter I must offer another description of the origin of the universe, in comparison to the information I have presented. "At the briefest instant following creation all the matter of the universe was concentrated in a very small place, no larger than a grain of mustard [the 'grain of mustard' was an ancient colloquialism for the tiniest imaginable speck of space]. The matter at this time was so thin, so intangible, that it did not have real substance. It did have, however, a potential to gain substance and form and to become tangible matter. From the initial concentration of this intangible substance in its minute location, the substance expanded, expanding the universe as it did so. As the expansion progressed, a change in the substance occurred. This initially thin noncorporeal substance took on tangible aspects of matter as we know it. From this initial act of creation, from this ethereally thin pseudosubstance, everything that has existed, or ever will exist, was, is, and will be formed." This quote is from Nahmanides, written in the 13th century in *Commentary on the Torah*, Genesis 1:1!! He was a Biblical scholar and commentator, and also a mystic, an early member of a branch of Judaism called the Kabbalah. I am sure you are as astounded as I am that a 700-year old description of the Big Bang is so accurate. No one knows if Nahmanides divined this from the Torah alone, or if his mystical experiences provided much of, or just a portion of this description (Taken from *Genesis and the Big Bang*).

As an aside, it should be pointed out that the Hindu and Buddhist versions of creation are amazingly similar to Nahmanides' version. "At the moment of creation, the universe is non-differentiated and non-material-like pure energy", followed by the appearance "of matter and differentiation." ("Before the beginning: The cyclic universe makes a return," Catherine Baker, *Research News and Opportunities in Science and Theology*, Vol. 3, No. 9, May 2003). I doubt if Nahmanides was aware of these theologies. The similarity of the versions suggests that the information obtained by Jewish mystics and Indian mystics through meditation is the singular 'information' available from that level of reality. I wonder if this corroboration between disconnected mystics can lead to a conclusion that this version is a "truth" implanted at the mystical level (See the discussion of other levels of consciousness and mysticism in Chapter 6).

Nahmanides' commentary on the Torah reinforces my insistence that the Bible be studied only from original sources, and from comments by the ancient sages, when comparing the findings of science with the Bible. Dr. Schroeder's two books, *Genesis and the Big Bang* and *The Science of God* provide an excellent starting point. As of this writing he has been an active scientist in applied nuclear physics for 40 years and has spent 35 years in critical study of biblical tradition. John Polkinghorne, a theoretical physicist in cosmology who became an Anglican theologian, is the only other person I know of with a similar dual background. From my viewpoint the fact that Biblical revelation and the recent discoveries of science provide the same description of the origin of our universe is profound evidence of my contention that the findings of science must lead to recognition of God and the wondrousness of His works. Polkinghorne has a similar conclusion: "I believe there are many other arguments for belief in God—including those from the intelligibility of the physical world and from religious experience...[They make] a cumulative case for theism. Thus, I believe that in the delicate fine-tuning of physical law, which has made the evolution of conscious beings possible, we receive a valuable, if indirect, hint from science that there is a divine meaning and purpose behind cosmic history." Here is a former scientist who understands the 'how' of the universe answering the 'why'. (*Beyond Science*).

Chapter 3: Is Life a Glorious Accident? No Chance

"A Glorious Accident" is the way Stephen Jay Gould viewed the arrival through evolution of conscious humans on Earth. Gould was the famous professor of paleontology at Harvard, dying in 2002, and a facile writer of many essays and books popularizing his thesis. We will begin to answer the question in the title of this chapter by examining his thoughts in *A Glorious Accident*, a transcription of a Public Television Series roundtable discussion conducted by Wim Kayzer (1997). Kayzer asked Gould: "You wrote: 'Through no fault of our own, and by dint of no cosmic plan or conscious purpose, we have become, by the power of a glorious evolutionary accident called intelligence, the stewards of life's continuity on earth. We did not ask for this role...but here we are.' What was that glorious accident?" I have abbreviated Gould's response, but with no intent to change his meaning: "The accident is 60 trillion contingent events that eventually led to the emergence of *Homo sapiens*. It's that no species now alive is predictable, and any species that exists does so by the merest good fortune of tens of thousands of antecedent events that went one way and not the other. If the dinosaurs hadn't died out, we wouldn't be here....There are six thousand species of mammals, none of which—outside the order of primates—is threatening to become a powerfully conscious species with this kind of strength and influence over the rest of the earth. If intelligence was meant to be, you'd think it would have evolved convergently in lots of other lineages. It's just a weird invention that developed in one odd species, [out of about] some 200 species of primates, living on the African savannas a couple of million years ago."

It is Gould's contention that the entire development of life in its earliest forms and the evolution into 'us' is entirely chance and accident. By contingent he means each step of the way is determined by a previous step, a very exacting process. And he quotes enormous odds against our happening along when asked if we re-ran the tape of evolution a million times or 100

70

million times: "Take groups of ten out a pool of a hundred, there's seventeen trillion groups of ten. So you never get the same result twice." And yet here we are, our consciousness and intelligence the result of our brain growing four times larger during the last two and a half million years of evolution, more rapidly than any other organ ever developed in the history of life. The rapid growth tapered off 250 thousand years ago (*On Human Nature*, Edward O. Wilson, 1978 and "The Emergence of Intelligence", William H. Calvin, in *Scientific American*, Oct. 1994). No one knows what mechanism drove the brain to enlarge that much or why it stopped enlarging. Calvin does suggest the environmental strains created by the appearance of ice ages in the same time period might have created the impetus for an accumulation of mental abilities that allowed greater flexibility and survivability. The language area in the brain appeared during the ice ages, as did the ability for rapid repetitive motions such as hammering and throwing (called ballistic movements). These would certainly appear to improve survivability. The Darwin scientists, like Calvin, constantly assume that new and threatening demands of the environment always drive new mutations creating species of higher complexity. Apes have only elementary forms of these ballistic movements; but they survived also. Why then were we so blessed? Glorious accident? Looks more like a miracle to me.

What can be seen from the preceding discussion is one Neo-Darwin Reductionist pattern of thought in evolutionary scientists: Evolution has created us against what appear to be insurmountable odds, yet we are *accidentally* here. Other paleontologists are not so sure that step-by-step contingency dominates evolution and suggest the odds against our evolution are smaller, making us less accidental (*The Crucible of Creation*, Simon Conway Morris, 1998). The debate in their literature is fierce; recent findings are disquieting to the view of gradual Darwinian adaptations from the earliest forms to us, the most complex. Scientists who study evolution routinely also presume that life originally appeared by accident or chance simply from chemical reactions. Darwin, himself, intellectually did not make that jump. He presumed an initial Divine creation, and then the mechanism of Natural Selection and other "means of modification". (*The Philosophical Scientists*, David Foster, 1985).

It is fascinating to me that current evolutionary scientists work at getting rid of Darwin's belief in a Creator. Stephen Jay Gould quoted Darwin's concluding lines in *Origin of the Species*, and deliberately omitted the phrase: "having been originally breathed by the Creator into a few forms or into one," taking God out of the conclusion altogether (Schroeder, *The Science of God*) (The quote is on page 19, Chapter 1 in this book.). Leslie Orgel, a research professor at the Salk Institute, in an article discussing the chance origin of life, noted that Darwin discussed the possibility of life arising spontaneously through chemistry in private correspondence, and therefore was "bending somewhat to the religious biases of his time" by putting "the Creator" into his concluding words (Leslie E. Orgel, *Scientific American*, October, 1994). They all read Darwin, they all revere him, and they don't want him to believe in God. What is most troubling to evolutionists is the issue of the origin of life. In order to satisfy their mindset of 'Any Theory But God', life *must* have appeared by chance. If life did not appear by chance, then God ordained life, and perhaps He is guiding evolution, ideas that scientists do not wish to accept and try to refute by their discoveries.

Let us then survey the odds for life appearing by chance. There is no question that organic compounds (life-forming chemicals necessary for life to appear) exist throughout the universe (Carl Sagan, *Scientific American*, October, 1994). Could those carbon-based molecules have coalesced by chance into living forms capable of reproducing themselves? The accepted definition of life requires the ability to grow to a certain size, to maintain the form, and to have reproduction. However, when life is studied at the biochemical level the definition of life gets a lot more complex. A living cell is 'alive' only after hundreds and thousands of protein molecules collect together and cooperate with each other to create the first definition I gave. Some of those protein molecules set up the structure of the cell; some form the organelles, the tiny 'organs' that help in the manufacture of energy and the creation of more protein molecules. Some of these protein molecules are 'enzymes', helping create and control the rates of chemical reactions. The enzymes are guided by 'feedback loops', a series of chemical reactions which analyze the concentration of cell products to guide rates of production. At the same time inorganic chemicals and ionic sodium and potassium are running in and out of the cell through pores in the cell membranes, processes mediated by chains of chemical reactions. All of this frantic activity is under the control of the genetic material in the nucleus of the cell, the huge DNA molecule, its messenger RNA molecules, and other DNA in the mitochondria (one type of organelle). It is from this huge web of activity that life truly arises, fulfilling the accepted definition I gave earlier.

In studying the mathematical probabilities, we need first to set time limits for the chance appearance of life to occur. The earth formed in a very hot manner from the clumping together of smaller bodies (planetesimals) in the planetary disc around our sun starting about 4.5 billion years ago. The earth started out with a surface of molten rock, and planetesimals kept arriving, boiling the oceans until 4.0 billion years ago. In his article Carl Sagan stated there is definite evidence that early bacterial forms were present by 3.6 billion years ago, and there is some evidence to suggest bacterial life as early as 3.8 billion years. As of 2003 there is active scientific controversy as to whether the early bacterial forms of 3.6 billion years ago, found in Western Australia, really represent life, but the findings are still generally accepted (scientificamerican.com/news, 3/7/02). These forms are called Stromatolites, "mineralized mounds of bacterial mats....visible to the naked eye," and are now dated at 3.5 billion years ago ("Questioning the Oldest Signs of Life," Sarah Simpson, *Scientific American*, April 2003). The 3.8 billion-year-ago discovery does not involve life forms but carbon isotope (^{12}C) evidence of biologic metabolism in Akilia, Greenland, and therefore a deposit from early life (*A Case Against Accident and Self-Organization*, Dean L. Overman, 1997). This Akilia area interpretation is highly controversial, but in another area of Greenland (Isua), a deposit of the same carbon isotope dated at 3.7 billion years ago is considered "well-accepted evidence." (Simpson, *Scientific American*).

These findings limit the time for life to appear by chance to 500 million years, and possibly as short a period as 200 million years. That time span may seem long to you, but after you realize what has to be accomplished, it is extremely brief. All life is managed by a huge molecule, the famous double helix DNA (deoxyribonucleic acid). In humans it contains 3.3 billion base pairs, the pattern of the pairs representing 30,000-plus genes of our genetic code. This microscopic spot (DNA) in a human cell is six feet long when straightened out, 1.0 to 1.5 percent representing the genes that manufacture proteins, the building blocks of living structures and the chemical processes (*Houston Chronicle*, 2/13/01). But we are looking at the end of the evolutionary development of DNA. What had to start life was a very small DNA in very simple bacteria.

The first issue is whether organic compounds capable of making up DNA were available at the time we are discussing, 3.8 billion years ago; and from research the answer is some were, but not very many of them. In 1953 Stanley L. Miller, working with Harold C. Urey, set up a chamber with the gases thought to be present in the primitive earth atmosphere, methane, ammonia and hydrogen, which happen to be the building blocks of protein. In the experimental apparatus water was heated at the bottom to arrange a circulation of water vapor. Electrical sparks crossed the chamber to act like lightening. He actually found 18 different amino acids (protein building blocks) in the watery gunk at the bottom that matched the pattern of amounts of amino acids found in the Murchison meteorite, found years later in Australia (Leslie E. Orgel, *Scientific American*, October 1994). Recent findings of astronomers using extraction analysis of meteorites, have identified 70 amino acids and other compounds; spectral analysis of light confirms that other organic molecules of various types useful to develop life do exist throughout the universe. However, the astronomers have found only eight of the 20 amino acids specifically used in life (Bernstein et al., *Scientific American*, July 1999). But even the presence of all these compounds does not guarantee spontaneous life because of the complexity of what must be organized to attain that goal.

One initial problem in the complexity of organization is the "handedness" of organic compounds (chirality). The molecules of each amino acid come in both right- and left-handed configurations, that is, they are mirror images of each other, just like your hands. When manufactured in an uncontrolled process from component parts the finished products will be 50/50 right and left. However, and this is a major point, all 20 amino acids used in life are left-handed. But in the oceans of the primitive earth the amino acids had to be equally right and left in distribution: the Miller experiment produced the same 50/50 distribution. The same consideration applies to nucleotides that make the codes on DNA and RNA (see below). All nucleotides manufactured in life are right-handed, although, following the chemical rules for the manufacture of organic compounds, they must have been equal in right- and left-handed abundance before life appeared on the young earth. If molecules that started life and controlled it fell together by chance, only one type of the handedness available had to be "chosen" somehow. Further, the nucleic acids called DNA are extremely complex, so that the "chance" appearance of life must be exceedingly small.

How complex is DNA? Imagine a ladder with the supports made up of long strings of DNA molecules (ribose sugar without an oxygen) held together with high- energy phosphate bonds that supply DNA immediate energy to do its work. The cross rungs are made of nucleotide molecules or "bases," compounds with one or two circles of atoms that can be manufactured from amino acids. In DNA these bases are the amino acids: adenine (A), guanine (G), cytosine (C), and thymine (T) and the bases of one side of the ladder bond to bases of the other support to make the cross rungs. Now twist this "ladder" around a central axis in your imagination and you have the double helix. DNA manufactures proteins, strings of individual amino acids, 100 in number or longer, to make a single molecule. A triplet of three bases is the manufacturing code for a single amino acid in the string of amino acids to be manufactured. For example AAC is the code for Asparagine, the amino acid that gives asparagus its odor. The triplet is called a codon. There are 64 possible codons, and 61 of them are codes for the 20 amino acids used in life. The other three are 'stop codes' marking the end of a protein string. (Lee Spetner, *Not By Chance!*, 1997) The information in DNA is estimated to be equivalent to about 20,000 rather long books in English (David Foster, *The Philosophic Scientists*, 1985).

The DNA can unwind itself, expose a set of its bases to RNA and instruct the RNA what protein product to produce. The various RNA types are basically messengers carrying instructions for protein manufacture. RNA looks like a single strand of DNA, with uracil (U) substituted for thymine in DNA. AAU is the RNA code for Asparagine. RNA strands consist of *ribose* nucleic acid, indicating that an oxygen atom has been added back to the ribose sugar of DNA which lacks oxygen, and therefore is called *deoxyribose* nucleic acid. All of this sounds simple, but it is much more complex. DNA sets up a special pattern for the RNA, much like a key fitting into the tumblers of a lock, but this key and lock relationship is conducted in three dimensions, not two, helping to shape the new protein. Further the electrical charges have to match, positive hooking up with negative, left-handed with right-handed parts of the molecule. This is a simple description of protein production. There is much more complexity. Somehow or other DNA guides the three-dimensional protein strand to be properly deposited in whatever structure is being produced or replaced, and since multiple cells are operating in the process, the DNA of each cell is also coordinating with the DNA of all the cells, usually perfectly. In computers run by humans we have garbage-in-garbage-out errors that run on average three percent. DNA cannot afford that level of error. The amount of information packed into DNA is simply enormous. Did it all appear by chance?

If life started by accident, by chance, it had to be a very simple life form. A simple bacterium, to fulfill the functions of life, must have between several hundred to a thousand genes in its DNA; there must be RNA, protein-synthesizing mechanisms, and especially enzymes, which are protein molecules that orchestrate the processes. Several authors with mathematical

DAVID J. TURELL, M.D.

expertise have calculated the odds to put together a bacterium by chance. David Foster used the DNA of T4 phage, a tiny living parasitic creature that attacks bacteria, because it is one of the smallest DNA's in existence, and small size permits a greater opportunity for chance to create it. He also presumed preexisting molecules of the codons, since Miller's research shows they might have occurred by chance, although none have been found free in the universe in astronomical research done so far. This presumption of preexisting codon molecules is a conservative approach that enhances the calculated probability of life forming by chance. Knowing the size of this DNA, he calculated 60,000 base pairs (remember, humans have about 3.3 billion), to guide the manufacture of the necessary 20 amino acids. Those base pairs must be formed into specific code patterns to manufacture the proper proteins. He calculated the specificity (read improbability) of getting the proper patterns by chance and his result is one chance in $10^{78,000}$!! That chance would be even smaller if he had not presumed the existence of necessary molecules to plug into the newly forming DNA. To make his point even stronger he calculated the odds of hemoglobin, the single very large protein that carries oxygen in our blood. At some point in our evolution mutations would have had to chance upon hemoglobin as a useful chemical. That chance was once in 10^{650}. Hoyle and Wickramasinghe (*Evolution from Space*, 1981), using slightly different assumptions came up with an improbability of once in 10^{850} for hemoglobin.

Hoyle and Wickramasinghe also looked at the simplest possibility for a protein related to life by chance, and calculated the odds for one functioning enzyme. That means getting the proper order into a string of amino acids from the 20 used in life. They estimated one in 10^{20}, but since a bacterium needs about 2,000 enzymes, the improbability jumps to one chance in $10^{40,000}$, if you want a whole live bacterium. Hubert Yockley disagreed with Hoyle and Wickramasinghe about their enzyme calculation. He is a leading authority on information theory and biology. He pointed out that not all amino acids would be equally available as H&W assumed. With that in mind he calculated the odds of the chance production of one specific known enzyme in living organisms and came up with the probability of 2×10^{-44}. (Overman). Michael Denton (*Evolution: A Theory In Crisis*, 1985) produces similar odds against the spontaneous appearance of life. "To get a [living] cell by chance would require at least 100 functional proteins to appear simultaneously in one place. That is one hundred simultaneous events each of an independent probability which could be hardly more than 10^{-20}, giving a maximum

76

combined probability of $10^{-2,000}$." Remember that the use of negative exponents represents *improbability*. Harold J. Morowitz, a biophysicist and professor of biology at George Mason University, made a similar calculation, which reduced much of the *chance* by assuming that a single-celled bacterium had broken apart its chemical bonds, and simply needed to reassemble itself. This is an extremely conservative approach to calculating the chance assembly of a living organism. The odds he computed against the cell reassembling were $10^{100,000,000,000}$. (Quoted in Overman). In comparison to these older estimates using actual primitive cells, Mullan has calculated the odds of the chance appearance of a theoretical, much simpler cell with only 12 proteins, each with 14 amino acids, using a 1.11 billion year time period. The odds he calculated varied from one in 10^{63} to one in 10^{100}, depending upon the degrees of complexity he considered (www.iscid.org, archives, 11/23/02).

These numbers from various authors approach infinity. The next thought brings us even closer to infinity. These calculations ignore the handedness of the amino acids available on the primitive earth (choosing only left-handed ones) and also the biologic process of "feedback", something available to judge the suitability of the organization of these enzymes. Simply throwing together one hundred functional proteins or 2,000 different enzymes doesn't guarantee life will appear. Those molecules have to work in a coordinated fashion. Now let us see if there has been enough time for the number of accidental chances to form life to approach infinity. Robert Shapiro (*Origins: A Skeptic's Guide to the Creation of Life on Earth*, 1986) calculated 2.5 times 10^{51} attempts to create life by chance during the history of the earth. He assumed one billion years as the time it took for life to appear, but we have seen that an average 300 million years is more correct. Recalculating his figures, to fit the shorter time span that has been shown to be available, reduces the possible attempts at producing life to 1.6 times 10^{41}. This is nowhere near infinity, and is nowhere near enough opportunities, compared to the infinite improbabilities just recited, for life to have had the probability of occurring spontaneously. Compare this to one chance in $10^{40,000}$ or any of the other improbable odds just presented. Bradley and Thaxton (quoted by Overman, pg. 62) conducted a calculation fairly similar to Shapiro, to test the odds for the random formation of one chance functional protein, 100 amino acids in length. They also assumed one billion years of time available, and further assumed that all the necessary amino acid molecules already were in existence, and further assumed a reaction rate of 10^{12} per second between those amino acids. The result they came up with was the impossible probability of 4.9×10^{-191}.

To put these odds or chances in perspective with mathematical theories of probability, the French mathematician Emile Borel proposed one chance in 10^{50} as a universal probability boundary, beyond which chance could be excluded. (*Intelligent Design*) William Dembski proposed a more stringent boundary, one in 10^{150}. (*Intelligent Design*, and more fully discussed in Chapter 7). Either way, when the odds for the accidental formation of life are combined with the odds for the formation of this universe as proposed by Roger Penrose, one chance in 10^{123} (see Chapter 2), there is no way that 'chance' has a chance to be the answer as to why we are here.

The molecular biologists have recognized the improbability of life starting by chance using DNA. They have seized upon proving the spontaneous generation of an RNA molecule, which is much simpler than DNA, and in some way could then create life. So far this appears to be an exercise in futility. Leslie E. Orgel titles his article in the *Scientific American* (October, 1994) "The Origin of Life on Earth—Growing evidence supports the idea that the emergence of catalytic RNA was a crucial early step. How that RNA came into being remains unknown." Again we are seeing the eternal optimism of the reductionist scientist. In 'catalytic RNA' he is referring to an RNA enzyme that actually could direct several processes, be reproducing of itself, and perhaps lead to life. In fact naturally occurring ribozymes (as RNA enzymes are called) had been discovered, but were capable only of "cutting and joining preexisting RNA." Orgel reports that some simple strands of RNA have been artificially produced in the laboratory, but after that nothing but disappointment: "After years of trying, we have been unable to achieve the second step of replication—copying of a complementary strand to yield a duplicate of the first template—without help from protein enzymes. Equally disappointing, we can induce copying of the original template only when we run our experiments with nucleotides having a right-handed configuration. All nucleotides synthesized biologically, [that is in nature], today are right-handed. Yet on the primitive earth, equal numbers of right- and left-handed nucleotides would have been present. When we put equal numbers of nucleotides in our reaction mixtures, copying was inhibited." He is telling us that RNA and enzymes or ribozymes must both be present to carry his theories forward. Several things have to be happening at once. The problem of the presence of right- and left-handed compounds appears to create more of an issue than just being limited to choosing one handedness over the other. And once again, the need for a feedback control, a way of managing and judging the results of several molecules working together is ignored. He finishes his article as optimistic as ever: "As chemists, biochemists and molecular biologists cooperate on ever more ingenious experiments, they are sure to fill in many missing parts of the puzzle."

Since 1994 research scientists have continued to attack that puzzle, but as you will see they haven't begun to solve it. So much is missing, and I am not sure that their beginning premise is correct. The odds of a self-replicating (copying) RNA molecule appearing out of nowhere and all by itself creating life as we know it, appears to be against all probability. And even if, against all probability, life arises in a lab, all that is proven is that the origin of life requires the intelligent design of a research scientist, not chance.

In April 2001 Robert M. Hazen reported in *Scientific American* (Vol. 284, No. 4) a theory and experimental evidence of how heated sea water near hydrothermal vents on the ocean bottom might have lead to the production of amino acids. In the presence of certain minerals found by such vents, "amino acids stayed intact for days—plenty of time to react with other critical molecules." 1990's studies at Rensselaer "found that clays can act as scaffolds for the building blocks of RNA...Once organic molecules attach themselves to a mineral scaffold, various types of complex molecules could have been forged. *But only a chosen few were eventually incorporated into living cells.*" (My italics). By 'chosen few' Hazen was referring to the left and right-handedness 100 percent choices that living organisms had made in RNA and DNA molecules. Hazen and his team next demonstrated that calcite crystal had electrical charges on specific faces of the crystal, which could sort out left and right-handed amino acids, with selectivity approaching 90 percent. Calcite was chosen because it is a major component of shellfish shells on the sea bottom. Their most recent work mimicked conditions at the ocean bottom: under extreme pressure and heat and in the presence of oxides and sulfides of iron, copper and zinc (found in such regions), with the addition of carbon, they produced "a rich variety of complex organic molecules."

Hazen's work is on 'prebiologic molecules," that is, those chemicals that could possibly lead to the molecules of life. At the other end of the process would be the appearance of the molecules of life, such as the type of "catalytic RNA" proposed by Leslie Orgel that we have been discussing. David Bartel and his group reported creating just such a molecule, a ribozyme, in *Science*, May 2001 (Vol. 292, Number 5520, pp. 1319-1325). This RNA catalyst can add 14 nucleotides or code letters to an existing RNA strand with 95 percent accuracy, by carrying the information from a pre-existing strand of RNA. Remember that three code letters are needed for each amino acid and it takes at least 100 amino acids to make a protein molecule. This is just a baby step, but the press release from the Whitehead Institute of M.I.T. (www.wi.mit.edu, 5/17/01) proclaimed that this discovery created "some of the strongest evidence yet to support the RNA world —an era in early evolution when life forms depended on RNA." Please note that such an 'RNA world' is only a theoretical proposal, yet the scientists' publicists assume that such a world *had to exist* in the past. To achieve this result Bartel tested "1000 trillion RNA's and found 65 that were more "efficient" in transmitting information by changing themselves. They then "evolved" these molecules and "found descendents that were 100 times more efficient." In the final step they again made "1000 trillion random RNA's go through test-tube evolution," and found the molecule described. Let's review the mathematics of this find to look at the possibility of natural chance turning up this particular RNA. A study of 10^{15} molecules; then intermediate refinement of the best ones; then another study of 10^{15} molecules to finally discover this one RNA molecule. Just one molecule in a manufacturing process guided by intelligent minds. Bartel was much more even-handed than the publicists in his comment on the study. "We will never be able to prove the existence of the RNA world…but we can examine the basic properties of RNA and see if these are compatible within the RNA world scenario." A perfectly reasonable statement.

Hazen's conclusions to his article give a fair overview of the way these scientists think about their problem of trying to create life in the laboratory. "It is clear that the origin of life was far too complex to imagine as a single event. Rather we must work from the assumption that it was a gradual sequence of more modest events, each of which added a degree of order and complexity to the world of prebiological molecules. The ancient earth suffered an embarrassment of riches—a far greater diversity of molecules than life could possibly employ. Minerals helped to impose order on this chaos. First by confining and concentrating molecules, then by *selecting and arranging* those molecules, minerals may have jump-started the first self-replicating molecular systems." (My italics). Hazen appears to be saying that the minerals possessed information, had minds of their own and knew how to do all this, whereas he is really a Darwinian who expects that this process had to occur by chance. The self-replicating systems "would not constitute life as we know it, but it could have, for the first time, displayed a key property of life. In this scenario, a self-replicating molecular system began to use up the resources of its environment. As mutations led to slightly different variants, competition for limited resources initiated and drove the process of molecular natural selection. Self-replicating molecular systems began to evolve, inevitably becoming more efficient and more complex." This is an entire flight of fancy. How did molecules make decisions to mutate? That is the province of genes, which don't exist in this setting.

One of Hazen's final statements is right on: "Scientists are far from creating life in the laboratory, and it may never be possible to prove exactly what chemical transformations gave rise to life on earth." Please recall that his approach is theorized to be the way to start a chemical process to create life, and how difficult it seems to be even though guided by an intelligent scientist. Add to this consideration how difficult it was for Bartel to find his ribozyme molecule studying over two quadrillion different molecules. Now recognize that all of this is supposed to have occurred by chance. And the entire process is not even alive at this point. Life requires DNA, enormously more complicated than RNA; life requires several types of RNA and an integrated group of cooperating 2,000 enzymes, as noted previously in this chapter. Life also requires accurate reproduction of the living organism. When a single-celled animal reproduces DNA is split into two copies, which must be exact, in order to produce two organisms that are completely alike, or there will be rapid changes in the species involved. Nature guards against this by providing proofreading within the cell (*Not By Chance*, Dr. Lee Spetner, 1997). All of these coordinated and integrated chemical parts *must* be in place to create a living organism, and the Darwin scientists claim this occurred by a hunt-and-peck chance system. Hazen assumes that life can occur from "a gradual sequence of modest events," all by chance. As a believer in the Darwin theory, he feels there was enough time for all those chance occurrences to somehow fall into place. Earlier in this chapter I indicated that life appeared within a 200-400 million year time period. Is that enough time, considering the odds against chance quoted earlier? To repeat myself, the odds of a self-replicating RNA molecule appearing out of nowhere and all by itself creating life, as we know it, appears to be against all probability. And even if, against all probability, life arises in a lab, all that is proven is that the origin of life requires the intelligent design of a research scientist, not chance.

Robert Shapiro predicted in his 1986 book, *Origins*, the approach current scientists would follow to create life in the laboratory; and he predicted failure. He proposed that when 'life' started in the pre-biotic era first "a hereditary system based [solely] on protein preceded those based on nucleic acids." Then RNA developed as a building material, gradually assuming the role of carrying the heredity. Finally DNA "in turn evolved, and became the genetic substance."(pg. 282). He then calculated the odds for "the appropriate subunits com[ing] together to form the first self-reproducing unit," the first step in his origin-of-life scenario. He imagined an extremely simple system involving only four amino acids, not the current twenty, and a cooperative group of ten enzymes. "One enzyme will be needed to control the entry of each amino acid into a protein that is under construction. Others might serve to provide a framework for protein synthesis, to help in making amino acids, and to secure a supply of energy." He assumed each enzyme would be 25 amino acids long, a very basic minimum to allow the molecule to perform the needed functions. (In nature they are usually over 100 in length.) "If we had to await the construction of this community by random selection from a pool containing only four amino acids, the odds of getting it right would be 1 in 10^{150}." And these odds are calculated ignoring the fact that only left- handed amino acids should be used. It does not appear to be Shapiro's opinion that life could begin by chance.

Stuart Kauffman, in *At Home in the Universe* (1995) holds a similar opinion regarding the improbability of RNA research finding the beginnings of life. He has an unusual background; having graduated from medical school, one would expect him to be doing research on people, but he is a member of the Santa Fe Institute, and is leading theoretical research into the attributes of self-organization within whole organisms, studying the science of complexity as applied to biology. His studies involve computer simulations, including the mathematics of the partial organization of chaos, phase transitions and autocatalytic sets. Phase transitions refer to changes in form either physically or chemically. They start slowly under the conditions driving the reaction and then suddenly move at much higher speed. A common example is turning water to ice: the environmental temperature drops to below 32 degrees, but the water temperature holds at 32 while enough energy is gathered (actually removed from the water) to crystallize the ice, which starts slowly, but then advances rapidly. Kauffman proposes that phase transitions help to create autocatalytic sets. These sets refer to masses of chemical compounds, which can react together to form other chemical compounds. Although no enzymes or catalysts are put into the mix to drive the reactions faster, some of the compounds undergo phase transitions, will "autocatalyze" and speed up the chemical reaction. These examples all show a degree of self-organization, that he is convinced is necessary to provide for the spontaneous appearance of life. To quote from his preface: "Natural selection [from Darwin] is important…Another source—self-organization—is the root source of order…The reductionist program has been spectacularly successful…but it has often left a vacuum…the complex whole may exhibit properties that are not readily explained by understanding the parts. The complex whole, in a completely nonmystical sense, can often exhibit collective properties, 'emergent' features that are lawful in their own right." After describing much of the same RNA research I have presented, he calls the advocates' theories "just-so stor[ies], in honor of Rudyard Kipling and his fanciful tales about how different animals came to be." He feels complex living organisms cannot possibly come step-by-step from "nude" RNA acting alone. I certainly agree. His preferred theoretical approach is: "Whenever a collection of chemicals contains enough different kinds of molecules, a metabolism will crystallize from the broth. Metabolic networks need not be built one component at a time; they can spring full-grown from a primordial soup. Order for free, I call it. If I am right, the motto of life is not We the improbable, but We the expected." "If ever we are to attain a final theory in biology, we will surely, surely have to understand the commingling of self-organization and selection." And here again, I agree up to a point. The mathematical improbability of life springing up spontaneously molecule-by-molecule leads to his logical conclusion that scientists using a step-by-step Reductionist approach in the RNA research will not be successful. But as a scientist he avoids the issue of the possibility of a divine creation.

Robert Shapiro, whose odds for chances to form life were quoted above, wrote his book in 1986 to make the same points as Kauffman, the same objections to the "just-so stories", calling them instead scientific mythology; and he has the credentials to be legitimately critical. He "is a professor of chemistry at New York University, an expert in DNA research and the genetic effect of environmental chemicals." (From the book cover) He literally tears into each experimental approach, including those of Miller and Orgel, explaining why each is a dead end, although he does not mention Kauffman's theories, which probably had not been fully presented at the time. Shapiro offers the opinion that "mythology has penetrated to such a degree that it is difficult to judge the actual extent of our scientific knowledge [in the science of the origin of life]." For example, "a sentence in a report of a NASA advisory panel [stated]: 'Many people feel that the efficient production of nucleosides is something that will be demonstrated sooner or later.' The approach, unfortunately, does not represent science, but rather a search for evidence in support of an established mythology." At another point in the book he says: "We have reached a situation where a theory has been accepted as fact by some, and possible contrary evidence is shunted aside. This condition, of course, again describes mythology rather than science." Shapiro recognizes that "evolution does not anticipate needs. It is unlikely that nucleic acids were developed with the hope that they would take over the genetic function at some suitable future date." He cannot support any current theory, but does offer some possible approaches of his own. He discusses the concept of "intelligent design", only to reject it. He imagines a time when most "reasonable experiments to discover a probable origin of life have failed unequivocally. In such a case, some scientists might choose to turn to religion for an answer. Others, however, myself included, would attempt to sort out the surviving less probable scientific explanations in the hope of selecting one that was still more likely than the remainder."

Something started life. It could not have fallen together by accident. There must have been an organizing force. There are only two choices for that force: some heretofore undiscovered property of chemicals to be able with extreme complexity to self-organize, or there is an outside organizer, perhaps God. An astute reader, at this juncture, is sure to be thinking: "Aren't you running afoul of the philosophic objection contained in God-of-the-Gaps, bringing in God to fill a hole in scientific findings, only to have to remove God when the scientists figure out how life got jump-started?" I don't think so. The recently discovered organizational character of chaos, which surprisingly does exist, can provide only a minute part of the overall complexity of life, demonstrated by the mathematical predictions presented earlier (James Gleick, *Chaos; Making a New Science*, 1988). The phase transitions and autocatalytic reactions Kauffman described do seem to point the way. But as he, himself points out, the mathematical improbability is enormous; he agrees life had to start at a very simple level with a primitive protobacteria. He uses the Pleuromona organism as his simplest form of life. It is equivalent to the T4 phage used by Foster to calculate those enormous levels of improbability. Kauffman quotes the same calculations of Hoyle and Wickramsinghe I presented, yet he predicts we will figure out the appearance of life following his theories. "Whether or not I am right that life started with collective autocatalysis, the mere fact that such systems are possible should make us question the dogma of a central directing agency. The central directing agency is not necessary to life. Life has, I think, an inalienable wholeness. And always has." That 'wholeness' can only appear when life has formed, not beforehand! His error is that he demands a "required" wholeness in order to form life. I think he is very optimistic, like most scientists raised in the era of reductionism. His major insights are correct: 1) there must be an "organizer" of some sort to create the complexity of life. He places that organizer within chemicals. And 2) the whole is much more than the sum of its parts and may be able to create organization above and beyond what might be expected, which for one example, explains why our brain creates consciousness and intelligence beyond our need to survive.

Consumed by his insights, in a sort of tunnel vision, he has lost track of the underlying complexity of life he, himself, points out. A basic living organism, a protobacterium requires about 200 different proteins and enzymes, each one over 100 amino acids long, all working together cooperatively in an organized manner, as previously described, with the enormously improbable odds calculated against this occurring by chance. For his scheme to work, he must imagine a group of 200 autocatalytic sets. These must work together and are required to develop an innate organizing intelligence to provide an output of all the proper proteins, each with only left-handed amino acids, and connected to right-handed sugars (ribose and dexoxyribose), thus somehow or other creating RNA and DNA. Kauffman, similar to most scientists, wants to grant a giant soup of chemicals the ability to assume an enormous complexity all by themselves, rather than considering the possibility that God formed the universe and either initially granted the organizing force to those chemicals, or that God continued acting after the universe was formed and was the organizer Kauffman and I agree had to exist. God may well be needed to fill this 'gap'.

There are two other considerations readers may have thought about in creating life on earth, solving the gap in scientific knowledge. How about using a simpler form than bacteria? Could viruses have started life? Viruses depend upon living organisms for reproduction and survival. They are not completely alive, by definition. If all truly living organisms died out so would viruses. They are not the answer. For creating life on the earth the other possibility is life hitchhiking in on a meteorite. It is clear that the conditions in the universe are uniform throughout its entirety. If life formed here, as it did, then life may have developed elsewhere. But remember, wherever life appeared, the enormous odds against life by accident or chance are the same as on earth, given the apparent uniformity of conditions in the universe. The possibility of life arising throughout the universe is the consideration behind SETI (Search for Extraterrestrial Intelligence), which is being conducted with large radio telescopes, and created the inspiration for the movie *Contact* with Jodie Foster. As of this writing there has been no contact. Recognizing the spatial distances in the universe, (the nearest galaxy residing two million light-years away, and since radio waves travel at the speed of light) and also understanding the narrow "window of opportunity" in time to form a sun and planet like ours, the likelihood of contact is slight and if it occurs, will come from our own Milky Way or perhaps the local galaxy group. The first conclusion to be derived from thinking about and analyzing the meteorite theory is we really may be the only folks around; our planet is so special it may have the only life at any stage of development. Secondly, remember what a shooting star looks like in the sky. Meteorites slamming into our atmosphere get broiled. Living forms would not survive, although as mentioned before, organic compounds are individually present in meteorites that have been studied, and conceivably could have contributed to providing the raw material of life. Please recognize that I accept the idea that life may have appeared and might still exist elsewhere in the universe. It is the arrival of the original "seed" of life, a form that started life here, that I doubt. Nor do I expect the arrival of super-intelligent alien forms. That assumes the development of a quantum gravity theory (now in research), which discovers a method of travel greater than the speed of light, the "beam me up, Scotty" approach of Star Trek.

The gap in scientific knowledge of life's origin persists. I want the molecular biologists and all the others to continue to research the problem of how life originated, even though the effort certainly appears to be mathematically futile in finding an accidental method. My reason is that it is exceedingly difficult to prove a negative. If life did *not* start by chance, then every possible experimental attempt to find an accidental start must be exhausted before everyone is forced to accept creation by an outside force. As Adler points out in *How to Think About God*, when attempting to inquire about something that cannot be explained by scientific investigation, and God cannot be, then the explanation of the origin of life may have to reside in "proof beyond reasonable doubt", not in an absolute proof. Rational philosophy and natural theology can only go that far, and these are the logical approaches I am employing.

Chapter 4: Is The Evolution of Humans a Glorious Accident?

As in the previous chapter, we will use as a counterpoint the theories of Stephen Jay Gould, who was convinced that we humans are a total accident. According to the odds, the probabilities, we shouldn't have happened but we are here. Gould is a good place to start. Not only are his ideas unique, they have provoked angry rebuttals from other Darwinists who feel he is attacking some of the basic underpinnings of Darwin's theories. I don't like Gould's logic and plan to rebut him also, while attempting to show that we are not accidental.

Before proceeding to discuss the proposal that the appearance of humans through the process of evolution is accidental, we will first look at the theories of how the process of evolution operated. I accept evolution as having occurred, and feel that what is debatable are the mechanisms by which it operates: 1) whether it follows an accidental purposeless path (the Darwin theory); 2) a path guided by pre-existing inherent evolutionary principles (intelligent design); or 3) by an immanent and/or transcendent divine force (operating within or without our reality). God is specifically implied in mechanism 3 and possibly inferred in mechanism 2. A question that is always in the background is: Did God set this in motion, with or without rules, and does He take part in the process as it flows along? Further, in this chapter I will show that the history of evolution does not follow Darwin's proposal that very gradual changes create the process. The flow of the history will be interrupted by side discussions when apparent defects in the original Darwin Theory appear.

In the last chapter bacteria were identified as the earliest life forms. They are unicellular, appeared possibly as early as 3.8 billion years ago, (*New York Times* on the web, "Dusted for Life's Fingerprints, Rocks Fail, Kenneth Chang, 6/4/02; *Science* Vol. 296, No. 5572, pp. 1448-52, Fedo & Whitehouse, 5/24/02) and certainly as early as 3.6 billion years ago; and they are still here. They are obviously very successful since 99.9 percent of all other species that have inhabited the earth are now extinct, of an estimated five to 50 billion species that existed at one time or another. The mean life span of a genus (a family of species) is 20 million years, another way of looking at extinction (David M. Raup, *Extinction, Bad Genes or Bad Luck?*, 1991). Bacteria have a marvelous degree of adaptation, as witnessed by the rapid way they have developed resistance to many of the antibiotics currently employed by doctors over the past 70 years. They have DNA, and continue their inheritance by cell division, by dividing in half. When they divide, both daughter cells have exactly the same DNA their parent had, and the parent has become both of them. In a sense, they go on living forever, but they cannot be especially creative and develop the degree of complexity the multicellular organisms have. However, they can exchange some segments of DNA, a process that helps them develop antibiotic resistance.

These multicellular creatures (eukaryotes) which arose somehow out of bacteria, multiply and reproduce through sexual activity, with each member of the sexual pair contributing one strand of DNA to the embryo for each chromosome. Receiving one-half of inheritance from each parent is what allowed the creation of the variety of life forms in evolution, through the combination of differing inheritances and also utilizing variations in the DNA from spontaneous mutations, changing one or more of the base pair codes. It also brought birth and death, which considering that it led to us, is a reasonable tradeoff. The mutations occur at random, slightly modifying the DNA and creating good, bad, and neutral (that is, unimportant) changes, in roughly equal thirds. Obviously, only if the mutation occurs in reproductive cells will the mutation affect the body form or the functional abilities of the species in a subsequent generation. A recent estimate of the mutation rate in humans is 4.2 per generation, of which 1.6 are bad and removed by natural selection. The remainder is equally either neutral or good. This rate of modification represents a change in a tiny portion of our DNA, which has 3.3 billion base pairs, and indicates how slowly evolution should be expected to move in humans (Eyre-Walker & Keightley, *Nature*, 28 January 1999). This mutation occurrence in DNA is the first principle of Darwinism, providing the variation in individuals, which is then tested by nature for its suitability for survival.

It must be made very clear that the understanding of how DNA works is very incomplete. The coding mechanism is clear, but the controls over putting together three-dimensional protein molecules to manufacture whole organs are not understood, although Hox genes thought to exert this type of control are found throughout several layers of evolution, from flies to mice. The DNA of single-celled amoeba is longer than human DNA, but most of it is non-functional. That means early DNA was larger than it had to be, as if preparing for the future. The same genes are used throughout evolution for similar functions, by all levels of complexity of animals. The pax-6 gene controls the development of eyes in flies and in humans, an example cited by many authors. The compound eye of the fly and the human eye are vastly different in construction, yet genetic control is quite similar. "What has quite unexpectedly emerged (from the study of evolution) is how seemingly very different organisms have in common fundamentally the same genetic information. Here is perhaps the central paradox of genes and evolution: vast contrasts in morphology [body type] and behavior need have no corresponding differences in the genetic code." (Conway Morris, *The Crucible of Creation*, 1998) Morris makes an educated guess that this master control gene, pax-6, originated over 600 million years ago as a control for light-sensitive organs, long before evolution decided eyes were needed.

Pre-ordained gene instructions and chance mutations, which change those instructions, are one side of the evolutionary process. The other side of the evolutionary process is Darwin's principle of natural selection. The organisms that are best adapted to the environment's changing challenges survive. This is the old adage "survival of the fittest" that everyone recognizes. Darwin himself, understood that Natural Selection was the "most important, but not the exclusive, means of modification." (Gould, *Scientific American*, Oct. 1994) There have been overwhelming natural disasters, including the giant meteorite that killed off the dinosaurs 65 million years ago (Chapter 2). David Raup answers the question in the title of his book, *Bad Genes or Bad Luck?*, by stating his opinion that most species appear to die out because they are unluckily caught by rapid adverse changes in nature, not that their genes are so bad. Still the major thrust of Darwin's ideas encompasses a gradual change in inheritance, which allows the best-adapted animals to survive and gradually mutate into a somewhat different form with slightly different capabilities. A major climatic change will kill off weak species and may drive the process into producing major changes in the organisms that manage to survive. This applies to both plant and animal kingdoms.

A major philosophic debate among evolutionary scientists is whether there is an underlying mechanism that drives evolution toward complexity, or is it an illusion that evolution appears to be programmed for complexity. From the time of Darwin until the present, the presentation of the theory of evolution has been that of a gradual process, one little step at a time toward increasing complexity in living organisms. It is Gould's contention that complexity is the natural result of life's initial condition: bacteria are the first and simplest form and so genetic changes had only one direction open, the direction of increasing complexity. At the same time he makes a great fuss over bacteria as being the most successful life form, having existed throughout the total history of life, and predicts they will continue to do so "into all future time so long as the earth endures." They do successfully live in every nook and cranny of the earth, on the surface and deep inside, in the most extreme conditions of temperature, and may make up the highest percentage of biomass on earth. "Biomass" is the concept of the weight of living matter produced on earth (Stephen Jay Gould, *Full House*, 1996). "Successful," I think is in the eye of the beholder. If bacteria are so successful, and they are, judging from the fact that they appeared with the onset of life and are still with us, then we must ask: why did complexity 'bother' to appear? Throughout evolutionary history, as Gould explains, successful species stop evolving: "We have no evidence that the modal form of human bodies or brains has changed at all in the past 100,000 years—a standard phenomenon of stasis for successful and widespread species, and not (as popularly misconceived) (sic) an odd exception to an expectation of continuous and progressive change." (*Full House*).

I feel Gould contradicts himself in these observations because of his underlying bias that each advance in evolution is an accident, contingent (dependent) on the last preceding accident, and therefore all advances in complexity are totally due to chance. He holds to the position that progress toward the more complex is only a passive reaction to the fact that anything less complex than bacteria cannot truly be alive. (Less complex organisms such as viruses are not truly alive, since they are really parasites, and could not survive without the existence of more complex life.) But that does not answer my original comment. Why should the evolutionary process bother to create more complexity if the initial species, bacteria, are so successful? Why wasn't there the "stasis" Gould describes in other successful species? By Gould's theory stasis implies no further complexity need appear. I believe increasing complexity is a built-in drive in the process of evolution.

Darwin in his concluding lines of The *Origin of Species* expressed his belief there was a push toward complexity in the evolutionary process: "As natural selection works solely by and for the good of each being, all corporeal and mental endowments will tend towards perfection." His opinion directly correlates with sacred theology, describing an attribute of God, Who provides good. Gould is forced, by his atheistic position, to characterize Darwin's statement as "expressing Victorian social preference". (Gould, *Scientific American* October 1994). To defend his viewpoint further, Gould presents in *Full House* scientific studies of both "passive" and of "driven" evolutionary trends, to support his view that evolution is a passive movement toward increasing complexity. He finds little evidence for "driven" trends. This attempt on Gould's part to assign a passive role to evolution is again completely contradicted by his own statement on the Cambrian period of evolution in the *Scientific American*. He discussed the rapid appearance of complexity and diversity in the 'Cambrian Explosion' 530 million years ago, when in a five million year period, all but one of the ancestors of today's multicellular organisms very suddenly appeared, after three billion years of primarily bacterial forms and a very few simple multicellular types. "The Cambrian explosion was the most remarkable and puzzling event in the history of life." Since he accepts a view of evolution as a passive process, depending upon an initial driving force of a chance and random appearance of mutations, followed then by the judgment of nature, it is no wonder he has no answer to the Cambrian explosion, which has all the appearance of extreme activity toward complexity. We will return to the Cambrian Explosion for a more complete discussion shortly.

The studies on passivity he presents ignore his own principle of long periods of 'stasis' for successful organisms. These studies imply that evolution plods forward slowly but steadily. Actually the fossil record evolution appears to go forward by fits and starts. In fact, Gould developed a concept of "punctuated equilibrium" to describe how unevenly evolutionary progress appears to proceed. In this theory (developed with Niles Eldredge) is the claim that most evolution is accomplished by large abrupt changes, after periods of 'stasis', not the gradualism of tiny changes envisioned by Darwin (Lee Spetner, *Not by Chance*, 1997 & Michael Denton, *Evolution: A Theory In Crisis*, 1985). The Punctuated Equilibrium Theory has four parts. "1. Most of the time natural selection does not cause significant evolutionary change, [but] acts to keep a species stable by weeding out individuals that deviate too greatly from the norm. [A species] may remain essentially unchanged for many millions of years." "2. Evolutionary change takes place in short bursts [of time]." 3. Isolated species evolve into new species by responding to adverse environmental changes in their habitat. 4. Only some new species survive, while others do not, as the specific species tries to maintain the integrity of its genetics as in point 1. This is called 'species sorting'. (Morris). This theory, discussed further later in this chapter, is an attempt to solve the complaint of critics of Darwin that very gradual transitional forms are never found in fossils. In science giving a poorly understood process a descriptive title gives that process an aura of explanation without explaining anything. It happens all the time in medicine.

One other odd quirk in understanding the process of 'complexity' in evolution is the size of our brain. As mentioned before it quadrupled in size very rapidly in 2.5 million years (Chapter 3), implying rapidly increasing complexity; but our brain is about ten percent smaller than the Neanderthal brain, the folks who died out 30,000 years ago as an unsuccessful species. The Cambrian Explosion appears 'driven' as does the development of our brain; these evolutionary activities defy scientific explanation, and we might ask why evolution has decided in a seemingly paradoxical fashion that our smaller brain is 'better', perhaps more complex, than the bigger Neanderthal brain?

I have presented this digression on evolution to clearly indicate to you that evolution is a theory, not fact, and there are all sorts of holes and inconsistencies in what is generally presented in schools and to the public. Is it passive, as Gould thinks, or is it driven to complexity, which is Morris' contention? (*The Crucible of Creation*). It is not clear-cut that the process functions all by itself. Other authors, Philip Johnson in *Darwin on Trial*, Michael Behe in *Darwin's Black Box*, Lee Spetner in *Not By chance*, and Michael Denton in *Evolution: A Theory In Crisis*, "[also] show how evolution is not a fact, but a theory. They expose serious scientific problems. They do not claim a more provable thesis; they simply state that 'we don't know' is intellectually preferable to insisting evolution is fact even if it means ignoring the evidence". (Rabbi Daniel Lapin, *America's Other War*, 1999).

Having now stated these objections and observations let's look at the history of evolution as currently accepted by science, facts only. In this way you are alerted to some of the disputed ideas in advance, which will help your thinking, but I need to warn you, as I have before, that I believe the process of evolution actually happened, while proposing that the mechanisms theorized by Darwin are not the way evolution has occurred. If the scientific findings, subjected as they are to intense peer review and criticism, are received with an open mind, they cannot be refuted. It is the interpretation of the causes of events that should be under debate. Those fossils that have been described really do exist. The fossils that appear to lead up to *us* exist. It is difficult to imagine a God, Who placed those fossils in the rocks just to fool us, or to test our faith. God is not disingenuous.

How complete is the fossil record? According to Raup it is "awful and superb at the same time. On one hand, only a miniscule fraction of past life has been fossilized (and found by paleontologists) (sic). On the other hand, we have tens of millions of excellently preserved fossils to work with. About 250,000 species have been described, named and located reasonably well in space and time. So, although the sample of past life is a small percentage of the whole, it is large enough to provide a lot of information." There are large gaps in the fossil story, because finding them is part knowing where to look, part luck, part hard work, and partially a problem of nature itself. It takes special physical conditions to trap organisms and preserve them. Luck has a great deal to do with it. An amateur fossil hunter in Australia looking "in pure quartz sandstone that rarely contains fossil remains" first found the Ediacaran fossils (simple multicellular forms) from 600 million years ago. (Raup). No professional paleontologist would have looked there.

Aging of fossils depends upon the age of the geologic layer they appear in and the use of radioactive carbon-14 dating, an accurate but not perfect technique that involves measuring decay of a form of carbon into another form. The general accuracy of carbon-14 dating has been substantiated by the method of uranium-thorium decay, with the two methods agreeing within 10 to 20 percent (Schroeder, *The Science of God*). And even more accurate is the rubidium-strontium decay "method, [which] gives self-calibrating and self-checking results" with an accuracy (I calculated from the example given) of plus/minus three percent (Miller, *Finding Darwin's God*). Not to belabor the point, there are several other radioactive aging techniques that agree with these.

As covered in Chapter 3, life began in the form of bacteria, 200 to 400 million years after the surface of the earth cooled, in a short 'window of opportunity'. "Thus life on earth evolved as quickly and is as old as it could be. This fact alone seems to indicate an inevitability, or at least a predictability, for life's origin from the original chemical constituents of atmosphere and ocean." (Gould, *Scientific American*). Nothing passive about that! The first multicellular (eukaryote) forms that have been found as fossils, appeared 600 million years ago, and are called Ediacarans, after the spot they were found in Australia. They constitute either a failed life form or may represent an early form of modern corals and jellyfish. They generally died out and were followed by odds and ends of minor forms. Morris suggests that a few of the Ediacarans survived into the next phase, the Cambrian Explosion as it is titled, and mentioned before. There were some relatively complex fossils, including seaweeds, fertilized animal eggs and embryos, and "surprisingly complex creatures", dating at about 570 million years ago (Precambrian) which have recently been discovered (*Scientific American*, April 1998). Prior to all these fossils is evidence of metabolic molecules that could only have been created by primitive eukaryotes – fat metabolism molecules in rocks 2.7 billion years old in Australia (Brocks et al, *Science*, 13 August 1999), 2.2 billion years before the Cambrian Explosion, which I will now describe more completely.

Suddenly, at about 530 million years ago, there was a five-million-year-long explosion of new multicellular complex animal forms from which can be traced all but one phylum (primary division) out of 35 now existing in modern animal life. Put in other terms, the 'explosion' represents a massive diversification in body forms in a very short period of time, not the gradualism usually associated with Darwinism and slow adaptation to nature. The paleontologists are absolutely convinced this five million period is valid and not the result of a gap in the fossil record. Whereas previous animals were soft bodied, these new animal forms had either external or internal skeletons. They were first found in the Burgess Shale high in the Rocky Mountains in Canada near Lake Louise, the subject of Gould's best-selling book, *Wonderful Life* (1989) and found by accident while building a rail line across Kicking Horse Pass.

Here among an enormous variety of animal forms the first notochord appeared in a tiny animal called Pikaia. The notochord is a primitive spinal column and cord, and the Pikaia are therefore thought to be the ancient ancestors of vertebrate animals including humans. This animal had a tiny brain along with its notochord, and its muscles are arranged in bundles or myotomes, just as our muscles are constructed. The basic body plan is that of the animal group Chordates, of which mammals are a part. In this tiny brain "were the first dim stirrings of neural activity that half a billion years later would emerge as full fledged consciousness." (Morris, *The Crucible of Creation*). Morris makes the point that a striking development in the Cambrian Explosion is the apparent sudden appearance of a substantial increase in neurological sophistication. "The appearance of the nerve cell must be regarded as one of the great steps in the history of life. This is because one path of evolution is then set toward the development of brains, presumably intelligence, and perhaps consciousness…The first two steps—

brains and intelligence— have been acquired at least twice in the history of animals." One phylum is the mollusks, typified by the octopus, and the other, of course, is the phylum of vertebrates, the organisms with a spinal column and an internal skeleton, that includes us.

The development of nervous tissues and brains in two totally different life forms such as mammals and octopi represents a principle in evolutionary science called convergence. It simply means that emerging life forms, probably due to their similar DNA patterns, will evolve body parts and organs that mimic each other, "despite having evolved from very different ancestors." Similarities in parts of seemingly unrelated animal types are extremely common according to Morris. Adapting to nature results in parallel solutions. Convergence is the answer to Gould's persistent statement that "if life's tape were rerun", Pikaia might not have ever appeared in the Cambrian explosion, and vertebrates including us, wouldn't be here. This is why Gould calls us an accident. He contends that since the Cambrian Explosion the number of phyla has markedly decreased from hundreds to the current 35, making evolution look much like a lottery, the survival of a phylum to be luck. By assuming a marked initial diversity that gradually becomes reduced during evolution, Gould makes evolution "the largest lottery ever played out on our Planet," (*Scientific American*, October 1994) and this results in protecting his view of his science from any outside influence or self-organizing principle, from any theological inference.

Gould's philosophic bias regarding evolution proposes that it is a process that gradually reduces the number of species to a few survivors. It may be based upon Gould's doctoral thesis on seashells. "According to Gould, the fact that there are thousands of potential shell shapes in the world, but only a half dozen actual shell forms, is evidence of natural selection. Not so, [according to theoretical mathematician, Stephen] Wolfram. He discovered a mathematical error in Gould's argument, and there are only six possible shell shapes, and all of them exist in the world. [He feels] you don't need natural selection to pare down evolution to a few robust forms. Rather, organisms evolve outward to fill all possible forms available to them. Complexity is destiny—and Darwin becomes a footnote. 'I've come to believe that natural selection is not all that important,' [Wolfram has commented]." Wolfram is a former member of the Institute for Advanced Study at Princeton. ("God, Stephen Wolfram, and Everything Else," Michael S. Malone, *Forbes ASAP*, 11/27/00) Criticisms from Wolfram cannot be ignored. He published his first paper in physics at age 15, and earned his

Ph.D. from Caltech at age 20, after working with and impressing the famous theoretical physicist and Nobel Laureate, Richard Feynman. At 22 he was awarded a MacArthur "genius" fellowship, and six years later created a very valued and widely used computer program, Mathematica (*NY Times* on the web, "Did this Man Just Rewrite Science?," Dennis Overbye, 6/11/02).

Morris, who also disagrees with Gould, notes, "Overall the evidence of diversity increasing throughout geological time is rather convincing... Nearly all biologists agree that convergence is a ubiquitous feature of life. What we are interested in is not the origin, destiny, or fate of a particular lineage, but the likelihood of the emergence of a particular property, say consciousness. Here the reality of convergence suggests that the tape of life, to use Gould's metaphor, can be run as many times as we like and in principle intelligence will surely emerge." And sure enough, after Gould used the Burgess Shale example of the Cambrian Explosion in his book, *Wonderful Life*, to support his contingency, or "lottery" contention, other Cambrian-containing shale sites were investigated and showed he jumped to his conclusions too soon. What turned up in China in 1995 was a fossil called "Yunnanazoon", probably a hemichordate, an unrelated and a more primitive form to our ancestor, Pikaia. Since then "large numbers of complete specimens of soft-bodies chordates from the Lower Cambrian Maotianshan Shale in southern China have been recovered", including "Haikouella lanceolata" (Chen, Huang & Li, *Nature*, 12/2/99, pages 518-522) and "Haikouicthys excaicunensis," which demonstrated a more complex head with eyes, and 'possible' nasal and ear areas, along with spinal vertebrae that were present in the earlier findings, reported by S. Conway Morris and his Chinese co-workers in 2003 (Shu, Morris et al, *Nature* 421, 526-529, 30 January 2003). Further examples of convergence.

Morris concludes his refutation of Gould's theories: "We might do better to accept our intelligence as a gift, and it may be a mistake to imagine that we shall not be called to account. We muddy the waters of the debate if we fail to acknowledge that the processes of evolution have metaphysical implications for us. This is because uniquely there is inherent in our human situation the possibility of transcendence. The fact that we arrived here via an immensely long string of species that originated in something like Pikaia rather than some other corpuscular blob is a wonderful scientific story, but is hardly material to our present condition." That is a very different approach from Gould's. Unfortunately, Gould is a very prolific and very gifted writer. He has succeeded in popularizing his viewpoint with the reading public to some degree, but Morris, one of the world's leading experts in the Burgess Shale and the Cambrian Explosion, is on the counterattack and is not willing to accept the atheistic approach typified by Gould.

With his belief in convergence Morris continued to investigate the Cambrian fossil beds in southern China and reported in *Nature* (11/4/99) with co-author De-Gan Shu their discovery of two definite vertebrate forms, fossil fish, one resembling a lamprey and the other resembling an early hagfish. Both fish were present in the early Cambrian explosion, according to the layers where they were found. These highly significant discoveries clearly put to rest Gould's contention of an evolutionary lottery, based on his proposal previously mentioned that if it were not for the appearance of Pikaia in the Burgess Shale we would not have appeared. It is clear that vertebral forms appeared in the Cambrian Explosion in several parts of the world, implying we may not have had a single ancestor, but several ancestor possibilities, following the reasoning of the theory of convergence.

I have shown you that evolutionary scientists do not march in ideological lockstep. The Cambrian Explosion must imply an inherent organizing principle to provide for such a rapidly advancing complexity. Could that principle have been arranged by God? Some scientists are beginning to wonder; some like Michael J. Behe, writer of *Darwin's Black Box*, are convinced. Morris, while offering some concluding remarks for his book, discussing the possibility of life elsewhere in the universe, suggests he is beginning to wonder: "Synthesizing the chemical building blocks of life is no guarantee that life itself is a preordained inevitability. Even if life is eventually created in the laboratory, this will be by conscious manipulation. What happened on the earth four billion years ago may have been very different." He seems close to reaching Stuart Kauffman's proposal that there are self-organizing aspects within the complexity of life (Chapter 3), and "suppose[s] that the far more complex phenomenon of life itself, defined as a replicating cell, was the product of a freak and extraordinarily rare event." He certainly does not consider us an accidental fallout from the process of evolution. Evolutionists offer the following alternatives to the proposal of an inherent organizing principle to drive complexity: 1) atmospheric oxygen levels were rising due to the increasing biomass of divergent plants, which allowed more vigorous metabolism and therefore more rapid evolutionary changes; and 2) perhaps the mutation rate was much faster during the Cambrian period. The first suggestion is a reasonable conjecture, but why did the rapid changes slow down so much after 5 million years, since the oxygen level did not return to lower levels, remaining the same until the present time. The second suggestion is totally unprovable.

There is further discomfort to the Darwin theory beyond the findings of rapid appearance of animals in the Cambrian period. "The story is the same for plants. At their first appearance the angiosperms [certain sexually reproducing plants] were divided into different classes, many of which have persisted with little change up to the present day. Within a space of probably less than fifty million years from their first appearance the angiosperms transformed the world's vegetation. Again, just as in the case of the absence of pre-Cambrian fossils, no forms have been found in pre-Cretaceous rocks linking the angiosperms with any other group of plants." (*Evolution: A Theory In Crisis*, Michael Denton, 1985. Dr Denton is a medical doctor and a molecular biologist.) The Cretaceous geologic period ended 65 million years ago coincident with the extinction of the dinosaurs.

Both the Cambrian Explosion of animals and the Cretaceous explosion of plants drive home the consideration that a drive to complexity is inherent in the evolutionary process. There "seems to [be] an inherent tendency to move toward emergent complexity, life, and consciousness." (Ian G. Barbour, *When Science Meets Religion*, 2000, pg. 112). This mechanism is somehow within DNA and recent research has revealed that some evolutionary change, especially more rapid change, is driven by mechanisms outside of DNA. Lee Spetner (*Not By Chance!*), a Ph.D. in physics who has studied Darwinism as a hobby, suggests, "that organisms have a built-in capability of adapting to their environment...Organisms contain within themselves the information that enables them to develop [rapidly] a phenotype [body type] adaptive to a variety of environments. The adaptation can occur by a change in the genome [DNA] through a genetic change triggered by the environment, or it can occur without any genetic change. For the organism to have this capability, it has to have in it the necessary information. No one yet knows how much capability of this sort is built into free-living cells, plants, and animals. The more potential there is, the more information the organism must carry" in its DNA and apparently outside of the DNA. Barbour makes the same observation (Barbour is a professor emeritus of physics and religion at Carleton College, Northfield, Minnesota.). "Some biologists have noted that the *internal drives of organisms* can initiate evolutionary changes." For example, "a few pioneering fish ventured onto land and were the ancestors of amphibians and mammals. Organisms themselves took new initiatives; genetic and anatomic changes followed from their actions (the so-called Baldwin effect). In such cases, random mutations in genes did not start the chain of events that led to change; rather, they served to perpetuate changes first introduced by *the actions of the organisms* themselves. This does not imply that the organisms were *trying* to evolve, only that purposive behavior as well as chance mutations set the direction of evolutionary change."

To illustrate this mechanism, and especially to show how rapid it can be, Spetner (pg. 205) referred to the work on guppies of David Reznick and his team at the University of California. They placed guppies, which lived in a river with predator fish that preyed on small immature guppies, into a river with a predator fish that preyed on large mature guppies. Within two years the guppies started to mature earlier and have many small offspring. They reversed the study and after putting different guppies from a river with a predator who preferred large mature guppies into a river with a predator that preferred the smaller ones, the guppies matured later and had fewer offspring, at the same rate as the guppies in the first part of the study. "The evolutionary rate calculated from this observation is some ten million times the rate of evolution induced from the observations of the fossil record [Reznick et al 1997]". (*Science*, vol. 275, pp.1934-1937). This study was done originally to look at a theory which said "that animals preyed on as adults will have as many babies as possible during their short life span, and will have many babies starting at an early age. Animals whose main predator attacks their young will take the opposite evolutionary tack. They have fewer but larger babies starting later in life." (*N.Y. Times*, "Theory of evolution experiment goes swimmingly," Gina Kolata, 1990).

The guppy study offers two possible explanations. "Reznick interpreted these changes as a result of natural selection acting on variation already within the [guppy] population. [Another] reasonable explanation is that the presence of the predator induced the changes in the individual fish," (Spetner) which the most recent research supports as the operative mechanism. "It appears that genes depend on the environment to give them 'go' or 'no go' signals." That is, the genes are turned on to be active or turned off to be passive by changes in the environment, which create chemical changes in the structure of living cells, which is then transmitted to the genetic material ("The Nature of Nurture: How the Environment Can Shape Our Genes," Sharon Begley, *Wall Street Journal*, 6/14/02; *The Dependent Gene: The Fallacy of Nature vs. Nurture*, David S. Moore, Ph.D., 2002). Philosopher of Science James Barham in a talk at Calvin College (5/25/2001) agrees: "We now know that cells are capable of regulating their own genomes

[DNA] in a functional, goal-directed manner. This means that [the concept] the organism is a machine controlled by the genome in the same way that a program controls a computer is out the window. What all of this means is that…we must proceed on the assumption that all DNA is functional and that…the inheritance of many functional capacities is not mediated by the chromosomes at all, but is carried out through the soma of the ovum." The soma is that part of the cell outside the nucleus. The nucleus contains the DNA (In the archives of www.iscid.org).

Science is constantly reporting evidence of this concept that living organisms can influence their own evolution and adaptations at a rapid rate. Here are two examples of ongoing research: Yeast, an extremely simple life form can quickly restructure its DNA when the glucose (sugar) it feeds on is scarce, causing it to absorb and burn sugar more efficiently. (Durham et al., *Proc. Natl. Acad. Sci. U.S.A.* 10.1073/pnas.242624799 (2002)) Secondly, rearing salmon in captivity, obviously a safe environment, results in the production of small eggs, which are less likely to survive in the wild than large eggs, the usual size produced by salmon in their natural environment. This "evolutionary change to [a] maladaptive state occurred in under 20 years." ("Rapid Evolution of Egg Size in Captive Salmon," Daniel D. Heath et al, *Science*, Vol. 299, No. 5613, pg. 1738, 14 March 2003).

Some or perhaps all of the control of gene activity may occur in parts of DNA, which previously has been considered "junk", making up almost half of all human DNA. The junk is sequences of bases that appeared earlier to have no genetic function until recent research has found hints of usefulness: Sections of DNA are found to be "conserved" (preserved) during evolution, that is, present unchanged in human DNA and in lesser forms, such as mice. Conservation implies usefulness for some function. One discovered function is repair of broken DNA and movement of sections of genes from one point to another. (U. of Michigan Health System, Public Release 5/12/02: *Nature Genetics*: June 2002,31:2, 159-165; also "Charting a Genome's Hills and Valleys," *Science*, Vol. 296, 5/31/02). Other recent studies have found the production of greater amounts of RNA than can be accounted for by the DNA in genes. RNA can act to regulate cell functions and form part of cell structure (*New York Times* on the web, "Citing RNA, Studies Suggest a Much Deeper Gene Pool," Andrew Pollack, 5/4/02). This RNA may guide the rapid evolutionary responses to nature, as in the guppy study. Many laboratories have jumped into research of the conserved 'junk' areas and have found the production of short RNA strands (21-23 code bases) of two types: micro-

RNA, which stops the production of protein, and RNAi which stops genes from working. Dr. John S. Mattick, a molecular biologist at the University of Queensland in Australia is of the opinion that this type of RNA "provides the complexity that separates higher life forms from simpler ones." (*New York Times* on the web, "RNA Trades Bit Part for Starring Role in the Cell," Andrew Pollack, 1/21/03). Further studies of DNA have also turned up two new amino acids, making a total of 22 found in nature used by animals to construct proteins (www.scientificamerican.com, 5/29/02). No doubt many more DNA functions will be found in what was thought to be unused portions of DNA.

Wm. H. Calvin theorizes that sudden environmental changes, for example, the ice ages, drove the development of big brains in humans, driven by the need for rapid adaptation (*A Brain for All Seasons: Human Evolution and Abrupt Climate Change*, Wm. H. Calvin, 2002). This is another variation on the findings of the guppy study. In his review of Calvin's book, Jeffrey H. Schwartz (author of *Sudden Origins: Fossils, Genes and the Origin of Species*, 1999) makes the same point: "Human evolution, like that of other organisms, is not a gradual transformation of form and behavior over time. Rather, like the shifts in the environments in which the organisms find themselves, evolutionary change is abrupt, even catastrophic." This is another example of two Darwinists agreeing with the punctuated equilibrium theory of evolution, not the gradualism described by classic neo-Darwinism.

Rapid change in evolution requires the utilization of massive amounts of information to create these sudden adaptations. These observations raise the issue: where did this information come from? First, is it possible it was it all in place when the process of the evolutionary mechanism started? Or, second, did it appear later on in DNA and possibly in the remainder of the reproductive cell created by chance mutation? All of this arrangement appears to be too purposive to assume that all the massive amounts of information in reproductive cells were deposited there totally by chance mutations. Spetner's review of the scientific findings concludes that individual mutations add little or no information in a slow chance process as proposed by Darwin. His opinion is that the information was present from the beginning of life (*Not By Chance!*). Overman agrees. Living animals are highly complex. Information theory requires that the level of complexity relates to the level of information content in a structure. This is defined as the "minimum number of instructions necessary to specify the structure. Structures…with high complexity [require] more information content which requires more instructions necessary to specify the structure. Highly complex structures require many instructions. Life appears to be formed only by a guided process with intelligence somehow inserting instructions into inert matter." Overman observes that most theoretical Darwinists do not understand information theory, confusing order with complexity. In simple terms order is repetition, nothing more. He claims this is the reason Darwinists conclude natural selection can somehow induce enough information into DNA. Information theorists strongly disagree (*A Case Against Accident and Self-Organization*, Dean. L. Overman, 1997).

Complex living structures appear to have been guided during evolution toward a specific goal. However, "natural selection, on the other hand, does not have a distant goal in mind, does not target any particular outcome and relies instead upon chance for innovations that are preserved by selection. In other words, the Darwin mechanism is extremely information-poor and relies upon chance to produce its information in small bits, by gradual steps. The problem comes when we find biologic systems that cannot be assembled by gradually adding tiny bits of information and require instead multiple coordinated changes before selectable advantage arises. These sorts of biologic structures require large amounts of information be generated in a single step. This is the key problem facing a Darwinian explanation, and is the reason why some doubt the efficacy of natural selection in producing these systems. The challenge and the essence of Darwin's theory, is to show that information can be built up gradually, step-by-step, from initial conditions lacking information". This is the major complaint of information theorists against Darwin theorists, and the major criticism that Neo-Darwinists refuse to consider (John Bracht, doctoral candidate, New Mexico Tech, www.metanexus.net, 5/29/02).

To continue the story of human evolution, we humans followed the Cambrian Explosion, but not directly, in fact over 500 million years later. As a dominant group the dinosaurs appeared roughly 200 million years ago and existed on earth for about 150 million years with an enormous diversity of species. Small mammals, the size of rats, coexisted, but did not advance beyond that size or complexity, until the dinosaurs were wiped out quickly and totally by a cataclysmic extinction, now thought to be caused by a six-mile-across asteroid that hit off the Yucatan peninsula 65 million years ago (*Rare Earth*, Ward & Brownlee, 2000). The explosive impact created a crater almost 100 miles across and threw so much debris into the atmosphere, the earth became thickly shrouded, creating the equivalent of a nuclear winter, and the temperature drop appears to have been the cause of wipe out the dinosaurs. The little mammals survived and evolved gradually into us. In Schroeder's book, *The Science of God*, he raises the issue of 'lucky us' or "divine retuning". After all, as he observes: "The asteroid gave life a chance to redirect toward the desired goal of a sentient, intelligent being able to absorb within it the amazing concept of ethical monotheism."

There have been five major extinctions among many smaller ones. Extinctions have played a major role in evolution. Showing how science advances, Raup, a leading expert in the study of extinctions, described in *Extinctions*, large impact craters that coincided with three of these major extinctions, but the lack of corroborating scientific evidence caused him to state that he could not accept a relationship. That is all changed. The crater causing the dinosaur extinction is now fully accepted. A large crater was subsequently found in Australia that coincides with the 'Great Dying', an extinction that caused a loss of 95 percent of all species at the end of the Permian geologic period, 250 million years ago. A lava flow may also have contributed to the 'Great Dying', with a release of vast quantities of gases into the atmosphere. A flow a mile deep and the size equal to one-half of Australia as been found in Siberia (*Science* Vol. 296. No. 5574, pp.1846-49, 6/7/02). And a crater in Quebec, Canada appears to have caused a major extinction 200 million years ago, at the end of the Triassic period. The two oldest major extinctions, 360 and 440 million years ago also appear related to craters, but no supporting evidence has as yet been developed (as of 2002). For the three most recent major extinctions, science is finding the corroborating evidence Raup wanted: A layer of iridium around the Earth of the proper date, microspherules of glass coming from melted rock, distorted quartz (called shocked quartz) in the earth's crust at the impact site, and the finding of exotic hollow spheres of carbon atoms, molecules called "fullerenes", containing examples of gases from outer space ("Repeated Blows", Luann Becker, *Scientific American*, Vol.: 286, No. 3, March 2002).

Raup looked at the safety of our civilization surviving an impact and quoted a study that estimated a major impact every 300,000 years. More recent estimates from various studies offer differing probabilities of different-sized collisions. Based on the number of craters on the moon, astronomers now estimate that major impacts, with asteroids measuring 3.1 miles across, hit the earth about 60 times in 600 million years, that is, an average of once in every ten million years. An asteroid this size would create a crater about 60 miles across (Becker). A study of near-Earth asteroids has reduced the estimate of their number to half (about 1,500), but the authors still suggest a 50 percent chance of a major collision every 500,000 years (*Nature*, 13 January 2000, pg. 165-166, Rabinowitz, Helin, Lawrence & Pravdo). Smaller space rocks near earth (in the range of 300-330 yards across) are estimated to hit the earth about every 20,000 to 30,000 years. One such projectile missed the earth in January 2002 by twice the distance to the moon. If it had hit it could have wiped out an area the size of a small city (Editorial comment by Sarah Simpson, page 82 within Becker's article). Raup and these other authors are estimating impacts from asteroids smaller than six miles (ten kilometers) in diameter. It requires a six-mile-across asteroid to create global effects similar to the one that destroyed the dinosaurs. We obviously need to catalog all the large asteroids that cross earth's orbit, a process that is occurring at this writing (2002), and learn how to change their course, if we want to avoid the dinosaurs' fate; and also catalog the smaller ones, which certainly can create major disasters if a populated area is struck. NASA hopes to have 90 percent of near-Earth asteroids identified by 2008 (Simpson).

There are events other than asteroid impacts that can affect evolution and life on earth. It was recently discovered that supernovae exploded near the earth about two million years ago. The evidence is the presence of several different layers of iron-60 in ocean bed samples found by a German research group. "Iron-60 is made by only one thing in nature, a supernova." Further evidence is the relative absence of interstellar gas and dust in our region of the galaxy, which the explosion would have blown away. This is exactly the same timing as the Pliocene/Pleistocene extinctions two million years ago. It is also the time that Homo erectus, our immediate human ancestor appeared. It is presumed that the explosions blasted away our ozone layer, opening up all living beings to intense radiation and ultraviolet solar rays. "'All sorts of mutational damage to animal's DNA would have occurred. New species could have emerged as a result. It is possible Homo sapiens may have been one of these,' said Dr. Narciso Benitez of Johns Hopkins University." ("How star blasts forged mankind," Robin McKie, *Guardian Unlimited*, 2/17/02, www.guardian.co.uk).

The universe is obviously a dangerous place, a point I have made before. The mass extinctions and the impact craters show evolution does not advance only through natural selection, but also through these accidental collisions, which obviously have a very substantial impact on all forms of life. Most of evolution does appear to be trial and error with some species lasting enormous amounts of time before disappearing. The Trilobites, a hard-shelled ocean-dwelling animal, appeared just before the Cambrian Explosion, consisted of a very diverse 6,000 species, and yet died out after existing 325 million years, by about 245 million years ago, as a result, it is thought, of competition from newly evolved fish.

Returning to the history of the evolution of humans, about 500,000 years ago, according to recent DNA evidence, the ancestors of the Neanderthals split off from the ancestors of *Homo sapiens*, us. The Neanderthals looked like the cavemen in the comic strip *Alley Oop*, larger heads and brows, smaller jaw, slightly stooped. Both groups appeared approximately 150,000-200,000 years ago, and actually lived side-by-side in Europe for 60,000 years, with the Neanderthals dying out 30,000 years ago. I have heard one television news report (July, 1999) of the discovery of a skeleton that suggested crossbreeding; most authorities in the past stated this didn't happen, but perhaps there was an occasional occurrence. In general the two populations appear to have remained separate. Although their brains were ten percent larger, it appears the Neanderthals lacked the mathematical and aesthetic capacity of our brains. They did practice burial starting about 100,000 years ago and the artifacts found at burial sites suggested they were religious. Their tools were sophisticated, but they never developed the capacity for art such as found in the Cro-Magnon cave sites of our immediate ancestors. Archeologist Alexander Marshack has found in a Cro-Magnon site a reindeer antler with markings that match the phases of the moon. Based on archeological comparisons the Neanderthals probably lacked literary and mathematical skills as well; their sites do not show any art or written symbols. (Michael Rothschild, in *Forbes ASAP* magazine. He is president of Bionomics Institute, San Francisco.) There is a major difference in the brains we are trying to compare. Our brain has an enormous aesthetic sense: think of music by Mozart or Beethoven; we have a tremendous mathematical capacity: look at the work of Einstein; we have an overwhelming sense of the sacred: "Men and women started to worship gods a soon as they became recognizably human: they created religions at the same time they created works of art. Indeed there is a case for arguing that *Homo sapiens* is also *Homo religiosus*." (Karen Armstrong, *The History of God*, 1993).

Our evolutionary appearance from primitive ancestors covered seven to ten million years and included a major change that involved brain size increasing four-fold in 2.5 million years. The Cambrian Explosion covered five million years. In the last chapter Stephen Gould told us that our appearance was an accidental result of "60 trillion contingent events" and if the tape of evolution were rerun he predicted 17 trillion tries would not come up with us. If our big-brained appearance is so unexpected, and the Cambrian Explosion is, to use his words, "the most remarkable and puzzling event in the history of life", what are the mathematical odds against these two events? After all, we are here. Those events occurred. Schroeder, in *The Science of God*, makes it clear that from a mathematical standpoint the odds are neither should have happened. In his calculations of mutation rates he uses facts and assumptions extremely favorable to evolutionary advances, and despite those very conservative assumptions he shows the odds are exceedingly small that either the Cambrian Explosion or our big brain should have appeared in the time allotted.

Let's take the Cambrian Explosion first. It happened about 100 million years after enough oxygen appeared in the atmosphere to support large-bodied organisms. One of the factors that limited development beyond bacteria for almost three billion years was the lack of oxygen. Oxygen, however, has its drawbacks. Think of the "anti-oxidants" that are now sold to slow your body's aging. Oxygen can be damaging to living molecules. One effect is aging. Another is injury to DNA, which must be protected at all costs. At the same time the living organisms were preparing for the Cambrian Explosion, protective mechanisms to repair DNA were put in place. It is possible that the rapid mutations that must have driven the Explosion were in part due to oxygen-induced DNA damage, and also may have resulted from an incompletely developed radiation-protective ozone layer. Schroeder's math calculates a need for "hundreds of millions of years" for the Cambrian Explosion that took 'only' five million years. Is there a possible explanation? The theory of evolution calls for mutations at random, and then a choice through survivability to nature's challenges. Schroeder's math is calculated according to this approach.

What he observes is that DNA must have been preprogrammed with regulatory genes. Regulatory genes produce a protein, which turns on production in some genes and turns off production on others. One example of a regulatory gene is the Pax-6 gene that literally must have been lying in wait over 600 million years ago, according to Conway Morris, long before eyes were needed, and then guided the development of very complex eyes in mammals, octopi, and even the compound eyes of insects. Since it controls all eye development found in evolution, it undoubtedly controlled the development of the two-lens trilobite eye. Raup (*Extinction*) tells us this arrangement "minimized spherical aberration" under water, and called its development a "system that in human terms would require a highly trained and imaginative optical engineer." Another example is the Hox genes. They play "very important roles in early development, defining especially the different parts of the body and its overall arrangement as a body plan." (Morris). Evidence in evolution suggests they appeared at least 70 million years before the Cambrian Explosion.

A final example of preprogramming or type of regulatory gene are the homeobox genes, which Jeffrey H. Schwartz describes as master genes, controlling many other genes at once. For example the same homeobox gene will produce a right chicken wing, and in a mammal will be responsible for the right front leg. Schwartz uses the 'homeobox' term to refer to all regulatory genes, including Pax-6 and Hox genes. Schwartz, in his own review of his book, *Sudden Origins: Fossils, Genes and the Emergence of Species* (1999), states that "mutations affecting regulatory genes (such as homeobox genes) can lead to animals with jaws filled with teeth, limbs and toes instead of fins, or eyes in bony sockets… It may take many generations for the mutation to spread silently, but, when it is expressed, the novel feature it underlies will appear in a number of individuals suddenly and if as out of nowhere." This is his explanation as to how species suddenly seem to appear, as evidenced in the fossil record, rather than the steady change predicted by Darwin. As previously discussed, very gradual transitional forms between species have not been found, although there are transitional species. Schwartz's interpretation supports the "punctuated equilibrium" theory of Gould and Eldredge against the Neo-Darwin approach of gradualism, their proposal that evolution is characterized by long periods without change, followed by brief bursts or episodes of many large changes, with the appearance of new species.

Support for the 'punctuated equilibrium' explanation is appearing in genetic research. In February 2002 a research team announced the finding that simple modifications [mutation] of the "Hox gene Ubx—which suppresses 100 percent of the limb development in the thoracic region of fruit flies, but only 15 percent in *Artemia* [brine shrimp]—would have allowed crustacean-like ancestors of *Artemia*, with limbs on every segment, to lose their hind legs and diverge 400 million years ago into six-legged insects." The chief scientist, William McGinnis, explained his findings: "The change in the mutated gene allows it to turn off other genes. Before the evolution of insects, the Ubx protein [produced by the gene] didn't turn off genes required for leg formation. And during the early evolution of insects, this gene and the protein it encoded changed so that they turned off those genes required to make legs, essentially removing those legs from what would have been the abdomen in insects. The kind of mutation that's in this gene is a so-called dominant mutation, so you only need to mutate one of the chromosomes to get a big change in body plan." (News release, "First Genetic Evidence Uncovered of how Major Changes in Body Shapes Occurring During Early Animal Evolution," University of California, San Diego, 2/6/02).

This discovery demonstrates a "general mechanism for producing major leaps in evolutionary change." (*Nature AOP*, Published online: 6 February 2002; DOI: 10.1038/nature716). The reader is aware I believe evolution occurred. I knew these mechanisms had to exist and that research geneticists would unearth them. However, the discovery raises more questions than it answers. How did the changed gene (Ubx) know *in advance* that its altered protein output would so beautifully coordinate all those other genes so that body form would jump from the multiple legs of brine shrimp to the six-legged form of insects? Genetic research supports my reasoning. The potential effect of a mutation actually depends upon the pattern of other genes present, and gene patterns vary among individuals. The new mutation may produce a good or bad effect, or no effect at all depending upon the gene pattern present. This obviously will apply to both single function and master control genes. "It is a network of genes, not a single....gene, that matters." ("DNA's Double Helix Isn't So Golden Now, But Happy 50, Anyway," Sharon Begley, *Wall Street J.* 2/28/03, quoting several leading scientists including Dr. Lee Hartwell, 2001 Nobel Prize winner in Medicine.)

Also, how did a brine shrimp survive with only six legs, which would tend to put it at a great disadvantage to other shrimp with all their legs? There had to be other simultaneous mutations in other Hox genes at the same time to make a changed but really functional animal who could then survive the challenges of natural selection. This assumption fits the fossil record, which shows jumps from one species to another and does not show the gradualism proposed by Darwin. Further, if these mutations occurred in *only one individual*, which is the way mutation appears, making a new species in that one individual, how did it spread to the whole original species to make the final modification? By definition one species cannot mate with another species, so the projection of this change throughout the existing species also implies a modification in reproductive capacity to allow the transformation.

To jump from one species form to another, it appears that DNA must come with a marvelously pre-planned "common set of developmental instructions." (Morris). If DNA came from 'a chance falling together of compounds', as discussed in the last chapter, where did this preprogramming come from? How do these regulatory genes, putting together complex parts, 'know' in advance of the trial appearance of these parts in nature, how they will work with or against the forces of nature and thereby improve the organism? Darwinism doesn't explain this.

As a brief aside, think about the operation of these master genes and the information they must somehow contain. If you have ever watched a building being constructed, I'm sure you are aware that there is a sequenced plan of action. Obviously, the foundation comes before the actual structure rises. Then all systems contributing to the finished structure must go into place without interfering with the placement of each other. For example, plumbing and electrical have to be put into the walls before they are covered with sheetrock. Painting is usually done before floor coverings, such as carpets are set in place, to avoid damage to the carpet. All very logical. All guided by intelligence, and by very complex three-dimensional planning.

Now imagine DNA in a fertilized human egg controlling the development of a fetus, creating a live baby. One cell splits in two, and at that moment literally this earliest of embryos decides which is right and which is left! Identical twins, who split apart at this moment, are usually born as mirror images of each other, one right handed and the other left handed. Spatial orientation from the very beginning, guided in three dimensions by DNA. As these first few cells divide, head and tail (in us the sacrum) and front and back aspects are chosen. Here the real work begins. Within a few days there is a tiny beating heart. Arteries and veins have to reach out to the forming body and limbs, and find the correct routes to reach all growing parts. Bones form; muscles must have the right attachments to them. The spinal column has a spinal cord within it, and nerves must reach out from it, similar to the developing arteries and veins, growing out to the proper destinations for later control of the body and also to provide pain, position and other sensations. And don't forget the digestive system hooking up to the liver, and the urinary system connecting the kidneys to the bladder. All of this going on simultaneously in three dimensions with chemical feedback systems checking everything, turning genes on and off simultaneously, and in a logical order protecting each addition from interfering with the next.

Research has demonstrated how this works. Arteries grow following the lead of nerves, developing along with the nerve branches, which appear first, the two branching systems thereby integrating together into the various parts of the body. The veins develop separately. The nerves appear to be the controlling tissue, since they also produce a molecule that encourages embryonic blood vessels to turn into arteries. One can imagine that the various tissues and developing organs produce substances to first attract the nerve growth ("Nerves Tell Arteries to Make Like a Tree," Greg Miller, *Science*, Vol. 296, pp. 2121-23, 6/21/02). Just imagine thousands of controlling molecules turning cellular DNA on and off in a precisely timed pattern. An absolute miracle initially created from two stands of DNA, one from Mother and one from Father, in each chromosome. How did all of this information become implanted within DNA in the time allotted for evolution to progress?

The answer is complicated and raises more questions about the genetic control of evolution than it offers. Not all the information to control embryo development is in DNA. Current research findings appear to show that DNA contains only part of that information and the remaining structures of the fertilized egg contain the other important developmental programming information. DNA is programmed to manufacture a supply of the necessary proteins for construction of the embryo, but the final location of those proteins is guided by the internal structures of the egg cell and by the cell membrane (covering). Each new cell formed is constructed in the same way. This non-DNA information is not passed through genetic DNA control nor does it rely upon DNA instructions. If the DNA of a fertilized egg is replaced with foreign DNA, development continues unchanged until the egg runs out of the new proteins that the original DNA should have been producing. Another finding in the newest research on developing eggs is that laboratory-caused mutations in the developmental genes generally result in changes that lead to death or deformity and "they never produce changes that benefit the organism."(*Signs of Intelligence*, edited by Dembski and Kushiner, 2001, Chapter 9 by Jonathan Wells, Ph. D., a postdoctoral research biologist at U. of California at Berkeley.) This means that a genetic mechanism through mutation to create new species has not been found and may not exist. Theoretically, only mutations in germ cell (sperm and/or egg) DNA can lead to a new species. If this research on embryonic development advances and confirms the early findings, it will disprove Darwin completely and raise the strong possibility of evolution advanced by mechanisms other than chance mutations. Darwinism has another problem with mutations. Mutation rates are known and if they, in fact, advance evolution, can they do it in the time intervals demonstrated by scientific research?

Returning to Schroeder's mathematical calculations, he used mutation rates to look at the possibility of humans appearing from a known ancestor of seven million years ago. His answer is the same result as in the Cambrian Explosion, "no way." Mathematically, using the most favorable assumptions for rapidly progressive evolution but also recognizing the randomness of mutations, our current human appearance would require "hundreds of millions of generations". He then suggests an alternative approach allowing 15 simultaneous annual mutations and the number of generations needed is reduced to 40 million! At 25 years per generation the seven million years allowed is still way too short. Again, Schroeder invokes the concept of preprogramming: "You just cannot win if the classic concept of *randomness* at the point molecular level of DNA is the driving force behind the mutations. Large groups of bases or even entire gene sequences must have been activated or inactivated simultaneously as units. Groups of genes used for one purpose must have changed functions simultaneously, with some genes waiting patiently and neutrally quiet in the genome for millennia until they received a genetic or environmental cue to join their redirected cousins". Evolutionary "processes [can] no longer be viewed as arising simply from random events. Our universe, tuned so accurately for the needs of intelligent life, indeed ticks to the beat of a very skillful Watchmaker."

Schroeder is implying that DNA is filled with information to guide evolution and to organize the work of master genes to control groups of subservient genes, creating major changes all at once. Schroeder's Watchmaker is the major issue in trying to study the mathematics of probability in evolution. Is the process totally a mechanistic arrangement, or is there an inherent program built-in by natural events or by supernatural (divine) intervention? Has supernatural intervention continued since life started? There is the evolutionist explanation of how all of this can occur by chance. I would be very remiss if we did not cover the opinions of Richard Dawkins, a professor of zoology at Oxford University, regarding the methods by which evolution progresses. He fiercely defends a mechanistic view of Darwinism that in no way allows the possibility of preprogramming within DNA, or the possible presence of a programmer, as inferred by Schroeder. He describes the Darwin mechanism as "the nonrandom survival of randomly varying replicators", more simply stated as the "random chance [of mutations] with nonrandom natural selection." (Pennock, *The Tower of Babel*, 1999). In "The Blind Watchmaker" (1985) Dawkins describes a computer program, which is designed to mimic random mutational changes leading to an advance in evolution. He used a random string of 28 letters in a series of computer generations and had the computer "[lock into place] 'correct' mutations (the correct letter in the correct position)" to create a previously selected verse from Shakespeare, "Methinks it is like a weasel." This was achieved in 45 generations, which had an 80 percent chance of occurring successfully, according to the probability equation Schroeder used in analyzing Dawkins's example. Schroeder's comment, also echoed by Behe (*Darwin's Black Box*), is "Dawkins's success at forming his sentence proves only that his computer is working correctly!" The point is simply that programming a computer toward a goal makes it reach that goal.

Remember that Dawkins approaches evolution by declaring that it starts with each random mutation, which is then in a subsequent step accepted by nature, resulting in a series of mutations (all at random), which are then organized somehow through their acceptance by nature. To me this is like pushing a rope and hoping that the distant end moves in a straight line! I realize that Pennock's and Dawkins's obvious response is that natural selection keeps the rope straight, through multiple trial and error sequences, sorting out good, neutral and bad mutations. That sorting, at random, adds to the size of the probability odds for and against success, especially if nature doesn't know where it is headed, a major tenet of Darwinian principles. Darwinism is initial mutation at random and a natural sorting out with no pre-planned sense of direction. This is a totally passive process!

Pennock has mounted a vigorous defense of Dawkins. Not referencing Schroeder at all in his book (to my mind a grievous oversight), Pennock pounces on Behe's objections. In the next paragraph after the 'weasel' example "Dawkins himself was careful to warn his readers that the analogy is misleading, and was meant to show the power of cumulative selection on random variations." 'Cumulative selection' is defined by Pennock as follows: "Evolution does not take giant steps in ten-league boots but rather takes many small steps, with natural selection operating cumulatively each step of the way." Referring to Hoyle's calculations of the possibility of life appearing spontaneously, (see Chapter 3) Pennock agrees, "the odds against a successful single step can be mind-bogglingly enormous." There is no question that breaking down the process of the appearance of life or the progress of evolution into successive coherent and cooperative steps will reduce the mathematical odds, if you forget the odds inherent in organizing those subsequent steps by chance so that all the new parts work together. In a sophomoric way, Pennock refers to Hoyle's calculations as "Hoyle's Howler": "Redo the calculations under the assumption of cumulative selection and the enormous probabilities shrink away." There are no such calculations in Pennock's book to illustrate his point. And further, Stuart Kauffman, another very respected scientist not referenced by Pennock, used Hoyle in his book, *At Home in the Universe*, to justify his lifetime of research into organizing principles inherent in the idea that the whole is more than the sum of its parts. And finally, another evolutionary scientist not mentioned by Pennock, Conway Morris offers his opinion of Dawkins and supports the point I am making: "His fundamental point of reference is the primacy of the gene. In this way, Dawkins takes a highly reductionist approach. Organisms are more than a sum of their parts, and we may also note in passing that the world depicted by Dawkins has lost all sense of transcendence." We must conclude that the scientists who study evolution show no unanimity of opinion in interpreting how the process operates. And several of them suspect some type of underlying programming principle.

Mathematicians have been struggling with the Darwin theory all through the Twentieth Century, trying to fit the process into the time scales available. When Darwin proposed his theory it was thought that the universe was eternal and time limits for chance did not exist. We now know that life appeared in a 200-400 million year window, and from the time of the Cambrian Explosion to the appearance of human beings is a little over one-half billion years. Darwinists have attempted to ignore the contraction of time available, but one of their own, the famous mathematician/population geneticist J.B.S. Haldane produced a theoretical paper which mathematically demonstrated that the time available is way too short. The paper concerned itself with the time involved in mutation rates that would produce a positive evolutionary change in a species to another species not just the simple variations that appear in microevolution (JBS Haldane, "The Cost of Natural Selection," *J. Genetics* 55, pp511-24, 1957). The problem he saw was the mutation rates of good, neutral, and bad were roughly one-third each (see page 89, where it is reported current human rates were found to be 38 percent bad). As a result it appears to be mathematically very problematic that a species could "acquire significant, adaptively beneficial mutations before being overloaded by harmful ones (what's called 'error catastrophe')." ("A Designer World," John D. Martin, Ph.D., 2002, www.boundless.org/2001/

features/a0000600.html). Geneticists produced papers for a few years trying to answer "Haldane's Dilemma" as the observation came to be called, but failing to do so, renamed the problem as "Haldane's Cost of Selection", and literally swept it under the rug (www.geocities.com/Area51/Rampart/4871/evolu.html; "What's Wrong With the theory of Evolution?", Tim Harwood M.A. (2001)).

About ten years later the Wistar Institute conducted a symposium uniting mathematicians and Darwinists in another attempt to find satisfactory mathematical formulas to fit the Darwin theory. The answer from the mathematicians was again emphatic. If the Darwinists were to insist upon random mutations to propel the evolutionary results now present, the time available was not long enough. They were told they needed a new theory; a system totally at random meant that the results which have occurred were totally improbable from a mathematical standpoint. Dr. Ernst Mayr, a noted Darwinist, answered the mathematicians in an astounding way, which demonstrates the evolutionist unwillingness to face the problem. "We have so much variation in all of these things that somehow or other by adjusting these figures we will come out all right. *We are comforted by knowing that evolution has occurred.*" (My italics; *Mathematical Challenges To The Neo-Darwinian Interpretation of Evolution*, Wistar Institute Symposium, 4/25-26/1966, pg. 30; out of print: available by request to Nina Long, nlong@mail.wistar.upenn.edu).

Yes, evolution has occurred, but the Darwin mechanism of random mutation with gradual change to new species (macroevolution) is obviously not correct. There are many examples of microevolution, the adaptation of a species under natural stress to the changing environment, without changing to a new species. The Darwin formula has no problem with this. What is at issue is macroevolution: the jumps from one species to another, the giant steps such as the Cambrian Explosion, the most dramatic one, followed by long periods of stasis, as Gould puts it, when evolution moves very slowly. As previously mentioned, Gould has referred to this as a "punctuated equilibrium", a proposal that many Darwinists feel is an attack on Darwinism. "Thus every once in a while a more complex creature evolves and extends the range of life's diversity…These additions are rare and episodic. They do not even constitute an evolutionary series." (Gould, *Scientific America*, October 1994). These jumps don't fit the Darwin theory. The most glaring defect in the original Darwin theory is that modern science has not found gradual stepwise transitional forms between species that

Darwin assumed would eventually be found by fossil hunters. Yes, there are some true transitional species such as a fish-like amphibian, Acanthostega, and these species lend strong support to the concept that evolution really occurred (*Finding Darwin's God*, Miller, pg. 40). "One species may appear to be descended from another, but the fossil record does not show how one evolved into another." (*The Evolutionists; The Struggle for Darwin's Soul*, Richard Morris, 2001) However, even transitional species represent giant steps between species. And of course, Darwin didn't know these giant steps would not disappear with further fossil gathering, as he anticipated they would when he wrote his book. He based his thoughts upon his observations and those of others of microevolution. To use Pennock's description of Darwin's theory: "Darwin expressed the idea of evolution that he had in mind using the formula 'descent with modification', by which he referred not to individual organisms or to modification of just any trait, but to *lineages of organisms, with common ancestors, descending reproductively one from another and changing over generations in their heritable traits.*" Darwin expected and predicted that transitional forms would be found.

As I stated in the beginning, I accept evolution as a factual process presented by science, just as Schroeder and Behe do. And I accept Pennock's point of view that scientific research must study natural and material things. Presenting the mathematics of the probabilities of events is to bring to focus the issue of evolution occurring totally by chance versus being guided in some way. The famous cartoon of a blackboard filled with math formulas, followed by a gap labeled 'a miracle happens' followed by more math, is not the way pure science can work (*Chalk Up Another One, the Best of Sidney Harris*, 1992). Science is not supposed to bring in God to fill the gaps. Science does create facts and does show how miraculous our existence really is. Therefore, science can be used by those who believe in a Deity to demonstrate His Works, actually strengthening their beliefs if necessary. By presenting scientists who question the Darwinian thesis and recognize that underlying programming may be in place, scientists who have strong mathematical objections to the idea of random progress, I have made it clear that the philosophy and/or theology of these researchers is not monolithically atheistic.

Further, it is obvious that there is no general consensus among the scientists in interpreting evolution in strict Darwinian terms. Conway Morris observes "there are two areas of contention: those of mechanism and those of implication. The first is a scientific problem, the second metaphysical." He spends the first 14 pages of his book discussing why there is no consensus! Schwartz's book, *Sudden Origins*, presents several hundred pages of the history of debate and contentiousness among evolutionists as a backdrop and reason for his presentation of his theory of homeobox genes creating new species, an unsolved problem in the theory of evolution. Many Neo-Darwinists do not accept Gould's punctuated equilibrium theory. Kenneth Miller opposes the idea quite militantly: "Despite Gould's efforts, however, punctuated equilibrium remains a controversial, even contentious topic among evolutionary biologists". (*Finding Darwin's God*). In the same chapter he spends 12 pages refuting Gould. Richard Morris spends an entire book of 262 pages on the subject of the controversies and battles among Darwinists, and especially the argument over punctuated equilibrium versus strict gradualism (*The Evolutionists; The Struggle for Darwin's Soul*). "The orthodox Darwinians believe that natural selection is by far the most important factor and that others are of minor importance. Gould and his colleagues prefer to look at evolutionary patterns in a more 'pluralistic' manner. They do not deny the importance of natural selection, but they maintain that other important factors are at work too." Just the point I am raising in this book. The Darwin Theory is incomplete. There are 'other important factors' at work, possibly theistic factors, although Gould will not accept the 'theistic' possibility.

As the reader must be aware at this point in the book, the Darwin Theory is in great difficulty when the fossil record is reviewed. The predicted gradualism does not exist. There are gaps between all species, whether transitional or not. There are enormous periods of time when species remain absolutely stable, not changing at all, then suddenly new species appear, as if out of nowhere. Traditional Darwinists have always claimed that the enormous amounts of time involved, over 3.6 billion years since bacteria first appeared, would allow for chance mutations and natural selection to have the time to make evolution work. But the sudden changes occur over short periods of time, much faster than known mutation rates should allow. Gould's 'punctuated equilibrium' is an attempt to account for valid scientific observations of the fossil record that set the Darwin Theory on its ear; and all he has accomplished is to infuriate traditional Darwinists. In an attempt to remain a Darwinist himself, Gould proposes that a small group from a species breaks off, enters a new habitat, and challenged by the new environment, in a series of gradual but fairly rapid mutations, rather quickly changes into a new species. "Because the changes occur so quickly, geologically speaking, there is no fossil evidence. Scientists once said that macroevolution is so slow we cannot see it; now the punctuationists tell us that it is too fast." (*Did Darwin Get It Right*, George Sim Johnston, 1998).

Punctuated equilibrium is an attempt to explain the fossil record. The theory may or may not be true. But the fossil record appears to be a direct refutation of Darwin. (Johnston) Darwin recognized the problem in *The Origin of Species*: "The number of intermediate varieties which have formerly existed on earth must be truly enormous. Why then is not every geological formation and every stratum full of such intermediate links? [This] is the most obvious and gravest objection which can be urged against my theory." (Harwood). The rapid appearance of new species is also a direct blow to Darwin's own statement: "If it could be demonstrated that any complex organ existed which could not possibly have been formed by numerous, successive, sight modifications, my theory would absolutely break down." (Quoted in *Evolution*, Michael Denton, pg. 213 and also in *Darwin's Black Box*, Michael Behe, pg. 39). Behe's entire book describing the intricate biochemistry of living organs as irreducibly complex is a direct attack on this statement.

How do strict fundamentalist Darwinists try to answer these objections? We have seen Gould and Eldredge try. Their proposal fits the fossil record but is it true? The Darwin scientists have tried to create life in their laboratories. No luck. They artificially alter genes and see offspring change. They estimate mutation rates to try and fit the time schedules seen in the fossil record. What they are forced to do is to try to imitate in their laboratories what they see in the history of evolution. But even if the experimental results *seem* to mimic evolution, that doesn't prove that is the way evolution happened. Darwin's theory is an attempted explanation of how past history occurred, and that raises problems. How do you prove history if you weren't there to observe it? The simple straightforward answer is you cannot.

All scientific theories are tested to see if they are 'falsifiable', that is, can they be proven or disproven. This requirement was added to the scientific method after it was suggested by philosopher of science Karl Popper (1902-1994) in 1934. All theories should allow the development of scientific testing. If a theory survives efforts to falsify it, it may be tentatively accepted (*Encarta Encyclopedia*, 1999). For example, Einstein's prediction that a speeding object experiences a slowing of time, seems against all common sense, yet clocks on satellites do run slower than clocks not in motion on Earth. Einstein's theories are provable, despite being so counterintuitive.

This cannot be done with Darwin's Theory of Evolution. It is "basically a theory of historical reconstruction [and] it is impossible to verify by experiment or direct observation as is normal in science...It is still, as it was in Darwin's time, a highly speculative hypothesis without direct factual support and very far from that self-evident axiom some of its more aggressive advocates would have us believe." (Denton) Darwin and his most ardent advocates actually have used a very illogical form of reasoning in attempting to support their theory. "The idea of survival of the fittest is entirely circular. Who survives? The fittest. How do we know they are the fittest? They survive. [Under this kind of reasoning] no matter what the complexity of an organism, a Darwinist can always make up an 'adaptive' story explaining its origin. Darwin was acutely aware that the edifice he had constructed was entirely theoretical. His claim was, not that natural selection had actually been seen to create new species, but that in theory it *could* create them." (Johnston). No wonder there are all sorts of just-so stories and proposals to support the Darwin theory, and all sort of controversy within the Darwin camp.

Moving beyond finding a lack of consensus in science, a look at the general population finds the same lack of consensus. There are three main areas of thought about evolution that can be identified: 1) those who feel the Darwin Theory of Evolution justifies their atheism; 2) those who feel that Darwinian theory of evolution attempts to destroy their religious beliefs; 3) and the middle road I follow, accepting the science, unthreatened by it and after studying the evidence presented so far, and as far as my thinking is concerned, coming to the conclusion that our appearance on earth is not an accident.

Our evolution appears guided, or as William Dembski terms it, we appear to be the result of "intelligent design". Evolution looks purposeful and directed toward complexity. Unfortunately purpose and direction cannot be directly proven. Evolution proceeds by fits and starts, long periods of 'stasis' and then sudden advances. All Darwinists accept that this pattern is true. The gradualism implied by Darwin's theory does not exist. His theory must be wrong. Other mechanisms to explain the history of evolution must exist. I have presented evidence that animals can partially direct their own evolutionary responses and that these changes can become inherited. Remember the guppies (Barbour, Spetner). DNA appears to contain information, which leads evolution into increasing complexity. I have demonstrated that it is highly unlikely that such a driving force appeared by chance. Recent research is beginning to show that large non-genomic sections of DNA have been conserved during evolution and functions for these sections are being discovered. Some of these areas apparently produce RNA which may have a regulatory function, rather than producing protein. These non-gene areas may be the mechanism for driving complexity (Forbes.com, "Scientists Ask: What is a Gene, Anyway?," Matthew Herper, 12.18.02; Nature.com, "Plans of mice and men," John Whitfield, 5 December 2002). The mathematical participants in the Wistar Symposium told the Darwinists that the amount of information contained in a single protein molecule was enormous, and they did not know how to calculate the massive information required to construct a complex organ containing many millions of those molecules (Pgs. 7, 96 of Wistar Symposium Proceedings). More recently, information theorists infer that the information required to guide evolution must have been present at the start, since the Darwin mechanism is too information poor, using random mutations as the sole source of information, to have provided the algorithms (sequential mathematical formulas) required to control the process (Dembski, Bracht). There is enough room in the unused portions of DNA (junk DNA) to store this information. Remember, the DNA of the one-celled ameba is longer than that of humans, perhaps as a plan to provide in advance the space to store this information as it developed or appeared during evolution. I foresee the time when scientists will uncover such organizing codes, finding that DNA is not simply a coding system to form protein molecules.

There is another piece of circumstantial evidence suggesting a pre-existing DNA guide for evolution to a planned complex end. Previously in this chapter the enormous planning involved in creating a fetus from an embryo was discussed. What should also be pointed out is that fetal development at times follows the evolutionary tree. Human embryologic development, for example, goes through stages resembling the structures of lower organisms on the tree, as if mimicking past ancestors from which humans descended during evolution; this fits the "common descent" portion of Darwin's theory. What also occurs is that fetal development in anthropoid apes (our closest cousins on the tree) goes through stages that resemble the features of the adult structures of man. As 50-day-old fetuses, chimps and other primates have brains as large as human fetuses, but they do not go on to develop as human brains do (*Scientific American*, July 2002, pg. 33, "Human Evolution, Food for Thought"). There are other similarities in the ape fetus to the human adult that do not develop in the adult apes: the round shape of the head; its position in relation to the spinal column; the teeth, the flatness of the face compared to the adult apes elongated muzzle, the position of the vagina (directed forward in adult humans and toward the back in adult apes), the large brow ridges over the eyes are absent in the fetus of the apes, but develop in the adult ape. There are other examples but these will do. Darwin's theory of evolution does not explain this. It is backward as compared to the common descent portion of the Darwin theory. If we descended through natural selection with modifications and branched off from the apes, why do their fetuses look like us? We should look like them. There are two evolutionary possibilities: first, human characteristics in ape fetal development might suggest an ancient human ancestor from whom all primates developed (Paul Carline, "Sit Down Before a Fact as a Little child," a commentary on G. R. deBeer's book, *Embryology and Evolution,* 1930, metanexus.net, views 2002, 05.30). There is no evidence of this, and I do not think there will be. As a second possibility, there may be a pre-planned set of instructions within so-called 'junk' DNA, which is programmed to produce humans (*Homo sapiens*) and the primates branched off from this prearrangement (See discussion of scientific findings in 'junk' DNA, page 101). That makes the best sense, and fits my contention that there is a built-in drive to complexity to produce human beings. As I have stated over and over, I do not think human beings are an accident.

Chapter 5: Our Hat Size Is Too Big for Darwin

This chapter explores the issue that our brain, during evolution, grew so large compared to our closest relatives, other primates, and what this extraordinary evolutionary development means in terms of the Darwin theory. The evolutionary record tells us that our brain grew almost four times larger than it was, in a period of 2.5 million years, as we developed from hominids to humans. There is no direct evidence that the trials of nature demanded that growth, but since the Ice Ages occurred in the same time period, some authors (especially William Calvin) have suggested a relationship, with more complex thinking and planning needed to survive the cold when it appeared. The overall changes in our ancestors, the genetic adaptations of the hominid line, "over the last few million years has actually been exceptionally rapid when compared to that of other mammals". (*The Paleolithic Prescription*, Eaton, Shostak & Konner, 1988). Unanswered is the obvious question: if our brain needed to grow to better survive the cold, why are there no other species that lucky? We appear to be something very special, or very lucky. "Such marked brain growth in one branch of a family of animals is quite rare. Usually, the same evolutionary pressures and constraints affect all the species in a family in much the same way so that the whole group steadily becomes more intelligent together." (*The Ape That Spoke*, John McCrone, 1991). The neurophysiologist, William H. Calvin in his book, *The River That Flows Uphill* (1986), raises the same point: "Why didn't some other primate double and triple its brain size too? Even if no one made it as far as we have, surely there would be some robust examples in evolution of bigger-is-smarter-is-better, demonstrating its efficacy for us to see. It doesn't take other examples of 200 percent. Even a 50 percent increase would help make the point. But none obliged." Calvin offers no answers to his rumination. Again why us and us alone? Actually the *Australopithecus* branch of our very early family developed a brain about 50 percent larger than ape brains and within an ounce or two of the size of the first of our line, *Homo habilis*; but the *Australopithecus* branch of development became extinct and only our line succeeded. Apparently a bigger brain doesn't always work out. The Neanderthal brain was about 10 percent bigger than our brain; they appeared on earth before us, co-existed with us, and yet they died out. The theory is we were more intelligent and drove them into regions where they had trouble surviving.

The real issue is: why is our brain so big and only ours? It didn't grow to match skull size; but the other way around, during evolution the skull must have expanded to allow the enlargement of the brain with its greater complexity, the only explanation that makes sense. Those two maneuvers had to be coordinated to work together. Our brain, about the soft consistency of custard wasn't going to stretch our bony skull plates. Babies start life with a head one-quarter the size of their bodies and the brain grows quickly, tripling in size by age six or seven, so that small children continue to have a bigheaded appearance. Body growth finally gives the head a one-eight proportion in adults. The baby's brain growing early in life does not get compressed by an unyielding skull. The skull bones are held apart by a softer tissue, which gradually adds bone to make the larger skull plates needed to create a solid container for the brain when brain growth is complete.

An additional problem involving complex coordination of changes in mother and child occurred during evolution. The female pelvis had to make required changes in its shape, which had to become more rounded and bowl-like for upright walking, as well as substantially enlarging the bony outlet and reshaping it to allow the birth of that bigger head. Our upright posture limits how large the opening can be. It also requires that the upper entry to the birth canal is oval in a side-to-side direction, across the body, and then in the lower portion it is oval in a front-to-back direction. The baby's head must twist about 90 degrees to emerge ("The Evolution of Human Birth," Rosenberg & Trevathan, *Scientific American*, November 2001). The coordination involved simultaneous changes in the fetus and in the pelvis, involving two different individuals (mother and child) at the same time linked by the necessity of birth through a bony circular pelvis. Could this occur all by chance mutations? Were there trial and error attempts at birth with an enlarging baby head pushed through a bony pelvis that had better be enlarging at the same rate?! According to Darwin's Theory, this is how evolution would have worked, if it were all by chance.

Size really is not the true issue. There are mammals such as whales, elephants and walruses with bigger, heavier brains (McCrone). Obviously, they are not as bright as we are. In the large mammals' brains roughly the same numbers of nerve cells, as in smaller mammals, are spread out in the larger size. Our brain, approximately four times larger than a chimpanzee's brain, is estimated to have only 25 percent more nerve cells (William H. Calvin in *Scientific American*, October 1994 and *The River That Flows Uphill*, 1986). But it is those cells and their intricate network of connections, and our gradual learning how to use our brain in all of its capacities, that has made us so intelligent compared to all the animals on earth.

Like the origin of life and the Cambrian Explosion, the appearance of the big brain is another major drive toward complexity, at a speed that belies Darwinian gradualism, and shows amazing coordination in managing all the related parts, especially enlarging the baby's head and also the mother's pelvis so everything fits properly. In a sense it is another of Stephan Jay Gould's punctuated equilibrium examples. This is an example of macroevolution, but without the gradualism Darwin anticipated. Microevolution is easy to demonstrate. It represents continuous adaptations by species to environmental changes: Darwin's finches in the Galapagos change beak-size from smaller to larger and back again adapting to changes in the seeds they feed on, caused by varying amounts of rainfall; the ground squirrels on the north rim of the Grand Canyon at 9,000 feet differentiate from the ground squirrels on the south rim at 7,000 feet as the canyon forms and separates them. Guppies change reproductive patterns over a few generations when challenged by predators. Moths in England change their color depending upon the density of factory smoke. On a trip to the Galapagos I have seen the sea-going iguanas, cavorting around the shorelines of the islands, perfectly at home on land and in the water. They look just like the iguanas of our desert southwest or Mexico who rarely see water. Their ability to adapt to water through microevolution is extraordinary, but real. However, the appearance of new species, macroevolution (the punctuated equilibrium theory) doesn't fit Darwin's theory. It is not his fault. He didn't know about the future events and fossils scientists of the future would uncover, and that transitional forms would not be found. The macroevolution evidenced in the five-million-year Cambrian Explosion simply does not fit the implied gradualism of Darwin's theory. I think he would be extremely surprised at the rapidity with which our brain grew, if he were alive today and reviewed the current findings of evolutionary scientists. Darwin returning to life might even come to doubt his own theory.

Darwin's theory is quite clear according to Paul R. Gross, emeritus professor of life sciences at the University of Virginia, who reviewed Behe's book, *Darwin's Black Box*, in the Wall Street Journal in 1996: "Natural selection does not operate 'by chance' in any ordinary sense. Changes in the genes do arise randomly: This has been documented as well as anything in science. But there is nothing chancy about what happens next, which is the survival and increase of what *works* ". The changes in animals or plants are dictated by the demands of nature, both old and new demands. That is why evolutionists invoke the Ice Ages as a possible driving force to produce a big brain. The issue comes down to this: was the brain we were given over the 2.5 million years it developed, the brain we 'needed' to satisfy the demands of nature 150,000 years ago when it stopped its enlargement? It is my contention that we got much more brain than we needed then or even now. We received a brain containing capacities that were not even discovered by us until the last 4-6,000 years.

To evaluate my contention that our brain was too large for our needs 150,000 years ago, we need to imagine living at that time as hunter-gatherers. Describing hunter-gatherers is easier than it might seem, for there are still such people on earth and anthropologists have extensively studied them. I am describing our species, *Homo sapiens*, at the beginning of our time on earth. In general the women do the gathering of nuts and fruit, and also of wild grains, while the men, either solo or in small groups, are out hunting. They lived together in groups of 20 to 50 individuals, five to ten families, and moved location from season to season both dictated by weather and by resource depletion. They developed a sharing of food and materials, as well as the protective function that a group could provide. After all, there were other tribes that might want to take what the group had. Leadership was very informal, and women played a very equal role to men, "generally exert[ing a] broad influence over decisions affecting themselves and the group, and assum[ing] roles of major importance within the economy and within the family." (*The Paleolithic Prescription*). The outright dominance of men over women is not thought to have occurred until the start of the Agricultural Revolution about 10,000 years ago. In this type of informal social structure conflict was occasionally severe enough to have resulted in homicide, as in our society now. Unresolved conflicts, if severe enough were solved by a dissident group splitting off and joining a nearby tribe that was friendly to them. The diet they consumed was quite good with a broad variety of proteins and complex carbohydrates, vitamins and minerals. The simple carbohydrates of our current diet just didn't exit, except as fructose (fruit sugar) and honey when gathered. The meats were lean and the roughage content high. The major job, maintenance of the group's diet was accomplished with just a moderate workload, contrary to what you might image, given our conveniences of today. With the appearance of agriculture, human size actually became smaller, and the work hours longer. This trend continued until the pioneer days in this country. Look at the small size of clothing and furniture in the museums for that period.

This description is not meant to present an idyllic existence. There were animals out there that could and did hunt and kill humans. Maasi children living in East Africa now under similar conditions have nightmares about being eaten by a lion. As mentioned above, tribes did attack tribes, and again, currently in Africa in the Sudan tribes still attack, kill some of the men and capture slaves!

These early hunter-gatherer *Homo sapiens* had to work out these patterns of cooperation I have described. They had to learn bit by bit that sharing benefited everyone. Evolutionary Psychologists have studied how this may have developed in early humans by using "game theory" as a construct of human interactions. This is a simple mathematical approach. A "zero-sum" game has a winner and a loser, as in an athletic contest: Mathematically assign a winner a plus-one point and the loser a minus-one point. The score in the interaction is zero. The Evolutionary Psychologists theorize that early humans may have created a 'non-zero-sum game', a social construction in which everyone benefited in a roughly equal fashion. Further, these scientists theorize that this was a learned process, not something instinctual (*The Moral Animal*, Robert Wright, 1994). The concept of this "game" in cooperation is simple: I help you to some of my food, and you are now one up on me. Next time around you have the extra food and on that exchange I am one up, but in reality we are even. Each of us wins; each of us has one point, which adds up to two. In chimpanzees this type of cooperation is observed, without language, but in humans language undoubtedly played a role. It is thought that morality and altruism had to be learned by trial and error through this 'game', but also by learning that "one good turn deserves another, as does one bad turn". Wright calls this TIT FOR TAT, and again is of the opinion that not a great deal of brainpower is needed to utilize this approach to altruism. These early social groups interacted and cooperated through "friendship, affection and trust—these are the things that, long before people signed contracts, long before they wrote down laws, held human societies together." (Wright). In a later book, *Non-Zero; The Logic of Human Destiny*, 2000,

Wright expands his theory, proposing that non-zero-sum interactions have allowed the increasing cooperation and complexity of the society we see today, a learned process, and I would add the thought that this advance was enhanced by the fact that we are hard-wired in our brains to have religiosity at an instinctual level, discussed a little further ahead in this chapter. Among early humans at least rudimentary language had to be used for these simple concepts to work. These groups had some rudimentary "music, art, oral folklore and ritual prominent in the lives of today's hunters and gatherers; they reflect great richness of imagination and demonstrate that the human inclination toward aesthetic and religious expression is universal" (*The Paleolithic Prescription*), but really not essential to survival, although certainly life enriching. These are attributes not seemingly required by the threats of nature.

Among hunter-gatherers hunting was a cooperative effort: there have been a number of findings of animals driven en masse over a cliff, allowing the hunters to browse through a pile of carcasses for meat and skins. Hand held stone axes and spears were invented, but bow and arrow was a much later arrival. This meant animals had to be stalked and throwing accuracy developed. The cooperating hunters had to plan their stalking strategy. Also, repeated hammering movements were required to break open husks, nuts, and perhaps shellfish, while grinding with a mortar and pestle required repetitive arm movements not quite as complex a maneuver as hammering.

There are many reasons why humans needed the bigger brain that developed over the 2.5 million years: the ability to develop language skills came with that brain and may well have helped in developing the cooperation necessary for group survival; and the athletic skills of throwing and hammering, referred to by the neurophysiologists as ballistic movements, were now possible and were helpful not only in hunting but in defense. What is surprising about early hominid evolution is upright posture and walking on two legs appeared first, as the earlier forms evolved, while the brain remained small. Upright posture with loss of arm strength reduced running speed and took away swinging through the trees. This made life a great deal more dangerous for these bipeds. They must have been under great pressure to learn cooperation for self-defense; they had to develop defensive and offensive athletic skills; they had to become inventive, creating spears and hand axes; and finally they had to develop foresight and the ability to plan strategies both on defense and during the hunt (*The Ape That Spoke*). Animals live in the present, even as intelligent animals as chimpanzees. Humans can plan the future. Humans are also inventive. They created clothing, woven baskets, leather sacks, and they learned to use fire and cook. The need for these capabilities, more than the stress of the Ice Ages may have helped drive brain development, but as I have noted before, it is still my contention that we eventually ended up with a brain that provided many more capabilities than we needed to survive.

Since the development of language started with an ape-like anatomy, and apes cannot speak, what was required were extensive anatomic changes in the throat, tongue and larynx, as well as enlarging the brain to contain areas to control tongue and lip movements to make a variety of speaking sounds and to develop an acoustical area for interpretation of speech. Chimps can make about three dozen sounds, while we are capable of hundreds. The physical changes required included a higher arch to the palate, a movement of the larynx (voice box) to a much lower position in the neck than it is in the ape. The tongue became much more mobile, the lips stronger, and throat muscles more powerful, allowing us "to 'bite' the air into a rapid series of vowels and consonants that make up speech." (*The Ape That Spoke*). The lower position of the larynx made it possible to choke on food or liquid that passed over the larynx, and required the development of a trap door over the top of the larynx, the epiglottis. The presumption among scientists is that language started with single grunted words for objects or actions. Gradually speed and sentences developed. We now can speak at a rate of 200 words a minute, while it is estimated, based on his anatomy that *Homo erectus,* 1.5 million years ago, possibly could manage "five or six words in five seconds" (McCrone), about 60 words a minute if *Homo erectus* was inclined to talk that long. While these physical changes to produce sound took place, there had to be parallel increase in the "hard wiring" of the brain to control the more rapid speech, a sequencing function to put the words in the right order, and an increase in the complexity of the auditory receiving areas in the brain to allow rapid interpretation of what was being heard. We know what we want to say and it all tumbles out seemingly effortlessly, but what happens in the brain is that a brief preview of the meaning we wish to convey flashes through our minds first and then the words pour forth! All of this coordinated activity of the evolutionary development according to Darwin, is supposed to have been handled by a process of mutations at random, and then a search for the best result among a large variety of differing results, while in the process of living and struggling with nature.

Chimpanzees use one sound at a time, repeating it for emphasis, if necessary. We use about three dozen sounds, "called phonemes. Their combinations have content: we string together meaningless sounds to make meaningful words. No one has yet explained how our ancestors got over the hump of replacing 'one sound/one meaning' with a sequential combinatorial system of meaningless phonemes, but it is probably one of the most important advances that took place during ape-to-human evolution." (*Scientific American*, Wm. H. Calvin, October 1994). Calvin's article is titled, "The Emergence of Intelligence", and along with a great many scientific authorities, he points to the development of language as the basic change that leads to our superior intelligence. Language gives us the ability to think in words, and especially in words that convey concepts, ideas that have no material form. Words like love, to express emotion; words like liberty, to express a state of being; or hunting, to express a plan of action. Our intelligence gives us foresight, and with foresight, planning the future. All other animals live in the present, reacting to the immediate situation. You cannot tell your favorite dog that you and he will take a walk in an hour. When he hears the word 'walk' he will immediately bring you the leash. Even chimpanzees, which love to eat termites, go to the termite mound first and then look around for a stick to put down a termite hole. They never bring a pile of sticks for the meal, while we put out forks before dinner comes to the table.

Calvin, a Ph. D., is a theoretical neurophysiologist at the University of Washington's School of Medicine. It is his theory that improved athletic ability paved the way for language development and intelligence. Ballistic movements, particularly "hammering, clubbing and throwing are essential to the manufacture and use of tools and hunting weapons." Apes have only elementary forms of these movements, while we are experts. During a slow movement, reaching out to touch something, there is little advanced planning by the brain. There is time to tell your brain to correct a course for your arm which you are watching with your eyes. However, ballistic movements are very sudden, "lasting less than one fifth of a second, [and] feedback corrections are largely ineffective because reaction times are too long. The brain has to determine every detail of the movement in advance. Hammering requires scheduling the exact sequence of activation of dozens of muscles. The problem of throwing is further compounded by the launch window—the range of times in which a projectile can be released to hit a target." Imagine a baseball pitcher throwing a 95 mile-per-hour fastball at the corner of the plate. Consider the complexity of the seven-foot basketball center, who jumps into the air to grab a pass, his back to the basket. Upon coming down to the floor, he immediately jumps up, twists his body and neck, eyes the basket, just a few inches larger than the ball, and with defensive players all over him, flicks the ball one-handed into the net. Calvin proposes that this sequencing mechanism for ballistic movements allowed us to develop the ability for rapid speech, and speech and ballistic activities probably evolved together as our brain enlarged. This athleticism when joined to our newly found language and intelligence allowed us to survive our vulnerable state as newly created bipeds, naked and slow moving.

There is another surprising facet to the process of evolution that turns up in the study of the development of language and intelligence. This is the appearance of organs appearing and/or becoming more complex long before their usefulness is applied in any useful way. The anatomy, which provided the ability to speak, was present for about half a million years in early Hominids, long before *Homo erectus* appeared and spoke in a rudimentary way. This anatomical change, mentioned earlier, involves a flexing of the bones of the skull base allowing the lengthening and dropping lower in the neck the pharynx (throat) and the larynx. The human larynx is lower than the Neanderthals' was, allowing humans a much better articulation of speech. Although the brain was enlarging and presumably increasing intellectual capacity, yet language is not thought to have appeared based on "the behavioral record" until one of our most recent ancestors arrived on the scene. Novel innovations, which appear in species long before they are used, are called "exaptations," or expressed another way in this case, "abilities that lay fallow until activated by a cultural stimulus of some kind." ("Once We Were Not Alone," Ian Tattersall, *Scientific American*, January 2000 and "How We Came to be Human," Tattersall, *Scientific American*, December 2001). Following the scientific approach in explaining "how" things happen, Tattersall offers the opinion that as brain and larynx developed, we humans passed a transition from nonsymbolic to symbolic thought, through a mechanism whereby "existing exaptations were *fortuitously* linked in some relatively minor genetic innovation to create an unprecedented potential." (My italics). And this is all by chance? I prefer to wonder "why" we should have been set up anatomically for language and symbolic thought well over several hundred thousand years before the need for such activity appeared. Fortuitously means accidental. It doesn't seem very accidental to me; it much more closely resembles good planning for the future.

There is another objection to Tattersall's interpretation of this exaptation. Tattersall comments that the human arrangement of the larynx "makes a vast array of sounds possible, [but] it also prevents simultaneous breathing and swallowing—thereby introducing the unpleasant possibility of choking to death." (Remember the Heimlich procedure?) To solve this problem in newborn human babies who must suckle milk and breathe at the same time, the larynx starts out high and descends lower in the neck, only after they are six months old and must learn to speak. If useless for hundreds of thousands of years, why were the changes maintained by evolution, especially with the threat of choking? (*The Ape That Spoke*). Evolution, driven by the demands of nature, is supposed, according to the Darwin theory, to look for proficient changes and to encourage the removal of superfluous ones. There appears to have been great planning for speech with the development of a trap door over the larynx, the epiglottis, to protect us from choking, and an appropriate progression of development to protect the newborn. Is this exaptation, and in fact all exaptations, God's planning? It is interesting that Tattersall, who is an ardent defendant of evolutionary theory, notes the dangerous aspects of laryngeal development, but is still willing to hold out exaptations as accidental parts of Darwin's theory. Contrast this with Mc Crone's description of the development of the capacity for speech earlier in this chapter. (*The Ape That Spoke*). His book reads descriptively, not as a defense of Darwin.

When *Homo sapiens* appeared 150,000 years ago, how much brainpower did those early folks need? They had to develop their athletic abilities to hunt and to defend, nothing as complex as basketball. They needed a rudimentary language for simple planning and cooperation. With the simple society that formed, they did not need concepts like 'life, liberty, and the pursuit of happiness', which are symbolic constructions required by modern societies populated by millions of people. Yet they were provided with a huge brain, a brain whose hidden capacities were not necessary for them to face the challenges of nature present at the time. They and we had to learn to develop those hidden capabilities. 30,000 years ago the Cro-Magnons in France produced sophisticated works of art on the walls of the Chauvet cave. Other caves had figurines, some of which are copied and sold today. "Burials from the period 40,000 to 10,000 years ago reflect a deeply spiritual side: these early *H. sapiens* offered elaborate grave goods to accompany the deceased in the afterlife." (Review by Donald Johanson of *Becoming Human: Evolution and Human Uniqueness*, Ian Tattersall, 1998, in *Scientific American*, March 1998). It should be no surprise that recent research in epileptics, who develop religious experiences during seizures, has identified a "God Module", a spot producing religious feelings in the temporal lobe of the brain ("Scientists and Religion in America", Larson & Witham, *Scientific American*, September 1999).

Why does 'survival of the fittest' require a "religious center" in the brain? I feel Darwin's theory does not completely explain it. E.O. Wilson, who is an atheist, feels he can justify the appearance of religion thru Darwin. He notes that, "religion is one of the major categories of behavior undeniably unique to the human species." [Tribal] "rituals not only label but reaffirm and rejuvenate values of the community." This obviously strengthens intra-tribal cooperation between members, and therefore, "the highest forms of religious practice, when examined more closely, can be seen to confer biological advantage." He then equates mythology with religion and concludes, "sociobiology can account for the very origin of mythology by the principle of natural selection acting upon the genetically evolving material structure of the brain." (*On Human Nature*, E.O. Wilson, 1978). Other experts both agree and at the same time disagree. Newberg and D'Aquili are both neurophysiologists and physicians, and in their book, *Why God Won't Go Away* (2001), describe their studies of subjects, during meditation, who practice mysticism, mapping the brain function during mystical religious experiences. They agree with Wilson by stating, "[among early humans] religion would serve to strengthen bonds between individuals and to encourage more peaceful and productive interaction in the community at large. Stronger social groups, of course, would mean better lives for clan members, which might ultimately result in higher rates of survival as well...evidence suggests that the deepest origins of religion are based on mystical experience, and that religions persist because the wiring of the human brain continues to provide believers with a range of unitary experiences that are often interpreted as assurances that God exists...It's very likely that natural selection would favor a brain equipped with the neurological machinery that makes religious behavior more likely."

Where they appear to disagree with Wilson is in their conclusion. Wilson never invokes God, they do. "Could it be that the brain has evolved the ability to transcend material existence, and experience a higher plane of being that actually exists? The mystics certainly insist that they have experienced just such a reality; a realm of being more real than the material world, [with] no clear boundaries between self and the universe, and ample room for the actual possibility of God. Science and common sense, on the other hand, tell us such a thing is not possible...our own scientific inquiry, in fact, began with this assumption. But science has surprised us, and our research has left us no choice but to conclude that the mystics may be on to something, that the mind's machinery of transcendence may in fact be a window through which we can glimpse of the ultimate realness of something that is truly divine. This conclusion is based on deductive reasoning, not religious faith [!]. We [are] left with two mutually exclusive possibilities: either spiritual experience is nothing more than a neurological construct created by and contained within the brain, or a state of absolute union [with the universe] that the mystics describe does in fact exist and the mind has developed the capacity to perceive it. Science offers no clear way to resolve this question." As scientists they struggle with the issue of God, but are forced to entertain the possibility of His role.

Religion is good for mankind and is needed, no doubt! If God is our Creator, the religious centers in the brain should be no surprise to believers. Science may not be able to resolve the question Newberg and D'aquili raise, but the existence of a brain capable of these religious experiences is very suggestive of God's contribution. These authors demonstrated that the temporal lobe is not the only location for religious experiences. There is a complicated set of interactions between the temporal lobe and several other parts of the brain during the mystical heights reached by meditation. Taking note of Gould's observation in Chapter 4 that there is no evidence the human brain has changed in 100,000 years, it can be claimed that this is a built-in mechanism, which early humans discovered how to use, when they found they needed it. Why not accept the idea that this mechanism was built into the brain as an 'exaptation', something to be used later as discussed earlier in this chapter? Wilson, and Newberg and D'Aquili, as scientists, are wedded to Darwin's concept of evolution: to fit their bias they prefer to believe that the ability to have religious experiences evolved. I think it is easier to explain as an exaptation, likely planned in advance by God.

To return to early human history, agriculture developed 10,000 years ago, followed by writing and written history 4,000 years ago. We then discovered simple arithmetic, and so forth. There is no point in my describing the whole of our cultural heritage as civilization advanced. Ian Tattersall, chairman of the department of anthropology at the American Museum of Natural History in New York, describes human uniqueness: "*Homo sapiens* is not simply an improved version of its ancestors—it's a new concept, qualitatively distinct from them in a highly significant if limited respects". Johanson is of the opinion our enormous intellectual and cultural capacities mean "we will not undergo any further speciation: our limitless cultural capacities permit cultural solutions to environmental changes." This means he thinks we are the end of the evolutionary line: we will have no further changes, no new species to replace us; just further improvement in the use of our brains and further expansion of our intellectual abilities. Johanson is a professor of anthropology and director of the Institute of Human Origins at Arizona State University, and the discoverer of one of our ancestors in Tanzania at the Olduvai Gorge. There is no other evolutionist who expresses this opinion. Calvin offers the following: In evolution, "human intelligence first solves movement problems and only later graduates to ponder more abstract ones. It is difficult to estimate how often high intelligence might emerge [in other species], given how little we know about the demands of long-term species survival and the courses evolution can follow." He raises the question: "Why are there not more species with such complex mental states?" And never answers it. We are as special as Tattersall tells us, and it seems we always were meant to be special and unique.

Ongoing research on infant and childhood development has demonstrated that talking to infants and reading to young children improves their I.Q. somewhat, by stimulating the brain to develop further than it would without that stimulation. Some of this may have gone on in the 150,000 years since our species appeared. We started with rudimentary language and increased athletic ability, and more than likely a degree of foresight and planning, which was obviously enough of an advantage to permit us to survive our slower running speed and loss of upper body strength. In the last 6,000 years or so we developed the ability to write, to read, and to do arithmetic and then higher mathematics; all were assigned to different areas of the brain, undoubtedly stimulating more complexity. The autopsy of Einstein's brain raised a chicken-and-egg type of question. His brain was 15 percent wider on both sides due to a one-centimeter enlargement of an area controlling "visual interpretations, mathematical thought and imagery of movement." (*Scientific American*, September 1999). As a child he was a left-handed dyslectic. Did his brain adapt to his brilliant thought processes, or did his brain start out with this very unusual anatomy permitting brilliant deductions to appear? The brains of geniuses usually look like brains of ordinary people. By whatever method the development conducted itself during the 150,000 years, we have expanded our original capacities into extraordinary mental abilities. We write novels, poetry, carve beautiful sculpture, create complex orchestral music, design complex structures and machines, and so forth, but you know the list as well as I. Much of these abilities come from our capacity to imagine what is not present, and has never been present. We invent the life and the people of novels; we create animals like mermaids, unicorns and centaurs. We live part time in our imaginations, and from that imagination spring forth ideas, plans, designs, philosophies of reality, and in fact, advances of our intellect.

And much of this is due to fact that we have consciousness. What is consciousness? It is simply that we are aware that we are aware. No animal has that capacity. They all live in the present. We are aware of the past and the present, and we can plan for the future. We have self-consciousness, a self-awareness that allows us to judge ourselves, to develop ethical and moral values for ourselves and in relationships with each other. Consciousness leads us to wonder what is over the next hill, and has made us explorers and searchers. We are constantly striving to learn why we are here, how we got here, and where we are going. As a result we study our universe and work out what makes it tick. We have sent men to the moon and automated probes all over our solar system. There are orbiting telescopes sending us undistorted pictures of the universe, sent out there because the images we receive through our atmosphere are distorted and not clear enough .We are constantly striving to learn, and the expansion of our knowledge in the last century is exponential.

Were did consciousness come from? Calvin tells us (pg. 30, *The River That Flows Uphill*): "evolution has no foresight, in the manner of human consciousness—it cannot plan ahead for something useful....Evolution selects useful features, based on *present-day* needs. If you don't have them when they are needed—well, it's just someone else's turn." Consciousness is more than just useful; it has been the vital engine in the creation of our current state of knowledge and civilization. In Calvin's view it just popped up, unexpectedly: "The key issue here is that old phrase: the whole is more than the sum of its parts. Consciousness is one of those things that emerges when you sum up all of those nerve cells [in the brain]. It's really an emergent property, one of those unexpected sidesteps in evolution in which a novel combination of preexisting things turns out to be handy for something completely new." (pg. 394). He sounds like Stephen Jay Gould: consciousness is just another 'glorious accident' following that amazing 'accidental' enlargement of our brain. Is evolution just one accident after another, or could 'design' be playing a role?

Calvin's concept of the "emergence" of consciousness from the matter of the brain comes from the materialistic approach of reductionism in science, and is explained as the whole apparently being more than the sum of its parts, a sort of 'miraculous' appearance, although no scientist would ever admit to entertaining miracles (See Stuart Kaufmann's discussion in Chapter 3). Brother Wayne Robert Teasdale, Ph.D., a Catholic theologian who teaches at DePaul University and Columbia College, objects strenuously to the concept of emergence of consciousness. He does not agree with the basis of the concept of emergence, which requires that the mind and the brain are separate, the dualism of the French Philosopher, Rene Descartes (1596-1650). "This split between mind and body is reported to our perception by our mind, that is, by our consciousness. When we examine this matter carefully what we notice is that everything—absolutely everything—depends on consciousness: our memories, ideas, perceptions, emotions, musing of the imagination, dreams, learning, thinking, our relationships, our experience of the natural world and the cosmos, the places we visit, where we live, the schools we've attended, the movies we've seen, the pets we have, the books we read, the sports we enjoy, cooking, eating, and love-making, all happen because we are aware…I have to be conscious to know I have a brain, and consciousness cannot be reduced to that which makes it possible. Let me express it as a principle: that which makes perception possible is the basis of all reality, because without it, there would be no reality for us". (www.META-LIST.org, METAVIEWS, 062, 2000). This is a powerful definition of consciousness and it shows just how special we are for having it (Teasdale's concepts of a universal consciousness are presented in Chapter 8).

Mathematician Roger Penrose in his very complex book, *The Emperor's New Mind* (1989) discusses whether artificial intelligence can ever be created with our level of consciousness. His answer is no. He does not think a complex mathematical "algorithm can evoke *conscious awareness*." He is one of the world's leading mathematicians, and as the Rouse Ball Professor of Mathematics at Oxford, worked with Stephen Hawking on the mathematical understanding of the universe. In his mathematical way he lists functions of the mind needing consciousness as: common sense, judgment of truth, understanding, artistic appraisal, all a part of judgement-forming (his term). It is the automatic functions that do not need consciousness: those that are programmed, algorithmic, instinctual.

Like many thoughtful scientists he wonders about consciousness and why we have been given it: "What *selective advantage* does a consciousness confer on those who actually possess it?" His answer, put simply, is that our consciously aware ancestors could imagine what their prey might be likely to do next, and gain advantage. By the same token, when our ancestors were themselves the prey, they could imagine what the predator might try next and find an evasive action that worked. He suggests there is a deeper reason for consciousness to appear: "Alternatively, perhaps there is some divine or mysterious purpose for the phenomenon of consciousness—possibly a teleological one not yet revealed to us—and any discussion of this phenomenon in terms of the ideas of natural selection would miss this 'purpose' completely." He mirrors Calvin's contention that consciousness arises from the complexity of the brain and is more than the sum of the parts: "The products of natural selection are indeed astonishing. The little knowledge that I have acquired about how the human brain works—and indeed any other living thing—leaves me dumbfounded with awe and admiration. The working of an individual neuron is extraordinary, but the neurons themselves are organized together in a quite remarkable way, with vast numbers of connections wired up at birth, ready for all the tasks that will be needed later on. It is not just consciousness itself that is remarkable, but all the paraphernalia that appears to be needed in order to support it!" Consciousness has arisen from an extraordinary design and Penrose looks primarily to natural selection, ignoring the possibility of a designer, although he does give some thought to divine purpose.

As a famous scientist and gifted writer, Paul Davies, who specializes in theoretical quantum gravity, comes closest to recognizing how unusual we are, how unaccidental we are, without invoking God, at the very end of his book, *The Mind of God*: "We have cracked part of the cosmic code. Why should this be, just why *Homo sapiens* should carry the spark of rationality that provides the key to the universe, is a deep enigma. We, who are children of the universe—animated stardust—can nevertheless reflect on the nature of that same universe, even to the extent of glimpsing the rules on which it runs. How we have become linked into this cosmic dimension is a mystery. Yet the linkage cannot be denied. I cannot believe that our existence in this universe is a mere quirk of fate, an accident of history, an incidental blip in the great cosmic drama. Our involvement is too intimate. The physical species *Homo* may count for nothing, but the existence of mind in some organism on some planet in the universe is surely a fact of fundamental significance. Through conscious beings the universe has generated self-awareness. This can be no trivial detail, no minor byproduct of mindless, purposeless forces. *We are truly meant to be here."* (My emphasis). In another essay he writes, "If the universe were re-run a second time, there would be no solar system, no Earth and no people. But the emergence of life and consciousness somewhere and somewhen in the cosmos is, I believe, assured by the underlying laws of nature." His opinion is that the "laws of nature encourage matter and energy to self-organize and self-complexify to the point that life and consciousness emerge naturally." He predicts there is a "universal trend or directionality toward the emergence of greater complexity and diversity. The position I have presented is radically different. It is one that regards the universe, not as the plaything of a capricious Deity, but as a coherent, rational, elegant and harmonious expression of a deep and purposeful meaning." (Paul Davies in *Modern Cosmology & Philosophy*", Ed. by John Leslie, 1998). He disagrees with Gould that we are not a 'glorious accident', but at the same time he all but recognizes a Designer, and cannot bring himself to say so. Rupert Sheldrake in *A Glorious Accident*, 1997, calls Davies a "neodeist: if not God, then something fine-tunes all the constants of nature". It is truly amazing how scientists are afraid to admit they are not atheists. What else gives a universe 'a deep and purposeful meaning' but the works of God? Sheldrake, a biochemist at the University of London explains the attitude of scientists: "I'm oppressed by the sheer weight of scientific conformity. Billions of pounds are spent every year, there are hundreds of thousands of people whose jobs depend on this enormous institution. There's this huge bureaucratic system in place, and there are a lot of people within science who don't believe in it as it is now, but if you value your job and your career, it's better not to say so in public."

What our consciousness and our intellect have allowed us to develop, within the structure of science and mathematics, is a profoundly accurate understanding of how our living bodies work, how the universe works and what we see should leave us 'dumbfounded with awe and admiration'. Actually the advances in science and mathematics themselves should also leave us 'dumbfounded and in awe' of what has been achieved by humans in such a short time: "What science and mathematics, has so far achieved has been dramatic...The theories that are now available to us have an accuracy which is quite remarkable. But it is not just their accuracy that has been their strength. It is also the fact that they have been found to be extraordinarily amenable to a precise and detailed mathematical treatment." As this quote shows, Penrose is extremely proud of the mathematicians' prowess and their discoveries. These comments parallel those of Alan Guth quoted in Chapter

2, describing the extraordinary ability of mathematics to analyze the physical laws that rule the workings of the universe. Penrose is of the philosophic opinion that "there is something absolute and 'God-given' about mathematical truth. Real mathematical truth goes beyond mere man-made constructions. I cannot help feeling that, with mathematics, the case for believing in some kind of ethereal, eternal existence, at least for some of the more profound mathematical concepts is a good deal stronger than in other cases, [such as] the arts or engineering. There does appear to be some profound reality about these mathematical concepts, going quite beyond the mental deliberations of a particular mathematician. It is as though human thought is, instead, being guided toward some eternal external truth—a truth which has a reality of its own, and which is revealed only partially to any one of us." He has borrowed Plato's philosophy from about 360 B.C. Einstein put this same philosophic concept of mathematics very succinctly in 1921: "Here arises a puzzle that has disturbed scientists of all periods. How is it possible that mathematics, a product of human thought that is independent of experience, fits so excellently the objects of physical reality? Can human reason without experience discover by pure thinking the properties of real things?" Yes it can, and does (Quoted in *Beyond the Quantum*, Michael Talbot, 1986).

My interpretation is somewhat different. We have been given a gift with a purpose. We have been given the ability to develop a very powerful intelligence. Our curious and restless minds can search and explore, using the tools in mathematics and science developed over two millennia. This allows scientifically inclined people to seek out new discoveries through an intuitive process, predicting what will be found years before the actual experimental proof is available. It appears to me this is a major reason for the appearance of our big brain and consciousness. It is so we can understand and more fully appreciate the miracle of the construction of the universe, the miracle of life itself, and see the evidence for an intelligent design, for the handiwork of God. I view this intuitive process as nothing short of miraculous, and you will see why I feel that way through the examples to follow.

Einstein's General Theory of Relativity predicts many things about our universe, and one of them is that light passing by a massive object, such as our sun, will be bent. He uses a concept of space-time as four dimensions, which can be curved and distorted by large objects. He predicts that objects approaching the speed of light will find that time slows for them, but not for others not moving at that speed. An increase in the effect of gravity, a stronger gravity, will also slow the passage of time. His use of the word 'relativity' simply refers to the fact that every object in the universe is in motion and affected by its speed and by gravity, giving it an individual set of conditions. This means that an observer at any particular spot will see things differently that an observer in a different position, because the speed of the movement, using just that one condition in this example, will distort the observation. It is like the old example of the train whistle you may have learned in school. If the train is coming toward you, the whistle has one pitch; if it is traveling away, the pitch is different, adding or subtracting the speed of the train from the speed of sound. Einstein, using his intuition, combined with previous scientific observations and his knowledge of higher mathematics, conceptualized all of this without being able to see it, feel it or touch it. This goes entirely against what we experience on earth. Scientists have been able to make their minds comprehend what must be true, and not accept things the way they seem to be. Remember, it really seems that the sun circles the earth.

And scientists are human and don't always follow their own rules. Einstein made the following mistake: he published his Theory of Relativity in 1915. In 1917 Einstein developed further calculations from his original equations, which showed him the universe was expanding. Current belief in 1917 among scientists was that it was static, and he didn't accept his own findings, until a number of years later when astronomic observations proved the expansion (*The Science of God*, Schroeder).

In 1915 both the general public and the scientists were very skeptical of Einstein's predictions about the physical rules of the universe, but not Sir Arthur Eddington. He was a leading astronomer and mathematician and was convinced Einstein was correct. He placed expeditions in Brazil and in Africa during a 1919 total eclipse of the sun to photograph the position of stars during the eclipse, and again at night. The bending of light around the sun would shift their apparent positions, and that shift would be seen by comparing photographs. During the eclipse because of clouds, in Africa only two poor plates were obtained. In Brazil from 26 plates taken through two telescopes, one set of results was much smaller than Einstein's prediction and close to classical Newtonian theory, and the other set much too high for Einstein. Eddington, convinced his intuition about Einstein was correct, then studied the two poor African plates, and "using a complicated technique that necessarily assumed some of what he was looking for, and come up with a value pretty close to Einstein's prediction." ("Science in the Dark", Oliver Morton, *Wall Street Journal*, August 11, 1999). With this ambiguous result and "ignoring the set of observations that argued otherwise", Eddington created enough 'scientific spin', much like the political spin out of Washington, during a joint meeting of the Royal Society of Sciences and the Royal Astronomical Society, that they accepted his findings as proving Einstein's theory. Even with such ambiguous proof, the scientific world was willing to discard previous beliefs and critically accept the Theory of Relativity and use it in their scientific work. Although it seemed to defy what our senses told us, logical extension of mathematical calculations said it had to be so. Since then, Einstein and Eddington have been proven correct over and over by more advanced and exact techniques. In the 1970's radio telescope techniques demonstrated the bending of light within one-tenth of one percent of the prediction (*Einstein's Universe*, Nigel Calder, 1979).

To my mind, intuitive science is amazing. Discoveries are predicted by 'elegant' mathematical theorems and proofs, and years later the experimental results confirm the predictions. The aesthetic 'beauty' of the proof of a theoretical equation seems to tell the theoretical mathematicians their predictions and suppositions will eventually by validated by experimental results. The ability of our intellect is staggering.

There are a host of other scientific predictions proven many years later. Finding an additional planet in our solar system was aided by a brilliant mathematical analysis. Most of the planets in our solar system were known in ancient times. Newton's calculations of their orbits, based on his theory of gravity, were in excellent agreement with the observed patterns. But Uranus was discovered in the 19th Century, and its orbit did not fit expectations. French astronomer Urbain-Jean-Joseph Le Verrier embarked upon a "delicate [mathematical] masterpiece of prediction." He assumed that there was a planet further out whose gravitational effect caused an alteration in the expected orbit for Uranus. Using Newton's formulas he calculated several properties for this 'presumed' planet and predicted the region *where and when* astronomers should look for it. Within a few years Neptune was discovered "precisely where and when Le Verrier said it would be." (*Faster Than The Speed of Light*, Joao Magueijo, 2003). In a way LeVerrier was lucky: Pluto, the last planet discovered in 1930, is so small its gravitational effect did not disturb his mathematical predictions.

In another example of brilliant prediction, Sir Fred Hoyle, a leading astronomer during the 20th Century, studied the chemistry of carbon; based on his knowledge that carbon was so common in the universe, and was manufactured from helium in huge stars that exploded, thereby spreading the carbon throughout the universe, he predicted how that manufacture was accomplished. Experimentation exactly proved his theory many years later.

Mathematical analysis of 'atom smasher' results in the 1960's predicted the presence of W and Z particles, having masses 80 to 90 times that of a proton. In the 1980's this prediction was confirmed (*The Mind of God*, Paul Davies). Alan Guth's inflationary theory, part of the current Big Bang scenario, predicted, in 1982, a pattern of "non-uniformity" of the cosmic background radiation left over from the Big Bang. Data from the Cosmic Background Explorer satellite (COBE), about 15 years later, fit the predictions exactly. "The agreement was gorgeous". (*The Inflationary Universe*, Alan Guth).

To survive the human race does not need all this brainpower and knowledge. At least not to handle life on earth. Yet we have this tremendous capacity to explore and understand our universe and how our bodies work, and in one very important way we do need this knowledge. We know now that asteroids and meteorites cross the path of the orbit of the earth. If we do not want to go the way of the dinosaurs, the orbits of those bodies must be mapped, and we need to be able to change their trajectories to protect ourselves. We are currently developing the capability to do just that. How did Darwinian evolution, which tests our bodies through the challenges of nature on earth, know we would need the capacity to change the solar system for our benefit? The answer to the size of our head does not lie in Darwin's Theory. Our intellectual capacity and our consciousness make the most logical sense when viewed as divine gifts.

Chapter 6: Hallucination or Glimpse of the Afterlife?

In my own search for God, one of the most startling experiences that encouraged me to pursue my quest were the patients, roughly a dozen, who told me about near to death experiences (NDE). There was also a friend, who sought my counsel because of my medical background, who had an out of the body experience (OBE) during surgery. Comprehensive descriptions of what these experiences are like will be given a little further into this chapter. Although I did not keep notes on these discussions with the patients, I do remember the details of those that impressed me the most. I was aware of such events from my own reading and from my medical background, and from having taken courses in 'death and dying' to better serve my patients. The description provided by each of these patients was dramatic, very impressive, and amazingly consistent in similarity. The change in attitude by each patient, in the way they approached their individual existence, was also very profound for them and instructive to me. The experience of each patient strongly suggested to me, and I know they felt that way, that they had had a glimpse of the afterlife while being so close to death. Frank J. Tipler in his book, *The Physics of Immortality*, 1994, devoted 36 pages to a discussion of an afterlife, as conceived of by the major religions of the world, covering both Eastern and Western theologies, to provide him with a means of proving that immortality might exist after our life on earth. It allowed him to try and present a mathematical proof and a proof from the science of physics, although he states very directly that he is an atheist.

I realize the thesis I have been presenting up to this point in the book is that pure science provides amazing insights regarding the origin and formation of the universe, and the miraculous way that living forms evolved and maintain their existence. In this way I have worked toward the philosophic proposition that the design we see revealed by science is extremely profound evidence for intelligent design, one of the approaches to a logical philosophic proof of God. In entering into this discussion of NDEs and OBEs, I know I am presenting information that is on the fringe of science. None of this is provable by experimentation, as was the information presented previously. This material depends solely on the testimony of individuals and a judgment of their credibility. The fact that thousands of such episodes have occurred, occasionally multiple times to the same person, the consistency and uniformity of pattern, lead me to conclude that the people who experience these events are not charlatans. The patients who spoke with me were not fanatical 'weirdly' religious folk. They were ordinary individuals who were profoundly changed by the event. There is no question in my mind that this information is worth studying and pursuing. Entering this area also requires a brief look at mysticism and meditation within the practice of religion, briefly thinking about psychic phenomena as related to theories that propose the existence of a universal consciousness, for which interestingly there is some scientific evidence. Psychic phenomena do not appear in any way to provide evidence of God. Meditation may provide useful evidence since the scientists who have made a study of these phenomena find that the meditative experience is very similar and often the same as the OBEs and the NDEs. Since critics of these events suggest the concept of 'hallucinations' to dispute the interpretations that are given to these experiences, the issue of meditation, or meditation-like state, which the skeptical critics invoke, and also psychic phenomena must be explored.

In the simplest terms, OBE is equated with the soul, or spirit, or self, (whichever word the person uses to describe the event) leaving the body and traveling, and then returning back to the body. The OBEr often observes his own inert body and the activities around it, if he has become unconscious or is anesthetized. He may simply travel away from his body and then come back to it. But at no time is he near death. An OBE may be the initial portion of an NDE, but in a complete NDE there follows an episode equated with experiencing the afterlife; an NDE occurs in a variety of ways, but is initiated by the event of 'almost' dying or actually being in a state of early death, and being brought back to life, usually through medical intervention. NDEs occasionally occur while not being seriously near death. These are not new phenomena, descriptions having been traced back into ancient times. They have always been with us. They have been reported in the history of ancient Egypt and Greece, Native American Indians, and Chinese, for example. Research among 44 non-Western societies found that all but three believed OBEs occurred. In another study of 488 world societies, 89 percent had "at least some tradition regarding OBEs." (*The Holographic Universe*, Michael

Talbot, 1991). Plato, about 300 B.C. reported a ten-day episode of Er, a soldier, who appeared dead for that length of time, but upon arriving home for burial, revived and reported, "what he had learned while on The Other Side." (*Beyond the Light*, P.M.H. Atwater, Lh. D.,1994). Although it is not clear from history that Plato was reporting an actual event, the concept of OBE was recognized at that time. The current incidence of OBE in the general population runs as high as 20 percent in some surveys, when people are asked directly about them. Often individuals are unsure of what others will think and keep the episodes hidden. There is nothing very scientific about these surveys, some of which report incidence in the eight percent range. Careful researchers in the field do think the rate is somewhere between those figures. Although some of the work has indicated NDE's may also appear at these rates, Susan Blackmore (*Dying to Live*, 1993), reviewed one study and thought the incidence was less than one percent. Other authors place the rate at 22 to 48 percent, when carefully defining the term 'near to death', not just using the patient's impression (Blackmore).

Defining OBE separately, it can occur spontaneously, in sleep, after drug usage, under anesthetics in surgery, or following a serious injury. Ernest Hemingway described his experience, after being hit with shrapnel in 1918, during World War I. "A big Austrian trench mortar bomb exploded in the darkness. I died then. I felt my soul or something coming right out of my body, like you'd pull a silk handkerchief out of a pocket by one corner. It flew around and then came back and went in again and I wasn't dead anymore." (Quoted by Atwater). Other well-known individuals reporting an OBE include Goethe, D. H. Lawrence, Jack London, and Aldous Huxley (Talbot). In a spontaneous episode, the person finds himself freed of his body, looking down at it, now in a weightless form that can travel through solid material and float about, above the earth surveying all below. The experiencers describe it as exhilarating, very pleasant, and are convinced it really happened. My friend, a woman whose OBE occurred during surgery, was frightened by the episode. The surgery was abdominal, and an emergency but not life threatening. She suddenly was floating high in the operating suite watching the operation performed on her. Afterward she asked her priest if she had done something wrong to have such an experience. Since these events are well recognized, he reassured her. I think she related the story to me for further reassurance. In her case the event was not interpreted as pleasant. Susan Blackmore had an OBE in her college days, induced by marijuana. She went floating out of the dorm, over rooftops, and then came back. At first she thought it was real enough, but subsequently checked the buildings' appearance, and found them different than her memory of the episode. She concluded it was an illusion due to smoking marijuana, but I imagine it stoked her interest into doing her current skeptical research into these phenomena.

OBEs, as mentioned before, do not raise an issue of afterlife. But they offer the suggestion that some part of us can leave our body; and could that part be our soul? There are opinions by some of the OBE experiencers that being out of their body is proof enough of an afterlife. There is no clear cut dividing line between OBE's and NDE's. An NDE starts by the person traveling out of the body, and surprisingly, may occur both near death and also while perfectly well. The following description (from Atwater) covers all of the possible parts of the event that have been reported, recognizing that the experience comes in many varieties including some or all of the segments. Perception becomes very sharp. There follows travel down a dark tunnel or through blackness, approaching a very bright light at the end of the journey, a loving light of warmth and peace. From the light will come friendly voices, people, beings, or even religious figures. Conversation or transmission of information may follow. There may be a visit or travel to an area or vista of great scenic beauty. Often there is a life review, in either direction, backward or forward. There may be a sense of receiving or understanding all the knowledge of the universe, a sense of timelessness, a lack of fear and a very deep sense of peace. There is a reluctance to return to one's body, and disappointment at being revived. A person who has had this experience often has a profound change in life style, a whole new philosophy of life. As described by Atwater positive changes include becoming more loving and generous, happier and more joyful. There is a heightened sense of knowing what is really important in life, a greater awareness of the needs of others. The person is no longer afraid of death, no longer restricted by religious dogmas, much more aware of "personal responsibility/accountability", and recognizes and "accepts a greater reality and the existence of God". (Atwater). There can be negative reactions also: Confusion about what happened. "Can you trust yourself"? "Disappointment with the uncaring attitude of others". Surprisingly, there may be depression and "an inability to integrate the experience into daily life." As a result there are counseling groups formed to help people with both positive and negative reactions, under the auspices of The International Association for Near-Death Studies (IANDS).

The people who have experienced OBEs and NDEs are convinced they are real events. Obviously, scientists have no way of directly proving the point, when all they can use is a personal description given by each person they interview. What has convinced some of the researchers that these events are real is the consistency of the descriptions. This requires the scientist to use his personal judgment as to the reliability of the person he is interviewing. A major point that will be presented later is the finding of convincing 'evidence' through confirmation by a third party of observed events during an OBE, or the OBE portion of an NDE. Obviously, the only way to confirm visits to the afterlife is for the experiencer to discover information not previously known, and to have that information confirmed, again by a third party. There are suggestive cases of this type, which will be presented shortly, and the ones I have chosen from the literature all seem to have a small to marked degree of confirmation. Whether any of these present absolute confirmation will be something for the reader to decide. Without evidence or third party proof, another problem is the mindset of the researcher: is the scientist an atheist or does he have a profound belief in God, to cover all extremes. Has the researcher had a psychic experience, or been out of the body? Those considerations will definitely influence judgment when having to psychologically evaluate information. Some people have had psychic experiences, most have not. And these experiences certainly are in the arena of 'psychic experience'. Since I have had, or been part of three psychic events in my life, I first need to describe each one, and my skepticism and possible explanations for them, allowing the reader to evaluate my objectivity in the area of psychic events before proceeding to discuss these phenomena further, as they may pertain to the afterlife.

Over 40 years ago, at about the seventh month of the pregnancy that produced my son, my Mother called from New York, 1,600 miles away from our home in Houston. She had a dream and had to tell me: My wife and I were going to have a son, and he would be named, "Jonathan Adam". Quite amazingly, I had already picked out the name for a son, "Jonathan Alan", based on the consideration that I was "David Joseph", two good Old Testament names, and in the Old Testament Jonathan and David were close friends, as I wished to be with a son. I did not remember discussing any of this thinking with my Mother prior to her phone call. My skeptical side tells me that I may have done just that in a forgotten prior telephone discussion. Recognizing that my Mother liked to be in charge, a good Jewish Mother in control, it is possible she picked up some hint from me in the past, liked the idea, and presented it to me as hers, from a 'dream'. At least she had a 50/50 chance on the sex of the baby; but, in dreaming of so similar a name, with hundreds of male names available, the odds are extraordinary. I remain very skeptical about this event, as to whether she really had the dream.

However, I'm not skeptical about the next event. It really happened, and I might have an explanation, unusual as it was. About 20 years ago, I was driving home from my medical office between 5:30 and 6:00 P.M. listening to a telephone talk show on radio with open subjects brought up by the listeners. My memory of this is very vivid: to this day I can show you the exact spot my car stopped for a red light. The lady told the talk-show host she had a remedy for severe sunburn. At that moment he told her to wait with her thought, and took a short commercial break. During the commercial my brain was on idle, until near the end when it suddenly flashed through my mind what she would say. She used a strong brew of tea, soaked a tee shirt in it, and put it on the victim, who would be greatly relieved. I had never heard of this approach before having my sudden thought. It made sense, as tea is a tanning agent. Just before the red light changed she was back on the air, stating the thought I had just had, exactly! For a moment I didn't start my car moving, stunned as I was. There was just a brief ride to the house, where I excitedly told my wife about it, and then my scientific mind tried to figure out what might explain the episode. Was I psychic or clairvoyant? The skeptic's explanation has to do with the time delay built into all talk radio. The stations, to protect themselves from what might pop out over the airwaves, use an eight- to 20-second tape delay in broadcasting the telephone conversation. When the thought jumped into my head, it was exactly during the time the lady was giving her statement over the phone. Perhaps the telephone line to the station was near my car, and I somehow sensed her remark. That in itself is very unusual, as I have never been able to "listen" to telephone lines either before or since this experience I had. At least it seems to me somewhat more reasonable than my "picking her brain" as she sat in her home across a number of miles in Houston. I have to accept that it is a psychic event I cannot fully explain away.

The last event occurred several years ago. I woke from sleep, not remembering any dream that might have been going on. Across from the foot of our bed were two transparent women, in dresses, dancing slowly to music I could not hear. I sat up to watch. They were bathed in the reddish light from a glowing clock with its two-inch numbers. They were separate from each other, each smiling, moving their arms and bodies. The figure on the right was my wife. But at the same time there was my wife next to my right side in bed, breathing easily and steadily, as if in a deep sleep. I have no idea who the other lady was. She was older than my wife, and slightly taller and heavier. It is hard to describe a transparent figure more accurately than that. I watched for what seemed several minutes, and suddenly they were gone. I did not see the figure of my wife come back to her body beside me. I think I was completely awake during this, did not feel disturbed or upset by the episode, just extremely curious as to why or how this happened to me. I did get out of bed briefly after this occurred to be sure I was awake. The next morning I asked my wife if she remembered anything, especially dreaming what I had seen. She did not remember what I described. She had nothing to add to what I told her, and had no idea, from my description, who the other person was. Back to my skeptic side, the simplest explanation is that it was all a dream and I projected those figures in a way that I thought they were real. We have all dreamed we are really awake, only to wake up and tell by the clock we have been sleeping. In this case it didn't seem like that. I woke up, saw the scene, and then I sat up in bed to watch. That is how I found myself as everything ended. As for the other woman, after all, strangers do appear in dreams as well as people we know. In psychic terms, I saw my wife's 'astral' body. It still seems entirely real to me, but was it?

By the time this last event happened, I had talked with many patients about their near to death experiences. I had changed from being agnostic to a believer in God and an afterlife, not at all influenced by these psychic experiences of mine, but because of what the patients told me, and the other reading, research, and logical thinking I had performed. I know these three incidents in my life happened. I didn't invent them, but they are not significant enough to influence my thinking about as serious and profound a subject as one's religious faith, and the profound effect OBEs and NDEs have on experiencers.

Although awareness of OBEs and NDEs was reawakened in the 1970s by research from Dr. Elisabeth Kubler-Ross and Dr. Raymond Moody, as I have stated, these episodes have a history over thousands of years. Modern medicine just wasn't listening (*Surviving Death*, Geoff Viney, 1994). I knew of Kubler-Ross's work while taking courses in death-and-dying to better understand and help my own patients. As I learned to counsel with my patients, and listen to them more closely, they told me of NDEs. Listening closely is important. If the patients feel your interest they bring out happenings they were not originally sure they wanted to reveal. Note that both Kubler-Ross and Moody are psychiatrists. Kubler-Ross was an agnostic who became a believer. (*Beyond the Light*, 1994) Dr. Michael Sabom, a cardiologist, was an out-and-out skeptic of Moody's reports, and told him so. Moody challenged him to ask his patients. Much to Sabom's surprise, Moody was absolutely correct, and no longer skeptical, published his findings of over 100 cardiac patients with such experiences, in his book *Recollections of Death: A Medical Investigation*, 1982 (quoted in *Surviving Death*). At this time (2003), there are hundreds of articles on the subject, covering thousands of patients and their single or multiple episodes. P.M.H. Atwater, Lh. D., is probably the most prolific of the investigators, having had sessions with about 3,000 people, and in-depth interviews with over 700. She has had three episodes herself, started out as a believer in afterlife and, of course, remains one. Susan Blackmore, a Senior Lecturer in Psychology at the University of the West of England, who states she is agnostic, with several books on OBEs and NDEs, is probably one of the most prominent skeptics, and considers both OBEs and NDEs hallucinations. She is a Fellow of the Committee for the Scientific Investigation of Claims of the Paranormal (CSICOP). CSICOP is an international organization with the express purpose of attempting to debunk any and all paranormal and psychic claims.

Until 2001 most of the books and research in this field have been tainted by skepticism. Certainly some of the scientists involved were psychiatrists and cardiologists, but others were lay people writing books describing their experiences with no way to support their claims. Most of the material involved interviews and reports months to years after the events. Many were third hand reports. Such research is suspect: "subjects [of this type] are 'self-selected'—people who already think something, not a random trial—and the delay means they may have had plenty of time to imagine things." (www.beliefnet.com, "What If It's Really True?", Gregg Easterbrook, 12/28/01). Lending an enormous amount of respectability to this field of research was an article in the prestigious medical journal, *Lancet*, Vol. 358:2039-45, December 15, 2001. What makes this study so special is that it was set up as "prospective" research; all survivors of cardiac arrest were interviewed as soon as they were capable of answering questions. From the answers the authors of the study received, they feel these experiences are real, are not hallucinations and require much more scientific study to arrive at some scientific explanation.

The cause of these experiences is currently unknown and the mechanisms are scientifically controversial. In any scientific issue that is under controversy, all sides must be presented. We will do that by quoting material from the opposite viewpoints, letting the reader decide for himself. I have reviewed many books about OBE and NDE published 15-20 years after the first material appeared, allowing for a better and clearer synthesis of ideas to be developed. I am convinced that ODEs and NDEs are important events that are not 'psychic' and suggest alternative realities and/or evidence of an afterlife and should be the subject of further research as real events. With my own experiences in mind, I still remain quite skeptical about psychic experiences, but considering the reports of police success in solving cases with the help of psychics, I maintain an objective outlook.

One of the controversies, of course, is whether these experiences are 'real' or just hallucinations. They are real enough to the person having the experience, but do these people really leave their bodies and observe something that can be objectively confirmed by others? I have collected cases from the literature that appear to satisfy these criteria. But first I wish to review cases from my practice that sharply caught my attention and stirred my interest. It helped me reach the conclusion that these are not hallucinations.

A female patient of mine came in somewhat late for her annual physical, delayed by having to care for her dying husband at their home and told me about his last day on earth. I had seen him for shoulder and neck pain several months before. A chest x-ray showed he had a massive cancer in the upper chest just below the shoulder. He was referred to the oncologists, but there was little to be done. On the last full day of his life he called her into their bedroom, and asked her to look out the front window to show her what he was seeing. There were people passing by in boats on a small river. She asked him if he recognized anyone. He knew all of them, and everyone was a dead person they both had known in life. This story set off the light bulb in my head. I had heard several NDEs by this time in my practice, but it took this information to make me realize that all NDEs I had heard about involved the dead, either known to the experiencer, or the person was a religious figure, known from history, or unknown and presumed dead. All the researchers in this field confirm that only the dead are involved, whether the NDE was truly experienced near to death or while in relatively good health. This is a point of great consistency: the persons communicated with are always dead. This story also interests me in how it parallels Greek Mythology: the dead were ferried in boats across the River Styx, a thought that occurred to me as my patient told the story. Another historical parallel I have since learned is the

151

Bardo-Thodol, the Tibetan book of the dead, which was an oral guide to dying in Tibet going back thousands of years, and reduced to writing in the ninth century. The description of visions at death it offers sounds just like modern NDE's (Viney).

Another patient of mine described his approximately six-year-old daughter's description of what she experienced while being in coma for a prolonged period after almost drowning in the family pool. She met and conversed with a white-robed religious figure, before returning to consciousness. While first working on this chapter, a ten-year-old shot himself in the head in Ohio. The family was told he would die, but four days later he came out of his coma and told his family: "I went to heaven and I saw Jesus. My grandfather came to me and told me to go back home. He said it wasn't my time." (*Houston Chronicle*, 9/3/99). Both of these accounts are completely typical stories of a child's experience as described in the literature. Usually they see religious figures, and a family member only if deceased. They never see their living parents. On rare occasion children, but not adults, may see a favorite teacher or playmate who is living (*Children of the New Millennium*, P.M.H. Atwater, LH. D., 1999, pg. 68).

As I continue to present stories like these, they will all sound generally the same. The real issue is what does this prove? Do these people come back from an encounter in heaven or with persons from heaven? The long human history of these stories and their consistency certainly would make one think they represent reality, not just wishful thinking that there is an afterlife for us. The skeptics who would deny this is real, and the scientists who deal in finding evidence of the truth, demand corroborating evidence. Such evidence must be external to the experiencer, must involve an object, a person or an event observed by the experiencer, and verifiable by a third party. I believe there is some solid evidence and now offer several tales from the literature that contains 'evidence'.

1) Michael Talbot, the author of several books on various aspects of science reflecting this area of research, recounts his own OBE as an adolescent. While asleep, he rose above his sleeping form and journeyed outside his house, through a solid glass window. He thought he was dreaming as he flew about. Somewhere near his house, lying in the grass was a book of short stories by the nineteenth century French author, Guy de Maupassant. He knew of the author, but the book he spotted had no interest for him, so he wondered why he was dreaming about it. He fell back to dreamlessness, but the next morning remembered the 'dream'. On the way to school a neighbor

stopped him. She was missing a library book after she had walked near his house. He took her to the spot where he had 'seen' it during his experience, and there it was! Talbot searched his memory to find some other explanation in order to avoid concluding he had an OBE while sleeping. Specifically he had not been in the area near the book while awake, and during the time it was lost. He had not recently communicated with the neighbor, did not know the book was missing and was not aware that she liked that particular author. He concluded that it could not be a series of unlikely coincidences and that he truly had an OBE during which he discovered the missing book. This case does not involve corroboration by a third party other than the neighbor, but I don't think a respected author of sophisticated reviews of science would deliberately invent a tale like this and claim it was true (*Beyond the Quantum*, Michael Talbot, 1986).

2) Kimberly Clark, a hospital social worker, was extremely skeptical of OBEs until her encounter with Maria, a patient who had a cardiac arrest and had to be resuscitated. After being revived, a short time later in the hospital Maria told Clark of being out of her body upon arrival at the emergency entrance, rising up to the third floor and seeing an old tennis shoe on an outside ledge of the hospital, with a small hole worn through on the side of the little toe, and a lace that was under the heel. She identified the maker of the shoe. Clark searched the hospital third floor, and had to find the shoe by pressing her face against windows until she spotted it. The shoe was retrieved and Maria's description was correct in every detail. "The only way she would have had such a perspective was if she had been floating right outside and at very close range to the tennis shoe. It was a very concrete evidence for me." (Clark, quoted in *The Holographic Universe*). Our resident skeptic, Susan Blackmore, noting this same story in her book, raises objections that are absolute sophistry, and well off the point. "Clark explains that this story served to legitimize Maria's experience, as if without it the experience was somehow invalid but with it the experience was 'real'. Of course NDEs should not need such legitimization for they are valid in themselves, as experiences." Of course the experience was 'real' for Maria. The proper issue to discuss is was *she really out of her body* in order to find the shoe? The evidence from Clark is clear: Maria was out of her body. Blackmore continued her critical comments by agreeing, "claims like this are extremely important if they are true. So is it true? This is, sadly, one of those cases for which I have been unable to get further information. Perhaps it may yet be possible but until then I can only consider it as fascinating but

unsubstantiated." It is not unsubstantiated! Clark reported her account in a book edited by Greyson and Flynn, *The Near-Death Experience: Problems, Prospects, Perspectives*, (1984). Dr. Bruce Greyson is a psychiatrist, and has been a very active leading research scientist in this field, and as of this writing is at the University of Virginia medical school. In medical literature an editor is (as Greyson was for the book) very careful to insert in a book he is editing, material he is convinced can be substantiated. How did Blackmore try to substantiate the story? She doesn't tell us. She could have contacted Greyson to have him confirm or deny Clark's tale, or tried to reach Clark for a direct interview. Michael Schmiker did contact Dr. Greyson and included this case in his book. Dr. Greyson could have denied the story, but obviously did not. Clark has repeated her story in *After the Dark*, pages 1-16 (1995) under her married name, Sharp (Michael Schmicker, *Best Evidence*, 2000). What Blackmore does is try to cast doubt and then immediately drop the subject after the quote above.

3) That Blackmore will contact other researchers is shown in this next story. A cardiologist Dr. Fred Schoonmaker had a female patient who was congenitally blind (blind from birth). She had an OBE during surgery and "correctly identified the number of people in the room (fourteen) and could describe the medical procedures. She could not, however, distinguish colours but could see forms and activities going on." (Blackmore). Of course, a congenitally blind person could not recognize colors, never having seen them. Schoonmaker was contacted by Dr. Kenneth Ring, a professor of psychology at the University of Connecticut, an internationally recognized leader in the field of OBE and NDE. The cardiologist confirmed the story, and Ring urged him to publish the three cases he had, but he never did. In personal conversation with Blackmore Ring said "Another intriguing, but in the end, useless anecdote. There has never, to my knowledge, been a case of a blind NDEr *reported in the literature* where there was clear-cut or documented evidence of accurate visual perception during an alleged OBE. I wish there were such a case—we'd all love it." (Pg. 133 in *Dying to Live*). The reader without scientific background will be confused at this point. Ring had the story confirmed by Schoonmaker. Why is it a "useless anecdote"? The key phrase is my italicized 'reported in the literature' portion of his statement. Among academic scientists unless one is willing to write material into the literature it becomes 'unsubstantiated'. It is not open to review by one's peers. This scientific ethic comes from the scientific method. The experimenter publishes his numerical results, his mathematics and his

statistical analysis. Other scientists can critically review the material and try to repeat it. If reproducible, it becomes accepted by the scientific community. Schoonmaker was a scientist, but as a private practitioner cardiologist and not being an academician he didn't feel it necessary to write a series of "case histories". Following academic ethics Ring and Blackmore are unwilling to use the story, but it certainly sounds valid to me, since Ring confirmed it by personal communication, and Schoonmaker had nothing to gain by inventing the story. This story is not an experiment to be reviewed and repeated and is not the sort of scientific report that requires the ethics of the scientific method. My partner and I, as private practitioners, conducted a 10-year study on the prevention of colon cancer, done for our own interest and the protection of our private patients. It was never published, but the results were just as valid as later published reports proved (My book, *Government by Political Spin*, 2000).

4) Kenneth Ring presented the following story in his book, *Life at Death* (1980), quoted by Michael Talbot in, *The Holographic Universe*. As a woman NDEr "found herself moving through the tunnel and approaching the realm of light, she saw a friend of hers coming back! As they passed the friend telepathically communicated to her that he had died, but was being 'sent back.' The woman, too, was eventually 'sent back' and after she recovered she discovered that her friend had suffered a cardiac arrest and was resuscitated at approximately the same time as her own experience." As meticulous as Ring appears to be, I would assume he confirmed this story. Ring continued his studies among the blind and published those results in *Mindsight; Near-Death and Out-of-Body Experiences in the Blind* (Written with Sharon Cooper, 1999). The descriptions given by people blind from birth and also those who became blind later in life are *exactly* the same as in sighted persons. These subjects claimed they could 'see' events around themselves during the experiences, returning to the blind state when they returned to their bodies. Several of Ring's subjects presented evidence of confirmation, but only one appears absolutely confirmed. The woman, because of a mistake during chest surgery, became, in a matter of about six hours, totally and permanently blind. When the doctors recognized her problem she was moribund and unconscious, and rushed out of the ICU to surgery. Her gurney passed by her former husband and her current lover. The men talked to each other but not to her. When she recovered from her emergency surgery, she said she was out of her body and saw both men 15-20 feet away from her gurney. Both men confirmed her story as to their

positions in the hallway. An issue, not commented upon by the authors, is that the men did speak while she was in that hallway. In her near-to-death state, unconscious and blind, did she hear their voices and somehow or other assimilate the information that they were present and remember it? Not likely. Her story is very exact: she even gave an estimate of how far away they were.

5) Dr. Michael Sabom, the skeptical cardiologist who was challenged to question his patients by Dr. Raymond Moody, became convinced of OBEs and NDEs by patients represented by the one in the following story. "I came to know this man quite well and visited him several times at his home. At no time did I find any indication that he possessed more than a layman's knowledge of medicine. It is evident that many of the details he recalled were given in response to my own probings and were not volunteered. I was also struck by his reaction to my inadvertent use of the word 'paddle' to describe the instrument that is held on the patient's chest during electrical defibrillation. 'Paddle' is a widely used term [by doctors] for these instruments and is so ingrained in my mind that I use it without thinking. The man demonstrated his unfamiliarity with this word, however, by his response: "They weren't paddles, Doctor. They were round disks with a handle on them. No paddles."

Blackmore does not mention this case, which gives a very clear example of how closely Sabom questioned his patients. Instead she attacks others of his cases, on such unsteady grounds as this: A man described in great detail the meters on the defibrillator used on him, unusual types of meters employed on such equipment in 1973 when the man was defibrillated. The man had never seen CPR performed. Sabom was absolutely convinced the man was out of his body in order to describe the events on the meters. Her attack: "From these [hospital medical] records we have no knowledge of what kind of apparatus was used, whether the needles did move in exactly this way at the right time and so on. Yes, the man gives a plausible account and it seems unexpected given his lack of knowledge, but without access to complete details of what happened (and these can never be obtained) we cannot know just how closely it really did fit the facts at the time." Sabom, a highly trained cardiologist, recognizes an older machine from the patient's description, and Blackmore doubts it. This is nitpicking. Sabom was perfectly familiar with these machines. In another instance she tried to refute his reasoning about the level of gases in the blood as they might relate to NDEs. The gas levels were relatively normal during this patient's episode. Blackmore expresses the opinion that "I cannot agree with his conclusion. In this special case it was quite likely that the man's brain, though not his arterial blood was suffering hypoxia [low oxygen] or hypercarbia [high carbon dioxide]." She does quote research that shows that arterial blood gases may not reflect the gas levels in the brain. I agree, but in this case the carbon dioxide level was actually somewhat low in the artery and the oxygen elevated as would happen in a patient given oxygen and recovering. Arteries deliver fresh blood. The sample was taken at the artery in the groin, over twice as far from the heart as the brain. Although there is no way of knowing for sure, low oxygen and high carbon dioxide in 'this brain' are highly unlikely at the time the arterial blood gas sample was taken, which was while the patient was still experiencing his OBE. Those figures more likely indicate that good circulation had been restored, allowing the lungs to lower the carbon dioxide that much. She has a right to her opinion, but she is a psychologist telling a trained cardiologist about the condition of his patient. She will develop unreasonable criticisms to maintain her skepticism.

Despite Blackmore's objections, Ring commented on Sabom's early work by stating that it was "the only evidence from systematic research in the field of near-death studies that suggests near-death experiencers can sometimes report visual perceptions that are physically impossible and not otherwise explicable by conventional means." (Ring & Lawrence, *Journal of Near-Death Studies*, 11/4, Summer 1993, pgs.223-229). Sabom, continuing his medical research, has meticulously attempted to provide verifiable evidence of these patients 'seeing' what they should not be able to see. In a more recent book, *Light and Death* (1998), he presents one case that appears to have absolute proof. The woman had a large basilar artery aneurysm, a blowout-type of bubble on an artery at the base of her brain. It was enlarging and threatening to burst. To remove it involved using profound hypothermia, taking her body down to 60 degrees Fahrenheit, stopping her heart and draining her head of blood! All so they could quickly move her brain aside and rapidly repair the artery, once all the preparations were in place. The chilling helped preserve brain cells, which otherwise would last only four minutes at normal body temperature. Draining the blood allowed the aneurysm to collapse so they could remove it at its base on the artery. They taped her eyes shut, and put molded earpieces in her ears, which produced clicking sounds to allow them to follow brain function by EEG. She was then anesthetized and put on a respirator. About 90 minutes after anesthesia was begun (it took that long to chill her body down to the desired temperature), the skull saw was used to open her skull, while at the same time the cardiac surgeon was putting cannulas (tubes) into her femoral (leg) arteries for the heart by-pass machine. She started her OBE with the sound of the saw. She heard the cardiac surgeon comment on the very small size of her arteries. She described seeing the skull saw for the first time while out of her body. Later when she recovered, she described the saw as looking like an electric toothbrush, with a notch for the blade, and being kept in a case that looked like a socket-wrench case. All of these observations were right on the mark, as was her description of the cardiac surgeon's comments about her arteries. She developed all this knowledge about her surgical procedure while fully anesthetized, her eyes taped shut and tight fitting earpieces clicking in her ears. This appears to be proof positive of her OBE. As the operation proceeded to the hypothermia portion, with her heart stopped and chilled blood pumped into her body, and finally, with no brain waves on the EEG, she entered the afterlife and saw deceased relatives. The exact timing of her hearing the saw and the comments about her arteries is clear from the operative notes. Obviously, the exact timing of her NDE cannot be determined.

6) Blackmore also denigrated the work of Dr. Elisabeth Kubler-Ross, whose early discoveries brought this whole field to the fore. After World War II Kubler-Ross was a professor of psychiatry at Chicago University Hospital, and began to counsel with terminally ill patients, helping them to come to terms with the idea of death. As Geoff Viney in *Surviving Death* reviewed her work: "An agnostic herself, Kubler-Ross had no illusions on the subject: as far as she was concerned death was an end to everything." She heard the stories of OBEs and NDEs and thought they were hallucinations. She then encountered several examples of patients who claimed to meet with "the ghosts of people that they did not know were dead. One notable case concerned the death of a young Indian girl who saw her father only seconds before drawing her last breath." Kubler-Ross knew the man was living somewhere in the United States, and in follow up discovered "that he was indeed dead, having suffered a fatal coronary only one hour before his daughter's moment of death." Blackmore noted that Kubler-Ross was sure NDErs "can see the world correctly, even if they are totally blind." And quoted Kubler-Ross: "We have questioned several totally blind people who were able to share with us their near-death experience and they were not only able to tell us who came into the room first, who worked on the resuscitation, but they were able to give minute details of the attire and the clothing of all

the people present, something a totally blind person would never be able to do." Rather than criticize as famous a doctor as Kubler-Ross in her own words, Blackmore quotes a "British commentator", author Ian Wilson: "Regrettably, Dr. Kubler-Ross has tended to be too committed to her patients to spend time publishing these cases in the proper depth to prove her point." Blackmore omits the credentials of Wilson, whoever he is, which should be provided to validate his opinion, committing the same error of which Wilson complains: not enough depth. This off-hand opinion casts doubt on the intellectual veracity of a highly respected academic physician, and is literally an insult. It is also another example of academicians wanting every last detail in print; as noted before, early studies in this field of research did not try to develop the type of documentation required by the scientific method. They relied on compiling a series of individual events often at long intervals after the occurrence. *The Lancet* study reported in December 2001, mentioned previously, made a completely scientific study of a group of patients with immediate interviews and analysis and will be presented more fully later in this chapter.

7) Dr. Raymond A. Moody, Jr., a psychiatrist who also holds a Ph. D. in philosophy, published the first book in the field in 1975, *Life After Life*, followed immediately by the book by Kubler-Ross. They worked simultaneously, but were at first unaware of each other. Blackmore quotes much of Moody's work in discussing the field, and is careful to pinpoint his reservations regarding attempts to confirm paranormal vision on the part of the OBEr or NDEr. "Moody is quite open about the problem. He explains that in a few cases he has been able to get independent testimony but in most cases the event is attested to only by the dying person himself and at most by a couple of close friends and acquaintances. He concludes that such corroborating stories, collected after the fact, cannot constitute proof." (Blackmore, *Dying To Live*). This sort of comment in his first book in 1975 is not at all surprising to me. He had opened up a new field of research and was 'feeling' his way along. All thorough scientists will express reservations of this type. However, his reservations have not stopped him from continuing to collect stories and to look for confirmation. In 1988 he published the following: A woman left her body during surgery and "floated into the waiting room, and saw that her daughter was wearing mismatched plaids. The maid had dressed the little girl so hastily that she had not noticed the error and was astounded when the mother, who did not physically see the little girl that day, commented on the fact." (*The Holographic Universe*, Michael Talbot,

from Raymond A. Moody, Jr. with Paul Perry, *The Light Beyond*, 1988). In this case there is only the maid for conformation, but put yourself in the maid's position. The maid would not forget something as startling as the mother commenting on a day subsequent to surgery about a clothing mismatch, nor would the maid make up such a story.

8) P.M.H. Atwater has done extensive research in the field for 20 years, with thousands of one-on-one interviews. She has a number of cases, which she feels have irrefutable external evidence as 'proof' of what she has been told by her subjects. I have personally discussed her work with her. Probably the most remarkable person in her book, *Beyond the Light*, is Dr. George Rodonaia. As a dissident in communist Russia, he was a victim of attempted assassination in 1976, run over twice by a KGB automobile, pronounced dead and taken to a hospital morgue in Tibilisi, Georgia, then a part of Russia. After being kept in cold storage for three days, his autopsy was begun by opening his abdomen. I have heard him very convincingly tell his story on television (9 AM, 2/1/00, KTRK Houston). Just as they were about to open his chest his eyes fluttered open, and the doctors, one of whom was his uncle, realized he was alive. As Rodonaia put it, "there were suddenly 13 converted Christians in the room." He could not speak for three days, but when he did the first thing he told them was to check an infant in the newborn nursery, the recently-born child of a couple with whom he was friendly. He knew the child had a broken hip, and x-rays confirmed this. He 'knew' because he had been out of his body while in the morgue, had visited and reassured the crying child by 'telepathy'. The child could sense his presence and stopped crying. "I was pure consciousness. I could be anywhere instantly, really there." He felt an overwhelming sense of love. He also had seen his wife arrange for his funeral, and she confirmed that he read her thoughts exactly. A husband reading a wife's thoughts is not proof, but a confirmed fractured hip is, and his wife confirms that incident. Dr. Rodonaia is a physician. Following this episode he became a psychiatrist and obtained a doctorate in theology, becoming a priest in the Georgian Orthodox Church. He is now a Methodist minister in Texas. Dr. Atwater is completely convinced of the authenticity of this story.

Dr. Atwater has more recently done extensive interviews with children who have had near-death experiences, and adults who had experiences as children. These 277 people are recounted in her book, *Children of the Millennium* (1999). There are several cases which seem to be proven, but in each instance the verification as written in the book appears to be primarily through the individual person, not third parties. However, Dr. Atwater has assured me by e-mail that the book contains "a whole slew of accurate and verified stories."

9) Michael Schmiker, an investigative reporter, reported a deathbed vision (an NDE) from 1924 in his book, *Best Evidence*. His book is a compilation of the best scientific evidence Schmiker could find to explain paranormal phenomena, such as ESP, deathbed visions and NDE, and other psychic phenomena. It included material gained from interviews with some of the leading university professors in the field. The deathbed vision was described in the book, *Deathbed Visions*, by Sir William Barrett (1926), a physics professor at the Royal College of Science in Dublin. His wife was an obstetrician who had attended a woman in childbirth. Although the woman had been in poor health during pregnancy, she delivered a child safely but died shortly afterward. As she was dying, she described to Dr. Barrett a vision in which she was seeing her father, who had previously passed away, and a beautiful world. Suddenly she was surprised by also seeing her sister Vida. Vida had died three weeks before, and the family had not told her because of her fragile health in the pregnancy. Schmicker felt this was extremely strong evidence since it was observed by a trained physician, who reported it immediately to her husband, another trained scientist. The case so impressed Sir Barrett, he found a group of other reports and wrote his book. Case 9 is one of the few I discovered that is like the study reported in *Lancet*. It fits the requirements of prospective research: an observation by a trained scientist, as close to the event as possible, with no chance for hearsay or memory embellishment of a period of time.

10) The *Lancet* report is authored by Pim van Lommel and included 344 consecutive cardiac patients who were successfully resuscitated in ten Dutch hospitals. Their overall findings and conclusions will be covered later. They describe one case of OBE, which apparently was the most striking of all their patients. He was found by passersby lying in a meadow, and brought to the coronary care unit cyanotic (blue from lack of oxygen) and comatose. A nurse removed his dentures so that he could be intubated with an endotracheal tube to his lungs to allow for artificial respiration. It took an hour and a half to resuscitate him to the point where he could be transferred to the intensive care unit (ICU), still comatose. A week later the same nurse was working in the cardiac ward delivering medicines. The patient immediately recognized her as the person who removed his dentures and placed them in a drawer on the "crash cart," a mobile cart carrying necessary bottles of drugs and equipment to deal with cardiac resuscitation. He "was also able to describe correctly and

in detail the small room in which he had been resuscitated as well as the appearance of those present", and as well as the appearance of the nurse (*Lancet* Vol: 358, December 15, 2001). The patient said that as he observed his own resuscitation "he had been very much afraid that we would stop the CPR and that he would die. He desperately and unsuccessfully tried to make it clear that he was very much alive and that we should continue the CPR." This is no doubt the most striking of the patients' experiences the researchers reviewed.

Why have I offered so many different reports with varying degrees of third party confirmation? Obviously, it is because this is an area that invites so much skepticism, and yet there appears to be more and more evidence that something very unusual is going on that cannot be dismissed out of hand. Actually there are many more cases with only a slightly less degree of outside confirmation. The authors of the *Lancet* study are totally puzzled as to the underlying neurological mechanism that creates these experiences, if, in fact, there is a straightforward neurological mechanism. "We did not show that psychological, neurophysiological, or physiological factors caused these experiences after cardiac arrest. NDE pushes at the limits of medical ideas about the range of human consciousness and the mind-brain relation." In their frustration at not being able to come up with a scientific explanation of their findings, they offer a very non-scientific theory. "NDE might be a changing state of consciousness (transcendence), in which identity, cognition, and emotion function *independently from the unconscious body*, but retain the possibility of non-sensory perception." (My italics). Transcendence is defined by *Webster's New Collegiate Dictionary* in three ways: as "extending or lying beyond the limits of ordinary experience, being beyond comprehension, or transcending material existence." In simple words, the Dutch physicians are proposing the possibility that a human state of consciousness can separate from the body and the brain and still function!! There is something very unusual going on during these episodes. Dr. Pim Van Lommel, the lead author of the Lancet article, offers an analogy to try and explain this phenomenon. "Could the brain be kind of a receiver (interface) for consciousness and memories, like TV, radio or mobile telephone? What you receive is not in the receiver, but electromagnetic waves (photons) are made visible or audible for your sense organs." What he is saying is that we are always surrounded by electromagnetic waves, but to pick up those signals we must turn on a receiver, a TV set, a radio, or a mobile phone. He implies that our consciousness is, somehow or other, "out there" waiting to be picked up by our brain. In this interview it is theorized that consciousness may pervade the entire body, and even though the brain is disabled during CPR, NDE and OBE experiences may be picked up from the body! ("The Heart of Death: An Interview with Pim Van Lommel," Jill Neimark, www.metanexus.net, Views 2002.01.14).

Since NDEs and OBEs are so unusual there is tremendous skepticism in the world about them. Why do I pick on poor Susan Blackmore? Because she devoted an entire book, and I think the only book in the literature, in a biased one-sided endeavor to claim that OBEs and NDEs are simply the results of a sick brain or a drug effect on the brain. She represents the skeptics in the world with closed minds, who are unwilling to look at current scientific efforts to understand these phenomena. Blackmore presents a very one-sided critique of all the material that was available at the time she did the research for her book (1993). Her own words explain why. "It is my contention that this 'real thing'—NDEs, mystical experiences and indeed everything on the spiritual path—are products of a brain and the universe of which it is part. For there is nothing else. I want to be quite clear. It is my contention that there is no soul, spirit, astral body or anything at all that leaves the body during NDEs and survives after death. These, like the very idea of a persisting self, are all illusions and the NDE can be accounted for without recourse to any of them." Her preface describes her philosophy. "There is no future heaven towards which evolution progresses. And no ultimate purpose. It just goes along. Yet our minds have evolved to crave purposefulness and cling to the idea of a self because that will more efficiently keep alive the body and perpetuate its genes. In other words, our evolution makes it very hard for us to accept the idea of evolution and our own individual pointlessness."

Her quote demonstrates her belief that our concept of having a "self", and therefore a soul, is an illusion of our minds. I could not live with such a bleak outlook of the meaning of my life, and most Western people agree with me. But we have to hear her. She is a leading critic of the work done in this field, and her challenges are important to evaluate the strengths and weaknesses of any conclusions we might reach even though she cannot be considered a true scientist. A true scientist would not be so biased. She employs Buddhist teachings to support her point of view. In this she is perfectly consistent with her personal beliefs. Buddhism does not have God, but levels of existence, and the theology reflects a pattern of relationship with the universe, partially as revealed through meditation. The experiences of NDErs are very similar, if not the same as those which are experienced by persons who meditate, and all researchers recognize that NDEs are like meditative responses. The experiences of meditation are therefore part of her book. Also, she did contribute some original research. Because of the religious differences between East and West, she did review the scientific literature studying NDEs in India. In her view, including a small study of her own, they are basically the same, with more dead people seen in the United States, and more religious figures appearing in India. Despite the marked differences in theology, NDEs are consistent throughout the world, an important point for her to establish, since she employs Buddhist mysticism and meditation in studying Western NDEs.

If she had wished to deal with monotheism, with Western theology, she would find that mystical Judaism, the Kabbalah, which began early in the Common Era, also has teachings revealed through meditation. The Kabbalah accepts the existence of the soul, God, and an afterlife, and is exactly the opposite of Buddhism. As Rabbi David Aaron explains in his book *Endless Light*(1997), about the Kabbalah, "according to the Kabbalah, when we pray we engage in a self-orienting experience. The words you speak—and they must be audible to yourself—act to arouse your self, your soul. This is directly opposite to the Eastern idea of meditation, which is emptying oneself of thought. Meditation is a calming of senses and emotions. But the Kabbalah calls for an intentional exciting of mind, will, and imagination. This is a very sensual understanding of prayer." I have used this as one example of meditation in Western thought. There has been mysticism in all the monotheistic religions. "Mystics throughout the ages actually report coherent and consistent observations of the transcendent, i.e. supernatural realities". Dr. Bernard Haisch, a high-energy astrophysicist, is the director of the California Institute for Physics and Astrophysics, and he believes mystics offer observations that are valid and must be included in any studies of reality, despite the discomfort of most scientists. As he describes himself: "As both an astrophysicist and a Christian I have no problem with evolution, a 15 billion year old Universe, a Big Bang and a Creator." (Website: meta-list.org, metaviews 006,2000).

What generates the NDEs reported by experiencers? Where do they come from? Even Blackmore agrees they exist. The issue is both a 'how' and a 'why' question, both scientific and theological. First, let me describe the process of dying from the medical standpoint. It is not an instantaneous event. It takes time. If the heart stops, in adults it takes an average of four minutes for the cortex (the outer, thinking layer) of the brain to die. Unconsciousness starts at 10-20 seconds, and the EEG goes flat, as the brain lacks oxygen and does not contain a reserve source. A person may keep up agonal breathing gasps somewhat longer, as breathing is controlled by a lower center that lives longer without circulating blood. If a massive stroke, for example, destroys most of the brain including the respiratory (breathing) center, it will take many minutes for the heart to finally slow and stop from lack of oxygen. You can see that there is time for OBEs and NDEs to occur. They have existed throughout history, when people spontaneously recovered from an injury or other life-threatening event, but now with medical resuscitation techniques, they are much more obvious. During resuscitation the brain is re-supplied with oxygenated blood and can start to function again. For this reason I am not so sure the brain and consciousness get separated 'transcendentally', as the Dutch physicians proposed.

Blackmore's theory about NDEs is called in her terms, "a dying brain hypothesis," basically a brain deranged by a lack of oxygen. She insists this places them in the medical scientific arena of 'hallucinations'. I agree with Michael Talbot's assessment that "although the orthodox [and skeptical] view is that they are just hallucinations, there is substantial evidence this is not the case." (*The Holographic Universe*). Blackmore agrees that these are not the usual hallucinations. First, they follow a consistent pattern in the majority of people who have them. Secondly they can occur in people who are not near death, in fact, people who are simply frightened by an event that threatens death. It is the unusually consistent pattern of NDEs that Blackmore tries to explain away throughout her book. Newberg and D'Aquili (*Why God Won't Go Away*) are quite clear in their opinion that these are not hallucinations. They equate NDE with a form of mystical experiences. "We do not believe that genuine mystical experiences can be explained away…as the product of other spontaneous hallucinatory states triggered by drugs, illness, physical exhaustion, emotional stress, or sensory deprivation. Hallucinations, no matter what their source, are simply not capable of providing the mind with an experience as convincing as that of mystical spirituality." The physicians in the Lancet report agree that induced experiences due to a sick brain (lacking oxygen, high in carbon dioxide) "are not identical to NDE. These recollections, however, consist of fragmented and random memories unlike the panoramic life-review that can occur in NDE."

To make this quite clear to the reader we need a medical discussion of hallucinations. By definition these are auditory, visual, olfactory and tactile, that is, hearing, seeing, smelling, or feeling, without true stimulation. They can occur when a patient is alert and fully oriented, or when ill, intoxicated by a drug, or near death from any one of a number of causes. They differ from dreams by being much more disjointed in the flow of events that are recounted afterward. Dreams tend to flow along much more logically, even if somewhat unreal, when compared to hallucinations. Hallucinations differ from delusions, which are ideas that do not fit reality: everyone in the world is plotting against me—the typical paranoid delusion of the schizophrenic patient; having the secret to control the world—a delusion of the manic patient. These are psychoses, or insanity in legal terms. Other terms to define are the companion mental states, confusion and delirium, which are as implied, both mental states that make no sense at all to the patient or the doctor, the latter a much deeper state of confusion. Hallucination seems real to the patient, just as NDEs are 'real' to the patient. The issue in studying NDEs, is whether the patient enters another level of reality and 'really' leaves his body. Dr. Moody is convinced after 20 years of research, "that NDEers have indeed ventured into another level of reality." He believes most other NDE researchers feel the same. "I have talked to almost every NDE researcher in the world about his or her work. I know that most of them believe in their hearts that NDEs are a glimpse of life after life. But as scientists and people of medicine, they still haven't come up with 'scientific proof' that a part of us goes on living after our physical being is dead. This lack of proof keeps them from going public with their true feelings." (Talbot, *The Holographic Universe*). Blackmore, in my opinion gives no answer to the 'consistency' argument that makes NDEs so special. Instead, she simply states: "indeed, the dying brain hypothesis accounts for it better." I thoroughly disagree, after reading her entire argument, but I have an even better reason for agreeing with Dr. Moody.

The definitions I have given of hallucination, confusion and delirium are neat textbook descriptions. In practice, in very sick patients they may meld into each other. During my 40 years in the arena of medicine, more than 30 years in private practice, I have seen, treated, and talked with many patients with hallucinations, confusion and delirium. The most well known example of these symptoms in patients is delirium tremens, described as follows: most readers have heard of the withdrawal symptoms of severe alcoholics called delirium tremens, so-named because they shake and are tremulous, but also because they have a mixture of confusion and hallucinations. The hallucinations usually involve hearing sounds or voices that do not really exist, feeling sensations that are not there, and seeing small animals, bugs and insects that even seem to be attacking the patient. What these alcoholics are hallucinating about seems real, in the present, and alive to them. The word 'alive' is the key to my reasoning. As stated, I have seen many hallucinating patients with all sorts of illnesses: drug effects and overdoses, liver and kidney failure, very high fevers, and so forth. What is striking, in relation to our current discussion, is the fact that these patients always imagine they are dealing with living beings, animals or people, and think the events are all in current reality. They do not leave their bodies or the earth.

By stark contrast the NDE folks, when they have their experiences, always, consistently, experience dead people, talk with the dead, be they ordinary people or religious figures. They never 'see' live people, unless they are experiencing an OBE in this reality we all inhabit. They may have a very accurate panoramic life-review. Many feel an overwhelming sense of peace and love. And they may, while exiting reality, have a sense of leaving the earth and joining in 'oneness' with the knowledge or consciousness of the universe. I didn't recognize this marked difference in my patients until I heard the story of the man who, just before he died, saw dead people he knew floating by on boats. Then it became very clear to me there was a distinct and highly significant difference between the NDE patients and all the others with hallucinations. Their NDEs are absolutely unique and extremely consistent from patient to patient, with the narrative flowing along very smoothly, in comparison to the usual form of hallucinations, which are extremely variable in content, and lack a consistent sense of narrative flow. Hallucinations are quite jumbled.

And this is why I agree so strongly with Dr. Moody, Newberg and D'Aquili, the Dutch physicians of the Lancet article and many of the other research scientists. There is no good neuro-physiologic reason why a sick brain should differentiate, so consistently, the experiences of those patients who have a close brush with death and a resultant NDE, from the standard hallucinations of ill people. As mentioned in Chapter 5, there is a center in the temporal lobe of the brain that produces religious experiences, the so-called 'God Module'. Newberg and D'Aquili describe many areas of the brain involved in mystical experiences during meditation, but their work does not provide a proof of a mechanism for the production of spontaneous NDEs and OBEs. Is there another special center for OBE and NDE, not yet discovered, but activated at certain times, or do these experiences originate in the God Module center of the temporal lobe? Having such a center makes better sense

167

than assuming, as Blackmore does, that a sick brain can so consistently produce the same event in so many patients with so many causes of being ill. If the God Module were found to produce NDEs, then the question becomes, why would evolution and natural selection have developed a center for religious feelings, or a center that appears to introduce an afterlife? Such centers are not necessary for survival. Yet humans have a God Module and many experience NDEs. We appear to have been given a special gift.

There is one other discovery the Dutch physicians describe in their Lancet article that strongly suggests NDEs are a special gift. Based on the interviews with patients, the NDEs described were scored as to 'depth' (how complex and complete they were): from no memory of one, 82 percent, deep, five percent, and very deep, two percent. The researchers found that the depth of the experiences correlated with mortality! Mortality while in the hospital or shortly afterward (30 days after CPR) occurred in 21 percent of all NDE experiencers, compared to nine percent in patients who had no NDE. And this was even more marked in patients with a very deep NDE, 43 percent versus the nine percent with no NDE. Does this infer that the brain 'knows' death is imminent? There is something very special, very unique in all of this.

All the research on this issue confirms the consistency of these experiences and dealing with the dead is part of that consistency. Blackmore's concluding refutations of the 'consistency argument' for NDEs do not include a discussion of 'why only dead people' in her presentation, although she readily admits, earlier in her book, the consistency involves the dead. She ignores this extremely important portion of the NDEs, because there is no answer for it, unless one or both of the two following propositions are true: 1) The newly-discovered religious area of the temporal lobe or a possible, but as yet undiscovered NDE area in the temporal lobe, were placed there by intelligent design to give us the religiosity we have and to show us the promise of the future or 2) we actually have the ability to visit our afterlife. This is my reasoning for believing Dr. Moody is much more likely to be correct than Susan Blackmore. My reasoning was developed before reading Blackmore's book, and it has been reinforced by the lengthy refutations in both Sabom's and Ring's recent books, published in 1998 and 1999 respectively. Both authors quote other clinical studies mimicking near-to-death states in volunteers which do not support Blackmore's contentions, and they also reference other authorities who have reviewed the issue and disagree with Blackmore. The physicians of the *Lancet* article discuss the possibility of 'transcendence." Newberg and D'Aquili conclude their book by suggesting that if the meditative "states that the brain makes possible are, in fact, glimpses of an actual higher reality, then religions are a reflection not only of neurological unity, but of a deeper absolute reality...There is nothing that we have found in science or reason to refute the concept of a higher mystical reality."

Michael Persinger, a professor of neuroscience at Laurentian University in Sudbury, Ontario, disagrees with Newberg. He has been conducting experiments "that fit a set of magnets to a helmet-like device, [creating] a weak electromagnetic signal around the skulls of volunteers. Four in five people report a 'mystical experience, the feeling there is a sentient being or entity standing behind or near' them. Some weep, some feel God has touched them, others become frightened and talk of demons and evil spirits. Persinger [feels] his research showed that 'religion is a property of the brain, only the brain and has little to do with what's out there'." ("Tracing the Synapses of Our Spirituality," Shankar Vedantam, *Wash. Post*, 6/17/01). Persinger in another interview offered the opinion "that there is no deity." And he added: "If you look at the spontaneous cases of people who have God experiences and conversions, their health improves." ("Spirituality and the Brain", ABCNEWS.com, 1/14/02). Persinger is stirring up an existing process in the brain, and I would persist in asking, why is such a mechanism in the brain in the first place? As he notes humans benefit from religious spirituality. I do not believe the presence of the mechanism is an accident of evolution.

Blackmore also has strong objections to the concept that somehow people leave their body. "Most 'something leaves' theories imply that whatever leaves should be detectable." She then describes a variety of experiments since the 1880s, which included such approaches as measuring the weight of the body before and after death. "Nothing can be reliably detected leaving the body during OBEs. Of course, the spirit or soul might be essentially undetectable but this further weakens the theory and makes it difficult to know what value it has. If whatever leaves is undetectable it follows that it cannot interact with the world." This is an interesting point, but indicates her lack of knowledge of the experiments in quantum particle mechanics conducted by Alain Aspect at the University of Paris-South. His studies, published in 1982 and fully accepted by the scientific world, clearly demonstrated that an individual quantum particle could be in two places at the same time. Amazingly each individual version of the particle 'knows' what the other version is doing, and this information is exchanged at faster than the speed of light!! This is known as "non-locality" and it represents conditions at the quantum level of reality that underlies the form of reality we experience. Non-locality has been "assumed to be a fundamental property of the entire universe." (*The Conscious Universe*, Kaftos & Nadeau, 1990). Aspect did his studies within the 50-foot space of his laboratory. Since then his findings have been dramatically confirmed in new studies over a seven-mile distance by Nicolus Gisin at the University of Geneva, (*The Non-Local Universe*, Nadeau and Kafatos, 1999) and an even larger distance of 30 kilometers (almost 19 miles) in a 1997 experiment (*When Science Meets Religion*, Ian Barbour). I certainly don't know if anything leaves our body, but these observations make it entirely possible that the energy quanta of our minds can be in two places at the same time! That is, simultaneously, in the body and out of it (See further comments about this subject in Chapter 7).

Blackmore also appears to be completely unaware of the theoretical mathematical research in particle physics and the energy makeup of our universe. In quantum cosmology, using what is called superstring theory, the mathematicians predict a ten- or eleven-dimensional construction of space, not the four dimensions used by Einstein. The theory is able to unite all the known forces, and, makes everything a construct and a portion of the space of the universe (*The Whole Shebang*, Timothy Ferris; *The Universe, the Eleventh Dimension, and Everything*, Richard Morris, 1999; and *The Elegant Universe*, Brian Greene, 2000). These extra six or seven dimensions, of which we are not aware in our three-dimensional state, are infinitesimally small, and are forms of energy, as is everything in the universe of which we are aware. It is fascinating to me that Atwater (*Beyond the Light*, pg. 96) describes an NDE of Nancy Clark, which includes the following observation: "I looked around and was awestruck at the multidimensional cosmos before me. I was aware of at least ten dimensions as opposed to our three-dimensional world." The mathematicians' intuitive calculations, although not yet scientifically proven, may have been already been 'seen' by Clark.

My answers to Blackmore's objection that the soul is not observed to leave the body are: 1) I have not seen any studies at the quantum level on the issue. How would scientists measuring quanta leaving our bodies identify them as part of our soul? Our soul may exist only at the quantum level of energy; and 2) it is possible the soul may enter one or several of the other predicted dimensions, and in fact, the afterlife may also be in one or more of those extra dimensions. The soul, therefore, may be undetectable in current science, but so are those extra dimensions; yet they are a part of our reality, can relate to it, and interact with it, according to the theoretical mathematics.

I have already shown that theoretical mathematical intuitions are eventually proven by science. Please give this proposition of mine some very careful thought. My guess is our life-after-life is not somewhere else. It is probably right here with us. Generally, in our three-dimensional form, we are not aware of it, but my theory suggests it is not difficult to cross over and come back at the quantum level, since quantum particles can be in two places at the same time.

In direct support of my theory is the work of the Monroe Institute in Faber, Virginia. Mr. Monroe has three patents on processes that use audio signals to help people reach altered states of consciousness, leading to OBEs. The technique trains people to alter their brain-wave frequencies to achieve OBEs under their own control. The head of a Zen Buddhist temple in Vancouver, Canada, is of the opinion that students at the institute can attain in a week what took him years of learning to meditate. (*Wall Street Journal*, 9/20/94). In the one-week course reported by the WSJ, 40 percent achieved OBEs. This is another refutation of Blackmore's position. In none of these OBErs was there a dying brain.

These extra dimensions may provide explanations for other psychic phenomena we all puzzle about. Can psychics reach the dead? I'm not sure of that at all, but there are convincing stories. The Monroe Institute provides the following tale reported by the Wall Street Journal: Katie McKeown, co-author of *Beyond IBM*, visited the institute after Louis Mobley, her collaborator on the book, unexpectedly died. A Mr. James R. Hoover, a DuPont manager—and skeptic—attended the same week as Ms. McKeown, and while in an altered state of consciousness spoke with Mobley. "He related the conversation to Ms. McKeown, who said that certain remarks could only have come from Mr. Mobley. That 'scared the daylights out of me', says Mr. Hoover. 'I still get chills thinking about it'." (*WSJ*). Another example: all of us have heard of police mysteries solved by the use of psychics. Therefore, although I have been somewhat skeptical, I am not about to deny psychic power as possibly being real. In fact scientific proof is under development. Dr. Haisch knows of U.S. government sponsored studies into psychic activity covering a 24-year period. Some of this has been declassified, after a review of these studies for the C.I.A., and then analyzed by Professor Jessica Utts, a highly qualified statistician who teaches at the University of California, Davis. "Using standards applied to any other area of science, it is concluded that psychic function has been well established.... It is recommended that future experiments focus on understanding how this phenomenon works, and on how to make it as useful as possible." (Website: meta-list.org, metaviews 006, 2000). It looks as if my skepticism should begin to yield to scientific proof, if my reliance upon the scientific method is to remain consistent. Dr. Haisch makes the point: "Rejection of evidence that cannot yet be measured with instruments in a laboratory is contrary to the scientific spirit of inquiry."

At the University of Arizona, professor of Neurology and Psychiatry Gary Schwartz has "explore[d] the question of whether consciousness survives death with the help of mediums (people who demonstrate unusual accuracy in describing intimate attributes of the dead to those who knew them well)." He does this by comparing "the brain waves and the heart rates of both the medium and the person for whom he or she is trying to contact the dead." He says his research "is actually a window or a doorway to a much larger spiritual reality which integrates ancient wisdom with contemporary science." His work has "require[ed] him to ask himself hard questions about science, faith and reason." "Survival of consciousness tells us that consciousness does not require a brain, that our memories, our intentions, our intelligence, our dreams, all of that can exist outside the physical body. That's the same idea that we have about God—that something that is 'invisible', that is 'bigger than all of us', which we cannot see, can have intellect, creativity, intention, memory and can influence the universe." He is an example of another respected scientist working on the edge of our reality (ABCNEWS.com, 1/14/02).

Another scientist who is actively doing research in energy fields in the universe and their possible relationship to metaphysics is Dr. Hal Puthoff, Director of the Institute for Advanced Studies in Austin, Texas. "Throughout mankind's cultural history there has existed the metaphysical concept that man and cosmos are interconnected by a ubiquitous, all-pervasive sea of energy that undergirds, and is manifest in all phenomena." He describes his work in Quantum Vacuum Energy and believes that his research will find "that all of us are immersed, both as living and physical beings, in an overall interpenetrating and interdependent field in ecologic balance with the cosmos as a whole, and that even the boundary lines between physical and 'metaphysical' would dissolve into a unitary viewpoint of the universe as a fluid, changing, energetic/information cosmological unity." (Website: META-LIST.org, METAVIEWS 084, 2000). Particle physics may one day prove that psychic phenomena are very real. This is not pie-in-the-sky material. This is the research of a noted scientist.

On the other hand, the ten-eleven-dimension theory may give an explanation for 'consciousness' and altered consciousness. In the last chapter, it was concluded that our very special mind and our consciousness, arose out of the whole of the brain, which is matter, but our *mind* is not matter. Perhaps our consciousness is in another interactive dimension, another plane of our reality. Kafatos and Nadeau, mentioned in Chapter 1, two professors at George Mason University, in their book, *The Conscious Universe*, have presented the philosophic idea that the universe itself is conscious and that humans can join that consciousness. Their argument is based on the non-locality findings in quantum research, previously described in this chapter. They state if the assumption is made that the whole is more than the parts, the "new relationship 'implies' without being able to 'prove,' that human consciousness participates in the life of the cosmos in ways that classical physics completely disallowed." They emphasize a science "not as a meaningless number crunching and equation solving activity." They wish it to "continuously emphasize the essential wonder and beauty of itself and the universe it describes…[As science recognizes the whole is more than the sum of the parts], science in no way argues against the existence of God, or Being, and profoundly augments the sense of the cosmos as a single significant whole." Recognizing that science is silent theologically, they offer the opinion that "it is time, we suggest, for the religious imagination and the religious experience to engage the complementary truths of science in filling that silence with meaning." (*The Conscious Universe*, 1990).

The Kabbalah, based on meditation and mysticism, teaches that there is a level in reality of collective species' consciousness, both animal and human, and, as I will show, this assertion is supported by science. For this reason "they teach that when you pray, you should not pray for yourself alone. You should pray with the collective needs in mind. When you make it happen, the life of hundreds of others is illuminated as well. [This] is how knowledge is transmitted. Once one person brings it into the world it is available to everybody." *(Endless Light)*. To make the point Rabbi Aaron tells the story of "The Hundredth Monkey." Biologist Lyall Watson in his book, *Lifetide* (1980, pg. 147), reported this research study: Researchers fed monkeys sweet potatoes by dumping them on a beach on a small island off Japan. The monkeys had never seen sweet potatoes before. They liked the sweet potatoes, but had no idea how to get rid of the gritty sand sticking to the potatoes. Finally one monkey dipped a potato in the ocean, and liked the sweet, salty flavor. She taught the trick to a few others and the idea gradually spread. Then the idea seemed to reach "critical mass", and suddenly all the monkeys on the island were using the washing technique. While the idea was spreading on the first island, researchers were beginning to deliver sweet potatoes to the beaches of other nearby islands and one colony of monkeys on the mainland. When the monkeys on the first island suddenly adopted the washing technique, "the troops of monkeys on the other islands and the mainland also suddenly and spontaneously began practicing the washing technique" much faster than the time it took on the first island (Also described by Michael Talbot, *Beyond the Quantum*, 1986). Watson did not know the exact number of monkeys it took to reach a threshold within general monkey consciousness, but called it "The Hundredth Monkey" phenomenon.

Research work on group-learning in rats was conducted by Harvard psychologist William McDougall, starting in the 1920's. He used a water maze, in which the rats could get out by swimming down a darkened tunnel rather than down a lighted route, which had an electric shock in it. By the twenty-second generation, the rats were learning the maze ten times faster. To discover whether this learning was passed on in the genes, he then tried unrelated rats, who also could negotiate the maze ten times faster. "The improvement seemed to manifest in the rat species en masse, disproving that the increase was being passed on genetically." (Talbot). Other researchers tried to disprove these findings, but to their surprise found their rats initially learned a similar maze about as fast as McDougall's twenty-second generation rats. More amazing, while McDougall did his work at Harvard, the other research was done in Scotland and Australia with "completely separate genetic lines, again demonstrating that the skill could not have been passed on genetically."(Talbot). These studies were reported in the British *Journal of Psychology*, a prestigious journal, in 1927, 1930, and 1938.

Findings of this type have been ignored by most scientists until Rupert Sheldrake began to study them. He is a professor of biochemistry at the University of London. He describes the habits of blue tits, a European bird, which learned in the 1920s in Great Britain to tear the tops off delivered milk bottles to drink the cream. The habit started in the southern part of England. By the mid-1930s it had spread all over Britain, at rates of discovery which were documented to accelerate faster than the initial spread and much faster and further than the blue tits could have flown. "Sir Alistair Hardy, a professor of zoology at Oxford, came to the conclusion that something like telepathy might be involved." (Rupert Sheldrake in *A Glorious Accident*, Wim Kayzer, 1997). Once the British blue tits started this habit then ones in

Holland, Sweden, Denmark and other countries began to do it. When the Germans invaded Holland in 1940, milk deliveries stopped, and started up after the war in 1945-1946. Since blue tits live only three years, none were alive that could remember the cream habit, yet in two to three years after milk deliveries began again, they were stealing cream again all over Holland. "The habit spread much more quickly the second time around than it did the first time." (Sheldrake).

Sheldrake reviewed the blue tit, the rat and the monkey studies in forming his theories, and has conducted his own experiments with humans, in an attempt to prove that a universal human consciousness might exist. A London *Evening Standard* crossword puzzle was given to Nottingham University students the night before it was published in London. They were given a fixed time to solve as many clues as possible, and then scored. Then a second set of students was tested with the puzzle later the next day after it had been published and worked by many people throughout London. The paper is not delivered to Nottingham, so the second group of students had not seen the puzzle. Their scores were 20 percent higher than the students tested the night before. There also was a control crossword puzzle given to the Nottingham students to provide a measure of individual variations in crossword-solving skills, and to further test the theory. The control puzzle was not published, and therefore was seen only by students. It was also offered the next day to the control students, and the student scores did not change, as there was no "universal consciousness" effect coming out of London, implied by the results of the first part of the study. Another study involved groups of adults he recruited. They were given three nursery rhymes in the Japanese language, one real rhyme, learned by Japanese children, and two invented by a Japanese poet. The adults "memorize[d] these rhymes by chanting them in the way children do. Later they were tested to see how much they could remember. They could recall the "genuine" nursery rhyme about twice as well as the others. This is the kind of effect one would expect" if there is a universal human consciousness (*A Glorious Accident*). Sheldrake's term for universal consciousness is "group mind."

Universal consciousness, human species consciousness has been studied at Princeton University. The title of the study is "Global Consciousness Project," and they have placed 40 random energy generators (REG) around the world with the random outputs reporting back to a centralized location to determine if disturbances in global human consciousness can alter the output of these machines, which are nicknamed "eggs". Recording started in August

1998. The dramatic events of September 11, 2001 occurred while 38 eggs were operating. The Project demonstrated marked changes with odds against chance of about 1,000 to one on the 11th. Recordings during organized silent prayer in America and Europe on September 14th showed significant changes, but less marked than on the 11th. The Project is very young, but similar changes have been seen during the funeral ceremonies of Princess Diana, around midnight on any New Year's Eve, the first hour of NATO bombing in Yugoslavia, and during some earthquakes (http://noosphere.princeton.edu/homepage.html).

Princeton is also the home for the PEAR project (Princeton Engineering Anomalies Research). In this study Dr. R. J. Jahn and others are using random energy generators and ask volunteers to try and influence the output from these machines, either under instruction as to how to try mentally change the outputs or by their own choice. After 12 years using over "100 individual human operators", they have shown absolute effects that are quite small, but statistically very significant, the odds for chance being about 10^{-13}. Overall studies have gone on for 18 years. These projects show that the human mind can extend out from the brain and influence the material world (*J. Scientific Exploration*, Vol. 11, No. 3, pp. 345-367, 1997).

The human mind can also project from the brain and affect dreaming. In the 1960's the Maimonides Dream Research Laboratory demonstrated just that. A psychologist spent the night in a room near the sleeping subject and concentrated on a picture. A group of independent judges compared the dream reports with an assortment of pictures, searching for a match. Elements of the paintings were observed to show up in sleepers' dreams about two-thirds of the time (*Healing Dreams: Exploring the Dreams That Can Transform Your Life*, Marc Ian Barasch, 2000; from an excerpt in *Science & Spirit*, vol. 13 issue 2, March April 2002.). Dreams may also carry urgent real messages: Barasch recounted the experience in 1943 of Dutch psychiatrist Joost Meerloo, who had "a vivid dream in which he had heard his brothers calling for help." He was on a troopship headed for Europe. His brothers were neurologically disabled and institutionalized in the Netherlands. Meerloo was so convinced they had fallen into Nazi hands, he got out of bed and wrote a dated note on the dream. "Two years later, in liberated Holland, he located records confirming that on the date of his dream, Nazi soldiers" had seized his brothers and sent them to be gassed (*Healing Dreams*). This is another piece of evidence that conscious thoughts can be transmitted over long distances, and can be picked up like a radio or

TV antenna, if the brain and/or mind are properly tuned in. Meerloo suggests that intimate relatives are more likely to receive these messages, but psychic communication between unrelated people also seems to occur, and re-enforces my opinion that there is a human species consciousness.

There is one other set of experiments that suggests a global human consciousness. I am referring to studies in intercessory prayer to influence medical outcomes. Unknown to the patients, groups pray for them and they are compared to a group of patients who did not receive such prayer, although their friends and family might have been praying for them, which also may have occurred in the first group. At the University of Maryland a review of 23 such studies showed that more than half "had a positive effect on patients' health." Prayer doesn't always work, but finding so many positive results are impressive. In December 2001 physicians at Columbia University reported their study of patients at a fertility clinic, prayed for by Christian denominations in the U.S., Canada and Australia. "The Columbia researchers expressed surprise at the magnitude of the difference [they found], saying they did not expect to find any benefit to prayer at all." Fifty percent of the prayed-for patients became pregnant, versus 26 percent of the others, with a total of 169 patients in the study (*New York Times* on the web, "Prayer Works, Jim Holt," 12/9/01). This is a highly significant finding. I do not know if God interceded or if this is a further effect of global human consciousness. Perhaps the patients sense that they are being prayed for, and this improves their outlook and feelings of optimism, which do influence medical outcomes (*Science & Spirit* Vol. 13; issue 1, Jan.-Feb. 2002, pp. 46-47).

Returning to Sheldrake to look at one other possible 'strange' phenomenon, he also champions the presence of "morphogenetic fields." By this he means a field similar to the one we can demonstrate around a magnet, but in this case it is applied to each specific species of animal. "Morphogenesis" is a biologic term referring to the three-dimensional formation of an animal from the fertilized cell. I have discussed in Chapter 4 the problem of understanding how DNA guides three-dimensional organization. It is his theory that a special "M-field" guides this construction and also the group mind in each species.

Sheldrake's work and his theories are very suggestive to me that there are other planes of reality in our universe. My theory is they reside in the proposed infinitesimally small 'extra dimensions' predicted by the theoretical mathematicians. In our three-dimensional state we are generally not aware of these planes, but they provide a locale for universal consciousness, OBEs and NDEs, allowing some of us to 'cross over' and then come back again. My philosophy professor in college made one statement during his course that has stuck with me and influenced my thinking all of my life. He observed that the universe is made up entirely of energy. He considered matter as energy on the 'outside', and our mind, our intellect, our consciousness as energy on the 'inside'. Our mind and consciousness are something more than the sum-of-the-whole of the matter and the electric currents of our brain. Perhaps they are contained in bundles of quantum energy, which can 'cross over'. Presently I cannot prove my theory, but it is as logical an explanation of all these phenomena as anything else I have heard of. And furthermore, if these other levels of consciousness exist, and there is certainly evidence presented here to support that assertion, then the gift of consciousness we have received through evolution assumes an even greater role than suggested in the last chapter. It raises the possibility that we will evolve to use an even larger portion of the estimated capacity of our brain, that use now thought to be about 15 percent of total capacity. We may eventually be able to enter the realms of OBEs and NDEs at will. Speculative, I admit, but possible.

Brother Wayne Robert Teasdale, mentioned in Chapter 5, feels we can enter other levels of consciousness now. He champions the use of mysticism in reaching these other levels, and the other realms of reality which surround us. "Everyone is a mystic by virtue of their existence, but not everyone knows it, or accepts it. Mysticism is the awakening to the interdependence of everything, and their unity in the fontal Source, the Divine. It is the endless horizon of essential, inward gazing connectivity. Mysticism as the direct, or unmediated experience of Ultimate Reality in Consciousness, is the goal of all knowing...Mystics and sages throughout time have taught us that an Ultimate Reality exists, more than exists, is all that there is, surrounding us on all sides. Now we can discern that insight in the utter truth and reality of consciousness itself, and its nature as caring, love, compassion, [and] concern. But the mystic sage doesn't ask us to believe this, rather we are exhorted to find out for ourselves through experience". (www.META-LIST.org, METAVIEWS 062, 08/10/00). Teasdale's definition of consciousness as being naturally caring, love, compassion and concern reinforces my belief that OBEs and NDEs are mystical experiences, not the result of a dying brain, and that these other levels of reality surround us and are accessible through conscious meditation. It is his point that our consciousness provides more than most of us realize.

Chapter 7: Belief in God Through Rational Philosophy

I am not a philosopher by training. I had one course in the subject in my pre-med years. Yet I wish to present logical philosophical arguments for a belief in the existence of God from the evidence presented in the previous chapters. To do that I am going to follow the philosophic reasoning presented by Mortimer J. Adler in his book, *How to Think About God, A Guide for the 20th Century Pagan*, published in 1980. Adler has been one of the leading philosophers of this country in the 20th Century, and his approach in this book is highly considered as an excellent exposition of how to approach thinking about God. I have no intent to plagiarize his work, but to use it for guidance. Adler was born in 1902 in New York City and was raised as a Reform Jew. He explains in his prologue that he left that faith after his confirmation at age 16, and after he married, with his wife and children attended an Episcopal church. He considered joining the Catholic Church, and then the Episcopal Church, but did neither. Although not strongly attracted to organized religion, as a renowned educator, in the 1930's and 40's he was an outspoken advocate of teaching absolute moral standards in the American classrooms, campaigning against the teaching of moral relativism, which began to appear in that period of time (Levy, letter to the editor, *Wall Street Journal*, 11/15/99). It was not until 1980 that he felt he could present a book, which would illustrate "a reasonableness of the belief that God exists." My background has some similarities to Adler. As I explained in the Introduction, I was raised as a Reform Jew, never left that faith, but wandered around for years as an agnostic, before recognizing the scientific findings and my own experiences in the practice of medicine that would lead me to God. I did not follow Adler's reasoning in my own decision, but having found his method, I will use it, give a synopsis of it for the reader, and follow his logic in presenting my arguments, which are based on the preceding material in this book. In offering a synopsis of Adler's presentation, the background of reasoning for each of his assertions may not be complete enough to convince the reader of this book. In that case I suggest obtaining a copy of his book, which is out of print, either from the library or a used book dealer.

Adler first defines terms, noting that "sacred theology" is philosophic thought based on Sacred Scriptures, in which in discussing reasons why God exists, the writers accepted from the outset the statements of those Scriptures as articles of faith, and in their writings assumed without question that He does exist. Adler's book was developed to convince "pagans" that a belief in God is possible. Late in his book he also notes "that there is a world of difference between *believing that God exists* and *believing in God*— confiding in him and having hope in him (sic)." Since his book was aimed at pagans, those in Western civilization who do not believe in the God of Judaism, Christianity or Islam, Adler employs what he terms "philosophical theology", or rational philosophic thought, based on reason, not faith, and also based upon our knowledge of ourselves and of the universe to reach his conclusion, "beyond a reasonable doubt that God exists." The term usually used is "natural theology", but he feels underlying religious beliefs may taint the works in natural theology. Since he attempted a totally rational approach to his task, and I am trying to do the same, I have named this chapter as using rational philosophy. In setting his rules for his argument, he defines God as a theoretical construct: "We cannot think of God as a physical object. Consequently, we must think of God not only as inherently imperceptible, but also as inherently undetectable. God cannot be thought of as physical, material, or corporeal. God's existence is both like and unlike that of other objects of thought the real existence of which we know either by direct perceptual acquaintance or by inference from empirical evidence. The real existence of God, being immaterial and incorporeal, must be imperceptible. It must also be unascertainable by scientific inference from empirical evidence, that is, evidence that we have through sense perception." Adler adds the following considerations: "God, not being corporeal or physical, cannot be a part of the cosmos. [Further], we must think of God as having an independent, unconditioned and uncaused existence. That which is independent, unconditioned and uncaused in its existence has its existence in, through, and from itself." God exists in and of Himself, and is therefore eternal, "everlasting in duration and non-temporal and immutable." In this way "God is in no way affected or altered by the existence or non-existence of the cosmos as a whole, totally outside of which God has independent existence." Since the cosmos (universe) has a finite existence, and God has, by definition has infinite existence, the universe is not God.

Adler preferred to make his job more exacting philosophically, by assuming in the beginning of his discussion that the universe (he always calls it the cosmos) always existed and always will. He purposely chose to ignore that it had an absolute finite beginning, which would require a causative agent, and "would be tantamount to affirming the existence of God." Instead he presented a reasoned argument that God is "necessary to explain why [the universe] continues to exist." His reasoning mirrors that of John Leslie mentioned in Chapter 2, that either God exists to create this universe or there exist vastly many, very varied universes. "That reason is to be found in the fact that the cosmos which now exists is only one of many possible universes that might have existed in the infinite past, and that might still exist in the infinite future. Whatever might have been otherwise in shape or structure is something that also might not exist at all." Our universe is by this definition a "merely possible universe." It is one of many possible universes that could have formed and then disappeared. But our universe, as a merely possible universe, "cannot be an uncaused cosmos." To paraphrase his reasoning, as a merely possible universe, it could be reduced to nothingness unless it was carefully designed to maintain its existence. Therefore, "a merely possible cosmos cannot be an uncaused cosmos." If it is made from nothingness, it requires a supernatural cause, to prevent it from returning to nothingness. "The cosmologic argument has now brought us to the conclusion that God exists not as the creative, but as the preservative cause of the continuing existence of a possible cosmos." Once he was satisfied with this proof of preservation, he then opened the discussion to a finite beginning for the universe, and presented God as the "necessary" Creator, which could provide a second proof.

Adler also uses Sir William of Occam's razor as I do: "[The razor] deletes from reality those hypothetical entities which we are not justified in positing." Or as I have stated it, don't add anything to your reasoning which is not necessary to reach a conclusion that appears to cover the known facts. Adler adds Occam's rule: "We are justified in asserting the real existence of unobserved or unobservable entities if—and *only* if—their real existence is indispensable for the explanation of observed phenomena." This rule allows his insistence that God exists, as an unobserved or unobservable entity, as well as validating the theorizing of mathematicians who predict the existence of particles or the presence of black holes, when those objects have never been directly observed.

It is now time to compare the material I have presented with the logical philosophic conclusions of Mortimer Adler. How well do the scientific findings and discoveries support the philosophy that a belief in the existence of God is reasonable?

Argument from first cause. 'First cause' is defined philosophically as the initial cause from which all else flowed; a first cause always had to exist, and be itself uncaused. Logically, if a first cause was caused, then it could not be the first cause. First cause can be applied to a single series of events or to all events taken together. What caused our universe to exist? What is the very first reason for it to exist? What is the first cause? We are here to observe our own universe and are compelled to try and answer those questions. We have seen that the existence of our universe revolves around two possibilities. Either this special universe was created by God, or there exist, or have existed, or will exist a tremendous number of universes, all differing from each other and from this universe, a special case permitting life, which allows us to be here. These proposed multiple universes are considered to be constantly forming, therefore, removing the need for a special creator of our 'special' universe, which eventually will appear with the luck of the draw. There are two objections to this: first, it is totally contrary to Occam's Razor. We have no way of observing these other universes, or proving their existence, and they are not necessary to provide for this universe that we know exists. We are not obligated to accept as possible everything our intellect can dream up. We can think of mermaids and unicorns, but they must remain imaginary. Secondly, it creates an imaginary game of chance for our consideration, which many scientists seem to prefer, setting us, the observers, up as "the winners in a vast and meaningless cosmic lottery. Invoking an infinity of unseen universes just to explain features of the universe we do see seems like overkill. Lottery theorists retort that unseen universes are better than an unseen God, but actually both explanations are equivalent in this regard. What we are trying to explain is how one particular, rather special universe is picked out from an infinity of also-ran contenders. The lottery theory amounts to little more than theism dressed up in science's clothing." (Paul Davies, *Forbes ASAP*, October 4, 1999).

If this is the only universe, it started just prior to the Big Bang. Alan Guth, quoted in Chapter 2 from his book written in 1997, tells us that the Big Bang Theory is a theory of what happened after the Bang, not of the Bang itself. The Bang is not described by the theory and its cause is unknown to science. The Bang occurred *outside* of time, *before* time! In 2002 Guth, Valenkin and

Borde produced mathematical proof that space and time appeared right *after* the Bang, and that there is a "boundary" or a true beginning to the universe, with the implication that there is nothing beforehand, nothing which can be investigated or found. There is no before *before* the Big Bang (Chapter 2, pg. 63). In his book he states that we appear to have gotten something for nothing. Although the universe represents tremendous energy, "the immense energy that we observe in the form of matter can be cancelled by a negative contribution of equal magnitude, coming from the gravitational field." It all adds up to zero, the "ultimate free lunch" mentioned in Chapter 2. I wonder if Guth still predicts that science will find a theory to explain this. Stephen Hawking has tried to explain the origin of the Big Bang with equations that involve "imaginary time", but that approach is as fanciful as anything else that has been imagined to get around the problem of something for nothing (Behe, *Darwin's Black Box*). William Lane Craig's article in *Modern Cosmology and Philosophy*, edited by John Leslie, 1998, also takes issue with Hawking: "The impression that Hawking's model is thoroughly non-realistic is heightened by his use of imaginary time in his final model of space-time. His model can hardly be said to have eliminated the place of a Creator."

There was another proposed theory, which appears to avoid the need for a creator: Big Bang, with expansion, and then contraction to a Big Crunch, only to be followed by another Big Bang. Each cycle is estimated to take about 200 billion years. There are two problems with this suggestion. First, as discussed in Chapter 2, in 1998 a mysterious force was discovered making the universe expand faster (Goldsmith, *The Runaway Universe*). Until 1999 science did not find enough matter to provide enough gravity to turn the current expansion process around. A series of experimental results reported from 1999 to 2003 by astronomers, studying the cosmic microwave background (CMB), appear to provide confirmation that the space within the universe is "flat", implying it will continue to expand, never contracting. The studies indicate that the "expansion is under the influence of a strange form of 'dark' energy that fills empty space and apparently acts against gravity." There is also 'dark matter'. This strange matter appears to supply enough missing matter to slow expansion, but not enough matter to then cause a contraction, because of the effects of dark energy causing expansion. One of the scientists, Dr. Mark Devlin of the University of Pennsylvania, commented: "These are completely different experiments with completely different calibrations [styles of measurement] and they fall right on top of each other." (James Glanz, "Shedding light on universe," *N.Y. Times*, 11/26/ 99). Renewed confirmation of these findings was reported in *Nature*, 27, April 2000, pages 955-959 by Bernardis and co-authors. Of extreme importance to us, it appears that life can evolve only in "flat" universes, the only kind that allows the appearance of carbon-based life (W. Wayt Gibbs, *Scientific American*, August 1998; also, Magueijo). Another example of a 'designer universe fine-tuned for life'.

In May 2002 yet another attempt appeared for a theory of a cyclical universe, using superstring/membrane theory. It was based on unproven, highly theoretical mathematics, and it has not yet been thoroughly investigated by the world's leading cosmologists to know if it possibly has any validity. It proposes cycles of trillions of years (See Chapter 2, pg. 64, Steinhardt and Turok). The second objection to these theories of Big Bang cycles, proposed to avoid the need for a creator, is a question that cannot be answered by science: what created the first Big Bang? It falls back to the unanswerable philosophic question: "why is there anything?", raised by Gottfried Wilhelm Leibniz (1646-1716).

As Paul Davies points out, in "the fifth century St. Augustine proclaimed that 'the world was made, not in time, but simultaneously with time.' In other words God is the creator not only of matter but of time as well." Jewish commentaries on Genesis from the same time period agree: prior to the existence of the universe, time did not exist (Schroeder, *Genesis and the Big Bang*) Biblical scholars predicted the Big Bang Theory 1500 years ago (Chapter 2). From this discussion I see no reason to disagree with any of the ancient biblical commentators. After all, current scientific theory confirms their opinions. Guth's scientific optimism aside, 'something' from absolutely nothing is patently impossible. His theories really involve a balance of negative (gravity) and positive (matter) energies. That may equal zero, but it does not represent 'nothing', which by definition must be absolute void, not the arithmetic result of a zero balance of forces. To be fair to Guth, he wrote his book using information available prior to its publication date in 1997, and he could not add to his negative and positive energies the energy of 'dark energy'. This was announced initially in 1998 with later further confirmation. It makes up roughly 70 percent of the universe and counteracts gravity, causing the continued expansion of the universe. This is an additional energy that results in a non-zero result to the sum of energies in our universe.

Guth's own statements actually refute his conclusions, from another standpoint, if he would only step back from his theoretical mathematical approach and apply some simple logic. "In our everyday experience we tend to equate empty space with 'nothingness.' Empty space has no mass, no color, no opacity, no texture, no hardness, no temperature—if that is not 'nothing', what is? However, from the point of view of general relativity, empty space is unambiguously *something* (sic). According to general relativity, space is not a passive background, but instead a flexible medium that can bend, twist, and flex." Guth calls space a 'false vacuum', in contrast to a true vacuum or an absolute void.

Our universe contains a space that is not an absolute void. It is actually a froth of quantum potentialities. Quantum particles pop in and out of existence all the time, so-called quantum fluctuations. When scientists make measurements, quantum potentialities pop into existence. Shimon Malin describes this in his book, *Nature Loves to Hide*, (2001). "In quantum physics, *measurements are creative* (sic): They literally create the electron [which they are measuring] as an actual thing, where, before the measurement, no thing existed." "An electron is moving toward a TV screen. Before impinging on the screen, the electron does not exist in space; it is merely a field of potentialities. At the time of impingement, however, it does actually exist; it is an elementary quantum event, an event in space and time." The quantum potentiality becoming an actuality is called 'a collapse of a quantum state.' "The collapse is a transition from potentiality to actuality. *Space and time refer to the ordering of things and events in the actual world* (sic). A potentiality, like a noumenon, is neither a thing nor an event; hence it does not exist in spacetime." A 'noumenon' is defined as "a ground of phenomena that according to Kant cannot be experienced, can be known to exist, but to which no properties can be intelligibly ascribed." (*Webster's New Collegiate Dictionary*).

By now you should be quite confused. Let's make it simple. Potential quantum forces exist, just not in the plane of reality (spacetime) that we experience in day-to-day life. They are somewhere else where we cannot directly appreciate them. Malin is a Professor of Physics at Colgate University. I view him as being just as confused as Guth. If quantum particles pop in and out of our spacetime, they must pop in and out of something. And that something is not the conjured up sci-fi parallel universes that are discussed. Malin makes the point that "the only universe whose existence is verified is the one we find ourselves in. The existence of others cannot be proved or disproved." Wherever quantum potentialities 'pop' from, it is 'somewhere' within our universe. It is an absolute characteristic of the universe we have been given. They do not pop out of 'nowhere.' Perhaps they come and go from the six or seven 'rolled up' dimensions described by superstring and membrane theory. Therefore, the space in our universe is false vacuum, not a true vacuum or an absolute void.

The concept of 'absolute void' raises one final issue about the Big Bang and expansion (without contraction) of the universe. What does the universe expand into? The answer, to be consistent with Occam's razor, is 'nothing', an absolute void. This universe must be all there is, and by definition there can be nothing beyond it. We cannot scientifically test this answer, since we are bound within the confines of the universe. To conjure up 'something' out there beyond our universe violates logic. Stating that this universe possibly came from a quantum fluctuation or collapse, as Guth has proposed, uses the knowledge we have of our space, and presumes that our space always existed. We have no way of knowing if that it is true. We can look back to the Big Bang, but not behind it, or before it. We can only presume the universe came from nothing. If this universe came from nothing and is expanding into nothing, the most logical conclusion is that this universe was created by a Creator, God, and it is the only universe in existence. It is the only apparent answer to "why is there anything." The last 50 years of cosmologic research have provided increasing evidence that this conclusion is warranted. It is a clear demonstration that the advances in scientific knowledge continue to increasingly reinforce a belief in God, a primary contention of this book.

Argument from Design. There are two aspects of this argument. The first is that the universe certainly appears designed for us, and secondly, living things are so amazingly intricate, they certainly appear to be designed. Chapter 2 describes the design of our universe, and the arrangement of the protective factors of the earth, allowing us to live here. Although I mentioned only a few, there are at least 20 major parameters (physical properties) and almost 80 minor ones that have to be extremely finely tuned to give us this very friendly-to-life universe in which we live. And further there are a large group of factors, which protect the Earth in our life-friendly solar system in a very dangerous universe. Imagine a control panel with a bunch of knobs each carefully adjusted to an exact spot on each dial to create our safe cocoon. The theoretical mathematicians have tried a new control panel, twirling the knobs, changing those values and find in their equations imaginary universes that expand too fast or collapse too quickly after the Big Bang that starts a universe. Only the 'tuning' present in our universe allows it to spread out homogeneously, form galaxies permitting the existence of an earth like ours, and last long enough to permit the appearance of life. This 'fine-tuning' generally meets Adler's requirement for the belief in the existence of God who is "required" to maintain the universe. Granted he presupposed a steady state universe, but only to avoid the issue of creation and creator. These 'laws" that run the universe maintain it. And as just discussed, this is a "flat" universe, which will slowly expand, existing forever, gradually burn out and become totally cold a hundred billion years from now.

In Chapter 2 I discussed the proposal from science and philosophy that the reason we have such a fortunate universe is that it is *the* lucky one for us out of an enormous variety of universes. In regard to this multiple universe theory, if you do any further reading in the philosophy of science you will meet the "Anthropic Principle." The principle states in simple terms something that is very obvious: if the conditions in the universe and on earth weren't just right, we wouldn't and couldn't be here. We are here so, of course, the conditions were right. This is the "weak form" of the Principal. It further states that the fact we are here to observe the 'fine tuning' creates no special reason to say that God did it. There are some proponents of the Anthropic Principle who offer a "strong form" of interpretation, which seems to state that because of the design of the universe, even if we were not here now, we would arrive someday ("Life, the Cosmos, and Everything," Bernard Carr, *Physics World*, October 2001, Vol. 14, issue 10; also, *Universes*, John Leslie, pg. 129). I do not see that the principle demands our appearance, just because the conditions allow us to appear (Leslie agrees). These arguments are attempts to show that the entire process of our arrival is all natural, and God is not needed. The weak form is used to insist there must be infinitely multiple universes, and by lucky chance our universe popped up all arranged for our appearance. Andrei Linde is the leading cosmologist favoring this interpretation ("Inflation, Quantum Cosmology and the Anthropic Principle," a chapter by Linde to appear in *Science and Ultimate Reality: From Quantum to Cosmos*, Cambridge University Press (2003); www.arXiv:hep-th/0211048 v2, 8 Nov. 2002). The Anthropic Principle is simply circular reasoning, not creating any new logical thought. Both Roger Penrose and Alan Guth feel that the Anthropic Principle is proposed only when cosmologists don't have a "good theory" or a "better explanation for something," (*Origins. The Lives and Worlds of Modern Cosmologists*, Alan Lightman and Roberta Brawer, 1990).

Under Darwin's theory everything happens by chance mutations, which are then tested by Natural Selection: if that is the case, why did we turn up, more specialized than required for survival by the theory? The logical choices to explain the fine-tuning under this approach are: 1) one very special universe created by God; 2) multiple universes spontaneously appeared, with one very lucky one for us, tuned just so, God not required. This position can be extended to an untenable suggestion, remembering Occam's razor: if it is insisted God is required, why would He bother to make many universes with just one designed for us; and finally 3) The universe we observe may really be different from that which we think we are observing. This latter idea comes from the study of quantum mechanics, in which the scientists find that everything at the quantum level is an average of probability; a quantum bundle of energy may be a wave or a particle, depending upon how it is measured. Therefore the observer actually influences the results of his observations! Further a quantum particle (a photon of light) has been shown to be in two places at once, and "knows" what its other "self" is doing at all times, and this information is transmitted at faster than the speed of light (The Aspect and Gisin experiments described in *The Conscious Universe* and in *The Non-Local Universe*, Kakatos and Nadeau; also discussed in Chapter 6). The speed of light is predicted by the Theory of Relativity to be the limit of speed for matter through space, but apparently this does not apply to quanta. What I have described is surprisingly absolutely true, even though it forced a disbelieving Einstein to offer the opinion early in the research, "God does not play dice with the universe." Later he did accept the findings.

The scientists who propose the Anthropic Principle avoid God by choosing interpretation choices Two and/or Three. My objection to the second interpretation of the Anthropic Principle is that it violates Occam's razor, by involving entities that are both unknown and imaginary and also not necessary to explain the principle. My objection to the third interpretation is that the quantum level of reality existed only in the earliest moments of the universe, as shown by scientists who break up three-dimensional matter in their 'atom smashers'. In general we live in a three-dimensional world, which is a creation of underlying hidden dimensions and quantum forces, forces that are not apparent in 'our' world. As I suggested in the last chapter, our consciousness, within our three dimensions, may be explained by an unseen and unappreciated reality in other dimensions at the quantum level. Near-to-Death episodes may come from these quantum dimensions and they perhaps are where the afterlife itself resides. However, it would appear that scientific measurements of our universe, in the three-dimensional state, are reliable representations of the reality we are able to experience. Just because the scientific discoveries regarding quanta are confusing, are not yet explained, and possibly can't ever be explained, should not dissuade us from accepting our reality, the one we are built for and adapted to, as real. Michael Behe in *Darwin's Black Box* refers to the Anthropic Principle and the multiple universe theories as silliness. I agree. It is a lot of convoluted philosophic rumination that leads nowhere except to avoid the simple possibility that interpretation number one is correct: one very special universe created by God. To repeat, nothing in the fine-tuning *demanded* that we appear; it *allowed* us to appear, and we did. What is wrong with suggesting that God guided the process?

The key in this argument is not the existence of design or fine-tuning itself, which is marvelous and caused the famous astronomer/cosmologist, Sir Fred Hoyle, to call it "a put-up job." The key is the designer universe *allows* us to appear, but we were not *required* to make an appearance. We were not 'expected' as Stuart Kauffmam put it in his book, although he uses that term to justify his theories about complexity. But here we are. Why? Life did not have to originate, but it did. If life cannot create itself from inanimate matter, and it certainly doesn't look like life is that sort of an 'accident' (Chapter 3), then it requires a built-in organizing principle which controls and drives the process, and probably drives evolutionary complexity as well. An objection to the design argument is that it uses the philosophy of teleology, the study of the reason or purpose behind what is discovered or described. Teleology suggests that, if there is obvious design that allows a beneficial effect, it must, therefore, have purpose and imply a designer. Skeptics argue that using teleology implies too much: if the design of the universe allowed us to appear, why can't it be considered just a lucky accident, the Gould approach, in which a designer is not necessary. That misses the point I just made. Yes, the designer universe allows us to appear, but it doesn't demand the second step, the fact we are here. Where does that impetus come from? No mechanism can be identified that makes our presence required. Yet we *are* here despite the enormous odds against it. Looking to God makes logical sense.

This is a similar approach to that which John Polkinghorne, the Anglican theologian and theoretical physicist (introduced in Chapter 1), makes in his book *Beyond Science, The Wider Human Context*, (1996). In his Chapter 6 discussion of our designer universe he proposes a "Moderate Anthropic Principal": "which notes the contingent fruitfulness of the universe as being a fact of interest calling for an explanation." He continues: "The evolution of conscious life seems the most significant thing that has happened in cosmic history and we are right to be intrigued by the fact that so special a universe is required for its possibility." He concludes the chapter by observing, "anthropic considerations are but a part of the cumulative case for theism. Thus, I believe that in the delicate fine-tuning of physical law, which made the evolution of conscious beings possible, we receive a valuable, if indirect, hint from science that there is a divine meaning and purpose behind cosmic history." (pg. 92). And I must again insist upon recognizing that we were *allowed* to appear by our universe, but not *required* to appear. That observation makes looking to God even more significant.

The issue of an underlying biologic design mechanism driving evolution is also an area of controversy between intelligent design proponents and their foes, skeptics and scientists. Here the arguments involve two different approaches to design. The first argument notes that evolutionary adaptations take on jerrybuilt appearances, supporting the theory that evolution is totally a natural process guiding itself by chance mutation and adaptation to nature's demands. Gould uses the Panda's "thumb" to make the point that everything about evolution is natural, using whatever expedient parts are available for the necessary adaptation. The second argument from evolutionists against intelligent design is the claim that some organs are not optimally designed, as a perfect designer should be expected to engineer. Before discussing both arguments, I remind the reader that I believe evolution occurred; higher animals did evolve from lower forms. To my mind the evidence is too overwhelming to consider alternate explanations.

The Giant Panda's thumb is a sixth digit, which allows it to manipulate bamboo, in order to eat the leaves, the animal's only diet. Why an extra digit, why not an arrangement like ours, four digits and an opposable thumb? Stephen Jay Gould in his book, *The Panda's Thumb; More Reflections in Natural History* (1980), explains the original five digits were all necessary for existing functions. Faced with the need for an extra digit, natural selection took a small bone from the wrist, rearranged some muscles and created a thumb. Gould's comment is, "if God had designed a beautiful machine to reflect his (sic) wisdom and power, surely he (sic) would not have used a collection of parts generally fashioned for other purposes." Michael Shermer in *How We Believe*, describes this as "an improvised contraption constructed from the history of what came before," and quotes Gould to enforce his thesis that God is not needed: " [This is] the chancy result of a long string of unpredictable antecedents, rather than as a necessary outcome of nature's laws." *But* there is a completely opposite interpretation, which is just as logical, or perhaps more so, as I view it. Robert Wright, in reviewing the panda's thumb argument, offers a marvelous counter: "if God were designing a machine that *designs* machines—if he (sic) were designing natural selection—he (sic) might well imbue this creative process with exactly the resourcefulness that the panda's thumb embodies…Natural selection, metaphorically speaking, seeks out and exploits technological opportunities, and it does so ingeniously, using unlikely materials when necessary. As Gould himself says, what is marvelous about the panda's thumb is that 'it builds on such improbable foundations.'" (*Non-Zero. The Logic of Human Destiny*). Gould and Shermer, using religions' definitions of the attributes of a perfect God, demand that to prove the existence of God, everything in the universe be designed in a perfect fashion and have 'optimal design.'

In a debating competition, this is simply a tactic of taking a definition to a 'logical extreme' in order to disprove it. It may not disprove anything. We all know that the universe is not perfect and that humans are not perfect. Must we then argue against the presence of God because everything is not perfect? Contrast this to the theory of 'intelligent design.' "Whereas optimal design demands a perfectionistic, anal-retentive designer who has to get everything just right, intelligent design fits our ordinary experience of design, which is always conditioned by the needs of a situation and therefore always falls short of some idealized global optimum." ("Intelligent Design is not Optimal Design," William Dembski, February 2, 2000, Discovery Institute, web site: www.discovery.org/new Articles). Dembski echoes Wright's thoughts, and I accept these interpretations as carrying the day.

There are many other examples of evolution not producing perfection, because what is available to be modified cannot allow perfection. Changing from four legs to the upright posture produced the following two instances of evolution using what is available, and therefore ending up with a less than perfect design. The human maxillary sinuses, in the cheeks under the eyes, have the drainage opening at the top, not an optimal arrangement. When the head is positioned on all fours, like four-legged animals, the mucous drainage is perfectly placed. The same comment applies to our lungs. In the all-fours position the bronchi (breathing tubes) drain perfectly toward the throat. However, nature has provided us with hair-like 'cilia', which sweep the mucous uphill to help with drainage, a very adequate solution although not 'perfect'.

Turning to the second argument about 'design' and the evidence for and against God, the eye is offered as an example of a less than optimally designed organ by proponents of the school of thought that evolution is totally a natural process. What they point to is the fact that the layers of the human retina are put in backwards (Michael Shermer, *How We Believe*). The rods and cones, the cells of vision are in the third layer, and must see the image focused by the lens through a second layer of nerves, and a first layer of blood vessels. There is a "blind spot" where the optic nerve appears just under the first layer. The contention is, a 'perfect designer' would have reversed these three layers. But let's stop a moment. Have you ever seen your blind spot, or those blood vessels? Our vision is perfectly adequate for our vision's function in aiding our lives and activities. (By the way, the blind spot can be demonstrated by a test called "field of vision", and a shadow of the blood vessels, looking like a road map, can be demonstrated by the following trick. In a semi-dark room focus your vision on an object across the room and have another person shine a very fine beam of light at an angle into one eye. With any luck you will see the road map.) And now the surprise: the eye of the octopus is 'perfectly designed,' with all those layers in the 'best' order, the sensory cells on top! (*The River That Flows Uphill*, William H. Calvin). This is a marvelous example of 'convergence', the appearance of comparable organs in very different branches of the evolutionary tree, as championed by Conway Morris (Chapter 4). Are we now to view God as the perfect designer for the octopus, but not for us? The vision in both species is precisely adequate for the needs of each species. Wright is correct. Natural selection is designed to use what is at hand in progressing forward. And Dembski's position is also correct in that the design of an organ is only required to adequately fill the needs of the species, and therefore, does not have to be a 'perfect' design. Since God is considered perfect, atheists and agnostics often raise the issue that His designs must therefore be perfect, as a way of refuting the existence of God. The point is illogical. God's perfection does not necessarily have to flow to His designs.

And there is one final consideration: So-called 'perfect design,' as described by the critics of the theory of intelligent design, may not, in fact, be the best design for optimal function. Research on the eye, reported in1999, suggests that the inverted or reversed design in the retina of the human eye actually provides a better blood flow with an increased supply of oxygen and nutrients for the very high energy requirements of the photoreceptor cells of the retina (*Signs of Intelligence*, Note 3, page 217). Simply put, the so-called 'imperfect design' of the retina provides for the best functional result, which after all is the major purpose of the design. Obviously, jumping to conclusions about patterns of design, without fully understanding the underlying effects on function, leads to very unreasonable criticism.

The battle between intelligent design proponents and defenders of Darwinian evolution evoke some strange accusations. In *Tower of Babel*, Pollack points out the names of intelligent design proponents, as if describing the enemy. He comments about Dembski's dedication "to the creationist cause" by noting that Dembski collected "multiple graduate degrees, in mathematics, philosophy and theology; so [he] will be fully armored and ready to ride forth." The implication is Dembski is educated for the wrong reasons, or that he need not have bothered to get those degrees because he is causing so much harm to 'true' science. What Dembski has is a Ph.D. in Mathematics and a Ph. D. in Philosophy, along with degrees in theology and philosophy. Quite an impressive collection.

Dembski's ideas, in my opinion, win the day. One of his approaches states: "There is no such thing as perfect design. Real designers strive for 'constrained optimization', which is something completely different." He quotes Henry Petroski, a professor of engineering and history at Duke University: "All design involves conflicting objectives and hence compromise, and the best designs will always be those that come up with the best compromise." Therefore, "constrained optimization is the art of compromise between conflicting objectives. That is what design is all about. To find fault with biological design because it misses an idealized optimum, is therefore gratuitous. Not knowing the objectives of the designer, Gould [and other critics are] in no position to say whether the designer has come up with a faulty compromise among these objectives." That sums it up: God does not need to be a 'perfect' designer, as long as the designed organs provide the needed functions to a necessary level of efficiency. Both the design of the universe and the design of biologic organisms are highly suggestive of intelligent design, and a designer, God. Suggestive, but not absolute proof.

Dembski also looks at the issue of design from a fascinating and I think brilliant mathematical/philosophical vantage point in his book, *Intelligent Design, The Bridge Between Science and Theology* (Discussed briefly in Chapter 3). He asserts that science is clearly capable, through the Reductionism approach, to define the degree of complexity of a biologic process or of an organism. By breaking down the process or the organism into component parts, it is possible to calculate the odds that the process or the organism were put together by chance. He calls this approach finding the "specified complexity". From his background in mathematical theory and knowledge of cosmology, he proposes that chance can be eliminated as a possible cause if the odds are less than one part in 10^{-150}. This he calls a "probability bound". If chance can be excluded by this method then intelligent design must be involved. This technique formalizes the material I have presented in Chapters 2 - 4, in which descriptions of fine-tuning and odds are presented from various sources. This technique, if accepted by the reader, appears to make irrefutable the probability of intelligent design operative both in the formation of the universe and in the appearance of life in single cells such as bacteria. The odds calculated for the formation of the universe and for the appearance of single-celled organisms demand this conclusion. When the additional complexity of millions of cells working together as human organs like the liver or the kidney is considered, although the odds of creating the complexity of such organs have not been calculated to my knowledge, the apparent odds require the conclusion that the process of evolution was helped by an underlying design mechanism.

Dembski has calculated the probabilities of creating a much simpler portion of a living organism, the bacterial flagellum. This hair-like structure whips the water and propels the bacterium like an outboard motor. It is made of 50 different proteins. To calculate the possibility of putting this organ together by chance Dembski breaks the process into three parts: 1) Selecting the proper 50 protein molecules out of the 4,289 proteins that make up the bacterium, E. coli. The odds are 10^{-66}. 2) Bringing enough copies of each protein to the proper location, 10^{-234}. 3) Properly constructing the flagellum out of the multiple copies of the protein molecules (over 20,000), 10^{-2954}. The three probabilities must then be multiplied, resulting in a final chance probability of forming a flagellum by an unguided Darwinian mechanism of 10^{-3254} (my calculation). This falls "considerably below the probability bound of 10^{-150}". (*No Free Lunch*, Wm. A Dembski, 2002, pgs. 289-302). Even at this 'simple level', a design mechanism seems required.

In fairness to environmental scientists, they feel they have two answers. First is an objection by Vic Stenger, Ph. D., Emeritus Professor of Physics and Astronomy, U. of Hawaii, to Dembski's probability bound. "Events with such [a] chance probabilit[y] occur all the time by chance. Just go to one of the web sites that provide perfectly random numbers and write down the first 150 digits from 0 to 9 that it gives. The specific sequence that results has a probability of 10^{150} to one against occurring by chance, yet it occurred!" (Discussion List on Physics and Cosmology, metanexus.net, 6/14/01). Stenger's statement is absolutely true, but it ignores Dembski's point. Dembski is not looking at random probabilities. He is looking at the specific organization of parts, which must be brought together to make a living organ or a living organism, which is why Dembski identifies this as "specified complexity", not at all a random event. To make this absolutely clear imagine dealing cards for Poker. Any combination of five cards in a hand has the same enormous odds against their appearance. But if in advance as the dealer, you predicted that you would deal yourself a royal flush in spades, and that was the hand you received, the other players would be absolutely sure you cheated, because the odds against your hand are so great. And that is what specified complexity implies, *required* appearance against enormous odds.

Secondly, the evolutionists say there was an enormous amount of time to allow for the development of life, two to four hundred million years from the time the earth was cool enough to allow for the appearance of bacteria, from four billion years ago to 3.8 or 3.6 billion years ago. Plenty of time for tiny steps to create living bacteria. And from that point on, there was plenty of time for evolution to develop humans. Their theory is that one tiny step at a time reduces the odds quoted in this book, a point that is mathematically true, if each step could immediately be able to work with previous steps. But what about the organization of those steps, which is the major requirement to create life, the working together of 100 or more proteins and enzymes? And so we circle back to intelligent design to organize those protein molecules into something that will become life. The odds to have this happen by chance are enormous, unless there are designing principles built into the process.

To summarize, "the world looks designed. If it looks designed, it could [reasonably] be equally explained by either the unconscious 'design' of natural selection, or the conscious design of a Creator." However, science is presented as discovering natural facts, and religion is seen as supernatural. "We have two options—one scientific and one religious—that [appear to] equally explain the observation of a designed universe. The so-called scientific argument is sustained simply by a bald assertion that nature did it and not by evidence that God could not have done it." ("Designed by Natural Selection", Gregory Kouki, www.str.org/free/commentaries/evolution/designed.html). Since God cannot be "proven" by science, and science finds all the answers, science will not admit to the possible existence of God. Given the equal possibilities, and the evidence that chance could not have created the design, I must favor 'design' by God.

Argument from Darwin. This section studies evolution and employs a review of scientific findings to suggest that God created the evolutionary process. We shall begin with the following self-apparent true statements. Proving or disproving Darwin's theory does not prove or disprove God. Darwin's theory and God are totally unrelated. What Darwin stated as his theory were his observations and conclusions concerning a process that may or may not have occurred. Darwin did not create the process of evolution. He simply stated his beliefs that such a process happened and was happening. Whether you feel Darwin's theory can be applied at all to the development of human beings is really a matter of how you think of the attributes of God, what you wish to believe about God and His works. There are four possibilities for the role of God in relation to the fact that we exist: 1) God does not exist and the entire process of the appearance of life and then finally of the human race is a 'glorious accident' *a la* Stephen Jay Gould; 2) God does exist, created life and coded DNA to control all of evolution from the beginning (Deism); 3) God does exist and has acted throughout time to guide DNA and to change the evolutionary process as required to eventually create us (Theism); 4) God does exist and created everything 6,000-10,000 years ago as we see it now, the position of the "Young Earth Creationists." I realize that there are also "Old Earth Creationists" who are willing to grant the age of the universe as accepted by the scientists. By accepting that point of view I think the Old Earth Creationists have an untenable position in trying to deny our evolution. The ape-like bones are there in ancient layers of the earth; the various isotopic aging techniques are multiple and confirm each other within narrow time limits and agree with geologic aging according to the layers in which bones are found. If Old Age Creationists accept the scientists' theory of the age of the universe and of the earth, they become very inconsistent in their beliefs.

The "Young Earth Creationists", on the other hand, have a very consistent belief structure based on the literal word of Genesis. I cannot quarrel with them: each person has a right to his own religious beliefs, and I do not have the right to attempt to change what any person prefers to believe. I have declared that I accept evolution as a process that has existed. I can see no way to refute the scientific evidence of microevolution, the modification of existing species. As yet scientific evidence can find no method in nature to explain macroevolution, the creation of new species, but the fossil evidence does present a progressive pattern of advance in complexity of form and capacity, and of physical and especially mental capacity.

Since I have already shown my objections to the first possibility, a 'glorious accident', and I have clearly demonstrated my reasons that creationism is wrong (possibility four), I am left with either possibility two or three to support. The material presented in Chapter 6 concerning the evidence for a continuous and currently present afterlife, implies God's continuing presence. It is difficult to imagine God initiating everything and then doing nothing further (possibility number two). However, Paul Davies, the theoretical physicist turned philosopher, has reasoning that is hard to deny for a "revised deism in which God designed the world as *a many-leveled creative process of law and chance.*" (sic, Barbour, *When Science Meets Religion*, pg.165). Davies has commented, "I'm sympathetic to the idea that overall the universe has ingenious and felicitous laws that bring life and indeed intelligence into being, and sentient beings like ourselves who can reflect on the significance of it all. It would be a very poor sort of god who created a universe that wasn't right and then tinkered with it at later stages." (sic) (*Nature, Design, and Science*, Del Ratzsch, 2001, pg. 198, note 19). Despite Davies' reasoning, I am more comfortable with recognizing that God's presence is continuous and active, making me a theist (possibility number three). God as a Creator only at the start, and then as an absentee landlord is termed deism, a pattern of thought that appeared in the 17th century. Theism is more popular in philosophic thought at present, but logical debate is not a voting popularity contest; use your own logic in choosing a position.

Darwin knew nothing of Mendelian genetics, which was in the literature, but not discovered until 40 years after Darwin published his theory. Genetic research and the discovery of DNA and how it works lead to Neo-Darwinism, an attempt to combine all the available knowledge. Darwinists have been seduced by the discovery of the structure and the function of DNA, in two ways. First, to them it explains how the Darwin theory works. Unfortunately, what is known about DNA at the present time does not explain everything. DNA is coded to designate amino acids to be added one-by-one to form strings of amino acids. These strings have a three-dimensional shape formed by the shape of each amino acid molecule and the electrical charges on those molecules. The strings can fit into each other like a jigsaw puzzle forming membrane sheets, muscle bundles, blood vessels, glandular structures and nerves, and so forth. As previously pointed out, it is the three-dimensional control of all these parts, as they grow and fit together into a body when formed from the embryo, that is not explained by a code for amino acids.

Newly discovered Homeobox genes ask for an arm or a wing, an eye or a leg to appear, but this amounts to calling for individual genes to supply the parts, and still does not present the spatial controls to fit everything together properly. Something "extra" arising from whole living organisms must be the answer. As Rupert Sheldrake has proposed, a morphogenic field, similar to the state of consciousness that arises from our brain, may be present at the quantum particle level to direct traffic. As Sheldrake notes, science has tended to ignore this aspect of nature by breaking everything down into parts, and then losing attributes of the whole that may control the whole (*A Glorious Accident*). The lack of scientific understanding of the control of morphogenesis (the manufacture and three-dimensional construction of living organisms) is not a proof of God. Beware of the "God-of-the-Gaps" mistake. What strongly suggests the role of God, as Creator is the seemingly impossible task of inorganic molecules coming together by accident, even in something as simple as a very simple ancient form of living bacteria. How did the individual parts of the bacteria know how to organize themselves into an outer membrane, and internal organelles, so the parts could work together to create a living form? Only if the sum of the parts as a whole create "something extra", to provide that control. Logically, it implies a creator to originally organize the parts. Here we are back to Dembski's intelligent design thesis: living organisms are too complex to pop up by chance.

There is a second way scientists have been seduced by the discovery of DNA. They approached DNA as a blueprint to the origin of life. As Robert Shapiro shows in his book, *Origins*, they created an extensive mythology, and for 40 years have struggled with the origin-of-life problem, and are no closer to a solution now than when DNA appeared on the scene. The reason is fairly obvious. They have worked from the top down, working backward from DNA to RNA, trying to find a simple group of molecules that would organize themselves into the ability to reproduce themselves over and over. Finally some small self-reproducing protein molecules have been created in the laboratory ("Life's Rocky Start," Robert M. Hazen, *Scientific American*, April 2001). Finding one molecule that can reproduce itself is the simplest part of the problem, especially when its manufacture is guided by a scientific intelligence. Remember those enormous odds of going from one protein strand to the roughly 200 different proteins and enzymes needed for one simple organism, organized to make it alive! Rather than turn to God, Shapiro, ever the scientist, optimistically expects some surprising discovery to pop up in the future, opening the door to a proper scientific understanding of the origin of life. "In the origin of life, however, if no surprises were forthcoming, that would be the most surprising result of all." Shapiro may represent the scientific community's atheism, yet there are 40 percent of scientists who believe in God.

A final observation is to recall the inadequacy of Darwin's theory to demonstrate the 'Origin of Species', even though he was sure it did. DNA has been found to control inheritance, and also control change and adaptation of species; that is, DNA has been shown to allow microevolution. Darwin assumed from his observations of species changing in response to nature, that gradually new species would appear. That jump in logic has never been proven. Darwin knew there were gaps in the fossil record of his day. There were no transitional forms showing a very gradual change from an earlier species to the arrival of a later one. He anticipated that those gaps would be filled in by future discoveries. To this date that has not happened. But that is what his theory requires, gradualism covering very minor changes in form and function until a completely different species arrives on the scene. What Darwinists can point to is the demonstration of transitional species forming branches on the evolutionary tree, but with full-fledged gaps between those forms. They *then* try to claim that this is proof of the theory, when obviously it is not. Kenneth Miller (*Finding Darwin's God*) puts up a facade of proof by describing a true transitional form, *Acanthostega*, a four-legged animal that "could breathe with its gills underwater, just like a fish, and could also breathe on land, using lungs." All well and good, but there are no fossils to show the gradual change from the pure fish form to this transitional form, and no fossils to fill the gap from 'four legs with gills' to four legs without gills. These gaps are still there, unfilled with the gradualism Darwin's theory requires, if the process of evolution is totally a natural unguided process.

As a way of denying that gaps exist, Miller also tries to refute Gould's punctuated equilibrium theory of sudden changes after long periods of "stasis" (no change), by quoting Gould's own work with the Bahamian land snail, *Cerion*. Over a 15,000-year period the shape and size of the shell gradually changed. But in my opinion this is no more a difference in species than the huge range of size, color and shape of the current types of dogs, domesticated over the past 15,000 years. It is adaptation of a species, but still the same species.

To understand how Darwin arrived at his theory let us look at one of his observations, the famous Darwin's finches of the Galapagos Islands in the Pacific. Their beaks have been measured over many years and the average size related to the seeds they eat. In very dry times the seeds are tougher and the beaks average slightly larger, presumably due to the ability to handle the tougher seeds; in wetter periods, there are more seeds, which are not as tough, and the beaks are smaller (Phillip E. Johnson, "The Church of Darwin", *Wall Street Journal*, 8/16/99). This process does not require mutations to appear. Any biological characteristic in a species is always variable, as not all individuals have exactly the same genetics. (Think of how humans vary in height.) Therefore, in the average finch population there will be a small number of individuals with larger beaks and a similar small group with shorter beaks. In the middle will be most birds with average beaks, all fitting under the well-known bell-shaped curve. Since larger beaks can handle the tougher seeds, in dry times more large-beaked birds will survive, shifting the average beak size in the larger direction, and, logically, the population of birds will shift back in wetter times to the smaller size. In the almost 150 years since Darwin started to watch the finches, they have fluctuated back and forth in beak size, but they are basically unchanged over that period, with no sign of a direction into which they might be evolving. Granted a fortuitous mutation may appear to help this mechanism of selection, but mutations are not needed for this species to adapt to the rainfall fluctuations.

I must now repeat that Darwin's leap of logic that new species should gradually appear has never been proven. And the reason is that his logic may be very wrong. The Theory proposes a process of mutation at random, with nature then deciding after the fact which mutation will be used; this is a backwards and therefore a passive mechanism which is obviously very weak. It works well enough for a species to make minor adaptations to changes in the environment, as shown by the finches, but is too weak a process to create new species by itself. There is a further weakness in this method: it is recognized that only 30 percent of mutations are 'good" (beneficial). The others that occur are either neutral or "bad". Darwin's Theory of Evolution is like "pushing a rope" which extends away from you and expecting the rope to progress forward as you walk forward. Evolutionists will counter with the claim that pressures from the environment will straighten out the rope, which is true in a way. In fact, evolutionists tend to make the Darwin Theory of Evolution actually sound active, which it is not: for example, in Chapters 4 and 5 is the theory that the Ice Ages were such an important stress, they *caused* our large brain to appear. Nature cannot demand the appearance of mutations that are beneficial. They appear totally by chance. Please understand clearly, the Darwin Theory, as proposed, describes primarily a passive process. If the 'right' mutations luckily appear, and remember, they are only 30 percent of all mutations, then the species survives the drastic changes in the environment—that is, if the mutations appear quickly enough. The rate of 'good' mutations is quite slow, making the speed of mutational change another important passive factor based on chance, and matched against rapid or slow environmental changes.

This is a very cumbersome process, which does not explain how the rapid changes in the Cambrian Explosion, occurred. Mathematicians have demonstrated that the Darwinian method of slow and steady advancement by random mutation cannot produce humans in the time allotted. It is just too slow, and information theorists state that not enough information can be generated to drive evolution at the rates seen. And yet there appears to be a "drive to complexity" apparently built into DNA, which has resulted in 5 to 40 million more and more complicated species now existing on earth, the survivors of 5 to 50 billion extinct species that existed at one time or another (Raup, *Extinction*). Further, animals can react to triggers in nature and create adaptations that are not the result of mutations, but are eventually passed on genetically. Where does the massive information come from to allow these adaptations?

The appearance of increasing complexity from unicellular organisms to multicellular is really very puzzling. As Gould has observed (Chapter 4), bacteria were the initial form of life and they are still here. He considers them the most successful of all living forms. Natural Selection, the major thrust of the Darwin Theory, implies that the most successful species survive. With such success by bacteria why should complexity in the form of multicellular forms be required to appear or bother to appear? Gould's reasoning is to observe that the only developmental direction available from bacteria, since they are the simplest life form, is toward complexity, which does not answer my question. If they are so successful why did they join together in multicellular forms? The teleologic answer, and one scientists use, despite their aversion to teleology, is multicellularity allows for sexual reproduction, providing more variation in offspring and an opportunity for a more useful choice in complexity. This answer implies purpose and design as teleology always does (see discussion below). As in the design argument, the appearance of complexity is *allowed* by the biologic laws of life, but does not appear to be *required*, which again suggests a "drive to complexity," certainly a pre-planning mechanism that would not be part of an accidental falling together of molecules to start life.

Would a natural accident that resulted in the formation of DNA have also provided the mechanism required to create this drive to complexity? That would be a truly amazing accident! It implies that DNA initially appeared containing a built-in mechanism for the purpose of creating gradually increasing complexity through the process of evolution. When discussing 'purpose' we enter the field in philosophy known as 'teleology', the study of evidences of design in nature, or further defined as "natural processes being directed toward an end or shaped by a purpose". (*Webster's New Collegiate Dictionary*, 1979). Since teleology implies planning rather than accidental advances through natural causes, scientists generally avoid this approach in thought, although they will employ it to seemingly defend Darwin, if they have to.

This issue of increasing complexity is another area where scientists have missed the point. They presume that increasing complexity *must* appear, but only by passive means. It is certainly true that scientists studying evolution have demonstrated that fossils show changes, which lead from more primitive species to more advanced forms. They have not shown the very gradual transitional forms predicted by Darwin, resulting in gaps between the fossil types. They have shown transitional species, but these species are still separated from other species by gaps. How do species jump these gaps that Darwin never envisioned? Perhaps evoking God to fill this "gap" in knowledge is wrong. Perhaps not. How are new species created? The discovery of Hox genes, as master controllers of other genes, and especially the Ubx gene (see Chapter 4), which allows the development of insects from crustaceans (shrimp, for example), partially answers that question, while raising the issue of how did the Ubx know in advance how to coordinate those other genes to create a jump to another species form that nature would accept, if evolution is so passive? But that doesn't really answer my original question, which is, why are more complex ones created? Are they necessarily better equipped for survival? Raup concluded that most species that became extinct had "good" genes, disappearing from "bad luck": for example, mutations not appearing quickly enough to catch up with rapidly appearing environmental changes. In a more recent book, Michael Boulter, a professor of ancient biology agrees (*Extinction: Evolution and the End of Man*, 2002). Their conclusions imply that more complex species are not guaranteed to survive. Currently science is so knowledgeable about living genetic mechanisms, can we expect that there is as yet an undiscovered natural process to create new species, a drive to complexity, somehow hidden in

DNA? If a pre-programmed mechanism to create increasing complexity is found in DNA, what is the reason for it being there? Is it present totally by accident? Not likely. Again, invoking the actions of God is not unreasonable, and is further suggested by the existence of exaptations.

Exaptations, discussed in Chapter 5, representing novel innovations in structure that are not employed for new functions for periods of hundreds of thousands of years, suggest a built-in mechanism which creates a drive to complexity, anticipating future needs for survival. That certainly implies design or planning, especially when one asks the obvious question, if animals do not need these unused organs currently to survive, why do they remain in an 'expectant' state? Why aren't they mutated away, if not immediately necessary or when they increase danger to the individual, as in the case of the human larynx, which developed lower and lower in the neck long before speech developed, creating a threat of choking to death? Again, the only logical conclusion is DNA or something else in the organism guides a drive to complexity, providing more orderly planning than the primarily passive process of Natural Selection. I would guess this is hidden in the "junk" areas of DNA regions that were thought to have no message at all. These DNA areas are now being shown to code for short strands of RNA (21-23 base codes) which control some aspects of cell and body construction and may be the source that "provides the complexity that separates higher life forms from simpler ones." (*New York Times*, "RNA trades Bit Part for Starring Role in the Cell," Andrew Pollack, 1/21/03; *Nature* 421, pgs. 231-237, 268-272 [2003]).

There is another way to think about DNA and the development of complexity in animals and plants. This is an approach which explains the major difference between Darwinists and the proponents of "Intelligent Design." In Chapter 4 it was mentioned briefly that the DNA of an amoeba is longer than human DNA, most of it non-functional (Page 90). One might view the large DNA molecule really unnecessary in the amoeba, but present from the beginning of evolution as a preparation for the events of the future, in a way an exaptation. To follow this line of reasoning, recall that DNA, as we know, is a code. The Darwin theory from this point of view is that chance mutations change the code causing complexity to appear, mediated by natural selection. In other words, the complexity is potentially there lying in wait for evolution to change the code. Darwin scientists presume that the mutations by altering the code, add information to DNA, thereby creating complexity. The Intelligent Design folks strongly question that assumption. They point out that it is more likely that the information necessary for the appearance of complexity resides in early evolutionary DNA, as in the amoeba, literally placed there when DNA first appeared, and changing the code brings out complexity through the effects of that intelligence. The ID scientists, using "information theory," claim that chance mutations cannot manufacture information, and that it had to be present from the beginning. Information theory is a recently developed branch of mathematical science (*No Free Lunch*, Dembski). Intelligent Design Theorists feel we must look for an "intelligent designer." If the ID point of view is correct, we must look to God. Now turn the argument around and assume that ID is not correct. What we are left with is the Darwin assertion that a miraculous six-foot long molecule appeared by luck or chance, and as a result of random mutations and natural selection altered its original form, creating all the diverse complexity we see today. Sounds liked a God-given molecule to me.

The complexity of living organisms that has developed is actually a further attack on Darwin. For the sake of this discussion I refer again to Michael Behe's book, *Darwin's Black Box*, which shows how gradualism cannot work to create the evolution of species. His viewpoint was offered in Chapter 1 as evidence of controversy among scientists. Behe was especially attacked by Robert T. Pennock in *Tower of Babel*, which attack I demonstrated was rather weak. Behe presents his concept of 'irreducible complexity', which is a powerful indictment of the gradualism required by Darwin. Darwin himself suggested the primary weakness in his theory: "If it could be demonstrated that any complex organ existed which could not possibly have been formed by numerous, successive, slight modifications, my theory would absolutely break down." (*Origin of Species*). Behe asks the question: "What type of biologic system could not be formed by 'numerous, successive slight modifications'?" And answers it with: "For starters, a system that is irreducibly complex, a single system composed of several well-matched, interacting parts that contribute to the basic function, wherein the removal of any one of the parts causes the system to effectively cease functioning. An irreducibly complex system cannot be produced directly (that is, by continuously improving the initial function, which continues to work by the same mechanism) by slight, successive modifications of a precursor system [an earlier form], because any precursor to an irreducibly complex system that is missing a part is by definition nonfunctional. Since natural selection can only choose systems that are already working, then if a biological system cannot be produced gradually it would have to arise as an integrated unit, in one fell swoop, for natural selection to have anything to work on."

What Behe is saying in plain English is the organs of the body have such complicated interrelated parts, and the biochemical functions of these organs have such enormously complex interdependent interrelationships among and between different chemicals, that to reach any kind of useful function, each particular organ had to appear totally organized from the beginning. There is no way that gradualism could work. Behe demonstrates in his book that living organisms are composed entirely of such irreducibly complex systems. It appears that Behe has successfully refuted the ability of the Darwin concept to allow the appearance of new species by the currently proposed methods of evolution. Despite these facts I still believe evolution occurred and we evolved. The scientifically demonstrated pattern of development and the geologic aging of fossils support the concept of evolution. What Darwin did was provide to science "a seemingly workable theory describing how a completely unintelligent process goes on in nature, creating all the wonders of life; a process in which spiritual/mental creativity was said to have played no part." (www.metanexus.net, views 2002.01.25, Don Cruse). This is the fallacy of Darwin. Nature did it all by chance. My thesis is just the opposite. Evolution occurred and required "intelligent design". It was planned and managed by God.

Argument from Consciousness. Consciousness is a special state of being: it is defined in *Webster's Collegiate Dictionary* as "the quality or state of being aware, especially of something within oneself; also, being conscious of an external object, state or fact, and characterized by sensation, emotion, volition and thought." I think if you go to the zoo, you will not see the monkeys or apes sitting and admiring a beautiful sunset. I know my dogs never notice anything like that. I am not saying that animal minds are totally blank. They have perception, recognition, and memory, and simple puzzle-solving capacity. They are conscious and they have a minimal sort of "mind", but it is all at a very simple and elementary level compared with the human mind and consciousness. Koko, the ape trained to sign hundreds of words, can put those words together into brief declarative sentences and brief requests at the level of a two-year old infant, all intended for the immediate present. Koko shows no deep insights, just immediacy in her concerns and responses. Our brains, with only 25 percent more neurons (nerve cells) than the chimpanzee brain, and with those neurons connected in the same patterns as in the chimpanzee, create a mind with enormous intelligence and with a consciousness that the chimpanzee shows no evidence of having.

Our consciousness involves being aware of our "selves"; we are aware that we are aware. It gives us the ability for introspection, resulting in doing things with our minds that have no relationship to our survival in nature; for instance, we wonder why we exist at all. To ruminate about ourselves, to philosophize, means that we understand concepts that have no material or physical presence. We all understand the meaning of words such as: "love", "freedom", "liberty", or perhaps "disappointment." Words such as these have nothing to do with survivorship in the wild. For each individual there is slightly different inner meaning, based on individual experiences with each concept. All through our lives our consciousness is fine tuned by our perceptions. This allows for a maturation of outlook that may greatly enrich our lives. Further, our consciousness enriches us in other ways. It gives us the aesthetic ability to wonder at the beauty of a sunset, a mountain range, or a landscape, to enjoy a musical composition, to be fascinated by a sculpture, to enjoy a painting, or to get all wrapped up in a book that can't be put down. Our consciousness has also given us an enormous range of emotions, which further enrich our lives, broadening the quality of our existence. "Animals may be consciously aware, yet it seems a blank kind of awareness. The animal mind [is] strangely uncluttered. There would not be the same churning of past thoughts and future plans that fill the human mind. There would not be the continuous chatter of our inner voice, nor the sudden breaks to reconsider our own actions as we switch from simple awareness to self-awareness." (John McCrone, *The Ape That Spoke*, 1991). Our brain gives us an astounding gift, consciousness, which is an enormous quantitative difference from the conscious state the animal brain gives animals.

Of course, a major puzzle for philosophers has always been, why has an inanimate universe developed animate organisms, and why one final branch, called human beings, of all the diverse developing branches of life, has ended up with consciousness, and is able to study the universe it arrived in? The same principle applies to consciousness as to our appearance. The universe is designed to allow life, and it appeared, but was not *required* to appear. Consciousness was not *required* to appear either in any living form, but it did. Why should that have happened? Why do human beings have this gift of consciousness, this ability to think so deeply and at the same time to have an aesthetic mental capacity, which turns life into a multi-faceted existence to be enjoyed, not just an exercise in survival?

Roger Penrose, the theoretical mathematician, feels that consciousness is so special and so complicated in origin, that he wrote his book, *The Emperor's New Mind*, to predict that computers, no matter how large and complex, will never develop consciousness from the artificial intelligence programs put into them. At the same time he wonders, as so many great thinkers have, why is there consciousness, why in us? "Consider the ruthless process of natural selection. The 'older' cerebellum seems to be able to carry out very complex actions without consciousness being directly involved at all. Yet Nature has chosen to evolve sentient beings like ourselves, rather than to remain content with creatures that might carry on under the direction of totally unconscious control mechanisms. If consciousness serves no selective purpose, why did Nature go to the trouble to evolve *conscious* brains when non-sentient 'automaton' brains like cerebella would seem to have done just as well?"

Paul Davies, who specializes in the theoretical field of quantum gravity, and in his writings presents a deistic concept of God, in *The Mind of God*, carries the meaning of consciousness further: "The existence of mind in some organism on some planet in the universe is surely a fact of fundamental significance. Through conscious beings the universe has generated self-awareness. This can be no trivial detail, no minor byproduct of mindless, purposeless forces. We are truly meant to be here." John Polkinghorne, the theoretical mathematical physicist who became an Anglican theologian, carries this 'wonder' regarding consciousness to the final step, recognizing God's role: "Our surplus intellectual capacity, enabling us to comprehend the microworld of quarks and gluons, [elementary quantum particles], and the macroworld of the big bang cosmology, is on such a scale that it beggars belief that this is simply a fortunate by-product of the struggle for life." (*Belief in God in an Age of Science*). And in his book, *Beyond Science; The Wider Human Context*, (1996): "I believe there are many other arguments for belief in God—including those from the intelligibility of the physical world and from religious experience—and are but a part of a cumulative case for theism. Thus, I believe that in the delicate fine-tuning of physical law, which has made the evolution of conscious beings possible, we receive a valuable, if indirect, hint from science that there is a divine meaning and purpose behind cosmic history."

Part of Polkinghorne's reasoning is taken from the opinions of Richard Swinburne, a British theist and highly regarded academic philosopher. Swinburne is an unusual philosopher of religion and some background is warranted before presenting his ideas. He is an evidentialist. They feel "that belief is justified only when evidence can be found for it outside the believer's own mind. He brings inductive logic to bear on questions of faith." Swinburne has gone so far as to apply a complex mathematical probability formula known as Bayes's theorem to propose that the Resurrection is probable to the 97 percent level (*N.Y. Times* on the web, "So God's Really in the Details?", Emily Eakin, 5/11/02). Swinburne also represents a continuation of the 17th century philosophy of John Locke: "How could sentience, self-awareness and free will arise in a purely material universe? They couldn't. Consciousness must have arisen from eternity, and the eternal mind must be God." ("Science Resurrects God", Jim Holt, *Wall Street Journal*, 12/24/97). Swinburne argues: "Why is intelligent life in special need of explanation? Why is there anything more to be explained if a Universe contains intelligent life than if it does not? Because, intelligent life is something which a creator God would have the power and abundant reason for bringing about, and so a phenomenon which, if he exists, would be quite likely to occur." (Richard Swinburne, Article 12 in *Modern cosmology and Philosophy*, ed. John Leslie, 1998). "If it is also (as the argument from fine-tuning claims) something not in the least likely to occur except as a result of God's agency, then its occurrence is evidence for God's existence." This is the conclusion of his book, *The Existence of God*, 1979.

Swinburne offers as God's reason for creating intelligent life the observation that it is extremely valuable and provides consciousness and the mental introspections that create our belief systems and our knowledge. "Knowledge is in itself a supreme good. It is good that there should be beings who understand this cosmic process and who reflect upon it. It is good that there be beings who can make a difference to things through their choice; they have purposes." He describes all the many good events that can come out of having conscious beings, beings who through their intelligence and insights can create positive differences in the world, a world in which we have dominion over everything, exercising our "indeterministic free will". (His term). "A God, who is by definition good, has abundant reason for bringing about human beings [with a] mental life." I find it very thought-provoking that he argues for a God who is good and causes good, in comparison to the reasoning that exists which claims to refute the existence of God because of the existence of evil in the world. He feels there cannot be a scientific explanation for the occurrence of consciousness, and adds: "science cannot explain why the organisms which evolution produced were conscious rather than unconscious robots; that fact provides a further argument for the existence of God." He concludes that the power of this world to produce intelligent life is evidence of the existence of God, "render[ing] the existence of God significantly more probable than not", meeting Adler's personal criterion of 'beyond a reasonable doubt.' This conclusion must be reached at a personal level for each of us, since there never can be absolute proof of God.

Swinburne's arguments from the 'good' caused by intelligence and consciousness, do not mention that consciousness provides for a predisposed religiosity. The religious center in the temporal lobe of the brain, and the mechanisms involving several other areas of the brain, outlined by Newberg and D'Aquili, create mystical and religious experiences during meditation, epilepsy and near-to-death circumstances. Evolutionary psychologists, or sociobiologists as they are also called, propose that this capability on the part of the brain evolved, because as everyone has recognized, religion is good for humans. However, there is no way to know just how or why this mechanism appeared. The sociobiologists are offering their usual 'just-so' Darwinian explanation, but our very large and complex brain, which contains this mechanism, developed 100,000 years before religious practice is thought to have appeared. Another exaptation, or good planning? Religion gives us a construct of purpose for our lives, a much more comfortable philosophical state of mind than considering the universe as purposeless, and it also provides a construct of universal moral and ethical values. Religion also provides the backdrop for altruism, without which characteristic humans could not cooperate as part of small or large groups.

Edward O. Wilson, the sociobiologist professor from Harvard is convinced that our religiosity was created entirely genetically as we evolved. "The highest forms of religious practice can be seen to confer biological advantage", by strengthening group cohesiveness with identity and purpose (*On Human Nature*, 1978). Therefore, he reasons that Darwinian evolution mixed it into our genes. I agree with his previously quoted statement that "the predisposition to religious belief is the most complex and powerful force in the human mind and in all probability an ineradicable part of human nature." Religious belief is a complex and powerful force, which, in view of the religious center in the brain, makes it seem that we were hard-wired toward religious experience at the outset, as an ancient instinct, not through Darwinian evolution. Group cohesiveness would certainly be helped by religion, but religion is not necessary for cooperation within a small tribe. The dangers from other tribes and man-eating animals would require learning to band together for self-protection (*Non-Zero*). Yet religion has always been an extremely important part of our behavior at all levels of civilization. Learned cooperation among tribal members undoubtedly accompanied the development of pagan polytheist religions in primitive societies, probably driven by our seemingly ingrained religiosity provided within our newly developed big brains. However paganism provided little of the aesthetic values found in the modern religions of today, which are only 6,000 years old. The demands of survival more than 6,000 years ago did not require religion at the aesthetic and sophisticated levels we have developed since then, matching the complexities of our advancing civilization. But paganism certainly met and satisfied the spiritual needs of the primitive tribes of the distant past as well as those in the present.

Wilson is proposing that we developed a religious instinct through evolution. Contrary to Wilson, I believe most of our original instinctual behavior has been greatly softened by the appearance of consciousness and our growing intellect and free choice, but not our religiosity. Just the other way around, religion has grown to be a much more important force in our existence as we have developed intellectually. Think about it. How much instinctual behavior do you think you exhibit today? Out-and-out instinct is hard to find in humans currently, other than obvious male-female personality differences, popularized in recent books. But people become emotionally distressed to the point of unreasonable actions in defending their religious beliefs. Just look at the 700 hundred year old mess in the Balkans or the continuous troubles in the Middle East.

Wilson tries to maintain that morality is also instinctual, that "innate censors and motivators exist in the brain that deeply and unconsciously affect our ethical premises." Robert Wright in his book, *Non-Zero*, fully disagrees, and presents our morality as a learning process, describing not instinct but instead his "game theory" of human psychological interactions, showing that as early humans learned to use their bigger brains, and as intelligence grew, we learned to work cooperatively with each other, because both sides could show a gain. His entire book explores that premise.

And I disagree with Wilson also. That is not how I was taught to think about the origin of morality in medical school. We are hard-wired with an area in the brain, which is reserved for our conscience, but that area must receive the teachings of right and wrong, the proper guidance from our parents and religious teachers by age twelve to fourteen, or we could end up as sociopaths, people with no conscience. Adults are responsible to pass along existing ethics to children, one generation teaching another. As a result morality and ethics have been very variable throughout civilization, depending upon the current state of public willingness to be more or less moral, but in the past few thousand years of advancing civilization, a progressively more highly-refined form of ethics and morality has replaced the barbarism that originally covered the inhabited earth. Civilized ethics and morality are a recent development, and considering all the atrocities occurring in the 20th century, ideal morality has not been fully accepted as yet by the human race. The advance which has occurred has been directly related to our developing religions and to their advancing intellectual theology, with accompanying ethics and morals, and in the West also directly related to the development of monotheism. Eastern religions, of course, without monotheism, have also advanced ethics and morals. Both types of religion have similar mystical and meditative experiences, only differing within those experiences by the influences of the underlying concepts of the religions themselves. Since religion is worldwide and so important to all human beings, I conclude that we were given religion very early in evolution to provide a basis for moral growth through intellectual development.

Obviously, without consciousness there can be no religion, which in a circular way brings us back to Swinburne's conclusions. Religion is a necessary good. It is very reasonable to assume that God provided consciousness and the programming of the brain to allow religious feelings and thought to develop as we evolved. In this way we were prepared for the absolute moral values so necessary to live by. Wilson, as an atheist, does not believe this (*On Human Nature*). Karen Johnson in *A History of God* strongly supports the viewpoint that humans arrived on earth programmed to embrace religion. In her Introduction she states: "Men and women started to worship gods as soon as they became recognizably human; they created religions at the same time as they created works of art. These early faiths expressed the wonder and mystery that seem always to have been an essential component of the human experience of this beautiful yet terrifying world. Like art, religion has always been an attempt to find meaning and value in life, despite the suffering that flesh is heir to. Like any other human activity, religion can be abused, but it seems to have been something that we have always done."

It is my conclusion that religion and consciousness, provided by God, arrived together as *Homo sapiens* appeared 150,000 year ago and grew in progressive complexity, culminating in the civilizing ethics and morals that have controlled our development into civilized societies over the past 6,000 years. Consciousness can exist without religion as in atheism. Religion cannot exist without consciousness. It is consciousness that must be present to give religion meaning and belief. They have co-existed and must co-exist to allow our approach to God.

Consciousness and religion must co-exist for another reason. Our consciousness, with our ability to plan, and with our broad range of emotions to react to others, results in our having freedom of choice and self-determination in our lives. Therefore each of us can produce good or evil. Our religiosity is a major aid in controlling the evil tendencies built into us. Stated differently, the gift of consciousness required a counterbalancing gift of religious feelings to control the potential for evil. That a perfect God would allow evil is called "The Problem of Evil", a major arena of philosophic discussion and a major argument offered by those who deny that God exists. As you will read in Chapter 8, I believe God intended that we have self-determination and free choice in our lives, as a means of allowing us to have the freedom to fail, to learn from it, and thereby to improve ourselves, and also 'prove' to ourselves that we are 'good', as well as proving to God we are 'good.' The fact that we have both consciousness and religiosity enforces the suggestion that this follows a plan of God.

This conclusion also applies to out-of-the-body and near-to-death experiences as described in Chapter 6. They mimic the religious experiences of mystics achieved through meditation, experiences that are the same all over the world. I have already expressed the opinion that this is a part of the religious hardware in our brain. Early mysticism developed in Judaism in the second and third centuries. Because it seemed to emphasize a gulf between God and man, it took until the twelfth century for it to be formalized as Kabbalah within the Jewish faith. The Western world has always been somewhat suspicious of something as mysterious as the experiences of mysticism, and somewhat afraid of it. "A journey to the depths of the mind involves great personal risks because we may not be able to endure what we find there. That is why all religions have insisted that the mystical journey only be undertaken under the guidance of an expert, who can monitor the experience, guide the novice past the perilous places, and make sure that he is not exceeding his strength. All mystics stress the need for intelligence and mental stability." (*A History of God*). Atwater in her book, *Beyond the Light*, does describe NDE experiences that were frightening to about one in seven experiencers, and Barbara R. Rommer, M.D. reported 17.7 percent "less than positive" to very frightening NDEs in the 300 people she interviewed, but the point of her book was that most of these events resulted in positive psychological and spiritual changes (*Blessing in Disguise*, 2000).

What is important is the fact that the vast majority of spontaneous mystic episodes, in the form of OBE or NDE, are extremely pleasant, and are not as 'dangerous' to the experiencers as the early mystics feared. Perhaps a religious mystic trying to force his consciousness to reach such an experience, can reach other dangerous areas that do not reflect the content of the NDE, while the spontaneous NDE is meant generally to be pleasant and informative. As I noted in Chapter 6, the NDE is an integral part of our consciousness, and there is no question that most often it is a very pleasant experience, and paraphrasing Swinburne, a very good thing, and therefore, an event, for good reason, added to the abilities of our consciousness us by God, perhaps as a means of bringing us closer to Him. The NDE is another very important piece of evidence to reach the conclusion that it is more reasonable than not to believe in the existence of God.

There is one final consideration regarding our consciousness. Would a loving God, intent upon *our* creation, create such a dangerous universe? This is another aspect of the Problem of Evil to be covered in Chapter 8. Our time on Earth is limited. Our sun can last only five billion years more. It becomes a giant red star and consumes the solar system before dying. There are asteroids 'out there' that cross earth's orbit and another major collision can recreate the circumstances that destroyed the dinosaurs 65 million years ago. If we have appeared by accident, as claimed by so many scientists, it is not surprising that these dangers exist and that there is no protection for our future. I think this is a most powerful argument against the existence of God. If God created us, why do we seem so unprotected? My answer is that the gift of consciousness, which seems to be an unnecessary addition to our capabilities for survival of the fittest, yet appearing as a part of the process of evolution, is a powerful argument for the existence of God. We are in an obvious sense very protected; our consciousness will give us the intellectual capacity to learn to destroy dangerous asteroids in the near future, and at the right moment arrange for a journey to another hospitable solar system, if one exists. God created us, and we have been given the capacity to protect ourselves through scientific space research. We can develop rocket science to knock the asteroids off course. Perhaps we can find a hospitable solar system later on. However, I don't think we are entirely on our own. Surely, if God created us, it was not an open-ended conception. He is with us and acts for us.

I think one can conclude from all the arguments presented in this chapter that it could be accepted beyond a reasonable doubt that God exists. This does not mean that a person must reach that conclusion. As Adler concluded at the end of the argument section of his book, one must be "persuaded that God exists, either beyond a reasonable doubt or by preponderance of reasons in favor of that conclusion over reasons against it." Adler stated that he was persuaded that God exists, based upon the one assumption that God is necessary to maintain the universe. He observed, however, that if the cosmos "initially came into existence out of nothing, the proposition 'God exists' can be established with certitude, for it is impossible that something could come into existence out of nothing without the action of a [pre-existing] creative cause." I have shown that a "first cause" must exist, and have added other factors, including the design of the universe allowing the development of life, biologic design seemingly pre-planned for increasing complexity, and the presence of consciousness, which other philosophers employ as a primary reason for the existence of God.

Chapter 8: Reflections on a Personal Theology

This chapter covers the reorganization of my thinking after completing the studies I have described in this book, concluding that not only did I believe that God existed, but that I wished to relate to Him in ways I had not done before. As an independent thinker I have my own judgment of the problems that are found with organized religion, and also the problems of discovering proper Bible interpretation. In the chapter I will discuss negotiating from reason to faith. I give my answer to the question of why there is evil in the world. I present my concept of how we are made in the image of God. I examine the foolishness of conflict between religions and the lack of tolerance. I discuss a solution to the battle between science and Creationists, to allow the proper teaching of evolution science in the public schools. And finally, there is a brief discussion of modern existentialist philosophy, which I feel is psychologically harmful, and how I think the material in this book offers answers to the harm. It is not my intent to convince you to think differently, or to change your beliefs. However, I have never thought it harmful to expose oneself to new or different ideas, to compare one's concepts to alternate approaches. This chapter allows you that comparison.

Organized religion and the independent thinker.

The main theme of this book is that, surprisingly, the discoveries of science when studied closely, and independent of religious texts, can lead a person to a belief that God exists. As Adler states, that is as far as philosophical theology (Adler's term) can go. In the last chapter I concluded there is sufficient evidence presented in this book to accept beyond a reasonable doubt that God exists. For some readers that may be the end of it: they may accept the conclusion or they may remain agnostics or atheists. They are not prepared to go further. For others, the evidence presented may have strengthened their pre-existing belief and helped them approach their religion in a state of expanded knowledge. For a third group, for the first time believing that God exists, they now must recognize they face the task of developing a system of beliefs. Therefore, there must be a secondary theme, just as important as the first, that a person should develop his own pattern or construct of personal religious belief, appropriate for that person and that person alone. No one should be able to tell you what to believe and make you believe it. Personal theology is too important to each of us, as adults, simply to accept a spoon-feeding of theology. I am not saying, don't listen to religious leaders, but quite the contrary. Approach religious leaders and ask questions. Read their books, and ask questions of yourself. They can instruct and teach you and will provide many valuable lessons, and much information you will need to formulate your own personal religious feelings. Nor am I saying do not belong to a religion. However, if you belong to a religious group, there is no harm in carefully studying its theology and sacred philosophy and then accepting it as you see fit. I know there are religions that insist a member must accept all of their dogma. If you are comfortable with that, it is proper for you. I am not trying to goad anyone into challenges against the religion they are in. I simply want to appeal to everyone to be thoughtful and get the most out of their personal beliefs and logical conclusions. On the other hand, if you do not now belong to a religion, develop your own religious philosophy and then find a comfortable religious group. Frankly, it is hard for me to imagine that you would be reading this book unless you wanted to understand fully why you believe what you believe, or wished to add further knowledge as you studied your beliefs.

Organized religion does have much to offer, but it also has many problems. First, we all know that God can be found and approached anywhere, not just in a religious building. The observant, praying individual does not need a special building. Once a group of human beings organize to build a building and organize a congregation, there will be human conflicts and errors in managing the business side of what now is a religious business enterprise. It is difficult to be in a congregation leadership position and accept the work to be done without expecting for oneself some secondary gain, in the form of recognition or praise from other congregants, when in fact the purist way to perform such duties is without expectation of any reward. It is the same as recognizing that the purest form of charity in anonymous. And as Jesus preached in Matthew 6:5,6: "When you pray, you must not be like the hypocrites; for they love to stand and pray in the synagogues and at the street corners, that they may be seen by men. Truly I say to you, they have their reward. But when you pray, go into your room and shut the door and pray to your Father who is in secret; and your Father who sees in secret will reward you." The purest religion is internal and personal, and how you live your life demonstrates the quality of your religious commitment.

The second problem with organized religion comes from the intensity of our religious feelings. Many authors and I believe those feelings must be instinctual, as important and as emotional as they are to us. That intensity, which I think is genetic, has made us as religious as we are, a situation that should be very good. But on the other side it makes various religions get into disputes with one another, and worse, into fighting and wars. As we all know, separation of church and state in this country came directly as a reaction to European state religions persecuting minorities over their differing practices and beliefs in God. The Crusades were a sin, the Inquisition a sin, the Irish conflicts a sin, and 700 years of Balkans fighting a sin, to name just a few examples during mankind's history of religious warfare. And in the East, the conflicts between Hindu India and Muslim Pakistan show that this is not just a monotheistic problem. Each religion is convinced that its theology is correct; that is the problem. God cannot approve of our battles over the proper interpretation of Him. Nowhere is a stone tablet, inscribed by God, Himself, with a simple paragraph containing God's exact instructions describing how we should approach Him and believe in Him in all aspects of theology. Organized religion always makes religious belief a great deal more complex than the Ten Commandments. It needn't be like that. Rabbi Hillel in the first century B.C. condensed the entire Torah into, "what is hateful to you, do not do to your friend. This is the entire Torah. The rest is commentary. Go forth and learn." (*Genesis and the Big Bang*). Or a century later during the Sermon on the Mount: "So whatever you wish that men would do to you, do so to them." (Matthew 7:12). This teaching is the primary concept of all western religion.

In terms of the proposals of this book to use the findings of science to approach God and more thoroughly understand His creation, there are no fossils stamped "Made by God", no layers of the Earth marked "Aged by God", to guide us. Therefore, there are no absolutely 'right' or 'wrong' religions in the way they view the theology of God and the contributions of science to the debate. Each religion's theologians present a reasonable point of view from that religion's perspective, but these are human interpretations, which means open to human error. Each religion's theologists are convinced that only they are absolutely correct, and as a result the tenets they create may be too rigid for the individual who prefers a freer pattern of thought. Chet

Raymo (*Skeptics and True Believers*) rejected the teachings he received at Notre Dame: "The text we used for my freshman theology class was Frank Sheed's *Theology and Sanity*, the thrust of which was that any sane person *must* be a Roman Catholic, so persuasive is the evidence for the objective truth of that faith." He studied science and left Christianity behind. Karen Armstrong, the former nun and author of *A History of God*, also lost belief in God: "The Roman Catholicism of my childhood was a rather frightening creed. I listened to my share of hellfire sermons. In fact Hell seemed a more potent reality than God, because it was something that I could grasp imaginatively. God, on the other hand, was a somewhat shadowy figure, defined in intellectual abstractions rather than images." She characterizes the catechism answer to the question, "What is God": "God is the Supreme Spirit, Who alone exists of Himself and is infinite in all perfection," as leaving her cold. "It has always seemed a singularly arid, pompous and arrogant definition. I have come to believe that it is also incorrect." Michael Shermer in *How We Believe* states that as a teenager he was a "born-again Christian" but in describing why he left Christianity he pointed to freedom: "It gave me a sense of joy and freedom. Freedom to think for myself. Freedom to take responsibility for my own actions. Freedom to construct my own meanings and my own destinies." Each of these skeptics could not tolerate the rigidity of the theology of the religion they left. Many religions may be too restrictive for the independent thinker. And it certainly is that rigidity of belief that leads to the intense intolerance between various believers of which we are all aware.

Which brings us to the third problem: how to approach the interpretation of the Bible, and how to combine religion and science in a reasonable pattern of thought? To study or even try to resolve the debate between Creationists and scientists, the interpretation of the Book of Genesis is of paramount importance for most people. The Bible represents the Word of God, and His instructions, but the interpretation of the original form in Old Hebrew presents a problem. The original five books of the Old Testament, the Jewish Torah, were written in Old Hebrew, with consonants only, and some accent marks. In studying those five books, it must be remembered to do it as directly as possible, employing scholars who know that form of Hebrew, and who use the ancient Jewish commentaries. Schroeder in *Genesis and the Big Bang* lists four biblical commentators who "have withstood time's test. [They] are accepted by Jew and Christian alike as guiding lights in the interpretation of the book of Genesis." He lists Onkelos, Rashi, Maimonides and Nahmonides, spanning time from 150 A.D. to 1270 A. D. One cannot go directly to the King James' Version and be assured of a proper interpretation. Old Hebrew was changed to Aramaic, to Greek, to Latin, and then to Old English before finally arriving at the modern King James form. Any modern translation must start with the original Hebrew version, which even today, is thought to be over 99 percent accurate in its portrayal of the original, despite being copied over and over by scribes through the centuries. Further, in Jewish tradition, these five books were given to Moses on Mount Sinai by God, with Moses writing as God spoke. Therefore, the Torah is considered by scholars to be like college lecture notes: not everything is present, and what is there is open to interpretation and expansion.

This raises the question of whether the three monotheistic scriptures are inerrant. That is, are the Old Testament, the New Testament, and the Koran (Qur'an) each the exact word of God. For many biblical scholars the answer is, no. The description of God is different in each scripture. That is why Karen Armstrong wrote her book, *The History of God*. As she traces the history of God in each of these holy books, the personality of God is very different, and as time passes and each scripture is produced, God changes. In the Old Testament God "chooses" the Hebrew tribe. He instructs them in war and helps them kill enemies. He appears to them in this reality (i.e. the burning bush). Although he preaches morality, he is warlike and vengeful. In the New Testament God's love for all people is shown, and His appearance in reality is accomplished through Jesus. He is not warlike and vengeful. By contrast, in the Koran God remains all-powerful, but is more remote, although He can be appreciated through the wonders of our reality that He has created. He communicates through the Angel Gabriel to Muhammad. Are all of these descriptions of the same God? Of course they are, as interpreted by the people who wrote each of these holy tracts. Divine inspiration was written down by humans, who modified the inspiration they received by their own point of view. This is why I feel the three scriptures are not inerrant in everything presented. This is why biblical scholars in creating modern interpretations use the time periods the scriptures were composed in and the surrounding attributes and mores of the existing civilizations to help in refining their decisions as to meanings. As the archeologists in Israel have shown, the Old Testament is generally historically factual, as is the New Testament.

It is on these grounds that I was willing to argue in Chapter 2 with the Creationist interpretation that the great flood of Noah was worldwide, and give my interpretation that it was local. How we think about God cannot depend on issues such as how widespread the flood was, for either interpretation cannot change our relationship with God. Yet the Creationists, to protect their version of a literal six-day creation, insist only their approach is correct, and everyone else is wrong. To reduce the conflict between religions, all of us must allow other religious groups the right to have their own variations in interpretation. No religion has an exclusive version of absolute religious truth. We all have part of the truth. Tolerating the beliefs of others by all of us is the answer. As Kitty Ferguson points out, you are your "own ultimate authority, [but that] doesn't guarantee that [you] have got it right. It doesn't make [you] THE ultimate authority. One of the assumptions of science and religion, that there is such a thing as objective truth, means that [you] might be dead wrong." (*The Fire in the Equations*). But don't stop searching and thinking. Be your own person and find comfort in your own beliefs. Competition between beliefs is totally unnecessary and unproductive.

From Reason to Faith

Having reached the conclusion beyond a reasonable doubt that one may believe God exists, is not the same as developing a relationship of faith in God, of believing in God's works, His love, and the strength He can offer. Again, referring to Adler, he regards this as a leap across a chasm, one across which "reason cannot build a bridge, however fragile and shaky that bridge may be." His play on the words 'a leap of faith' indicates one cannot jump from logic and reason to faith. We can use reason to understand a proper relationship with God, but we cannot use reason to reach faith. In the Introduction I noted that some people receive a gift of faith from their parents and accept it without challenge. I don't think faith, however achieved, varies in strength, but is the same whether achieved following search and reason, or received without question as a child. However, building strength in faith requires understanding the attributes of God and recognizing that simply declaring faith in God does not create a two-party contract. For example, on our side, we should accept responsibilities to moral lives, because that is the proper way to live, not because we expect a guaranteed reward. I have never accepted the idea of Heaven and Hell as standing for reward and punishment. That concept is a form of approaching God as a parent, who is teaching a young child right from wrong. It is adolescent, not adult reasoning. As a descendent of the Jewish people, I must honor the ancient covenant with God. As a result my definition of faith is perhaps more complex than most people would use. Not only is it "belief and trust in and loyalty to God", but it also includes being faithful, "firm in adherence to promises or in observance of duty." (*Webster's New Collegiate Dictionary*, 1979). My faith also includes that sense of duty, a duty to bring knowledge of God to the world. That is one of the reasons I wrote this book.

We know we wish to approach God with our faith, and we must use our faith in expecting His response to us. Since we cannot know God directly, we must make certain assumptions: He is the Supreme Being, omnipotent, omniscient and omnipresent. He is eternal, and always will be. "To acknowledge God's omnipotence and omniscience, as we must, is to acknowledge that he knows and understands us better than we understand ourselves, that nothing about us is hidden from him, and that, within the bounds of possibility, he can do with us what he wills. However, to acknowledge this is not to be assured that God is concerned with our conduct or cares what happens to us." (Adler). We cannot make the assumption that through prayer God will step into our lives and straighten out or solve problems. Therefore, we cannot take improper advantage of our relationship with God. For a sports team to pray to God for a victory in a game is to misuse faith in God. Praying for strength to play the best game you can is the only proper use of the prayer before a game. Prayer brings strength that will help facing and solving problems. Faith stems from an internally driven "religious belief in and worship of God draw[ing] its vigor and vitality from an article of religious faith that lies beyond the power of reason to do more than discuss. That article is belief in the immortality of the human soul and the promise of life hereafter." (Adler). And it is why I stressed so strongly the evidence presented in Chapter 6 of the Near to Death Experiences. If we have faith that God voluntarily created us and also has afforded us an opportunity for immortality, it means that we have faith that He does care about us, that He acts in a loving and benevolent fashion and that He is perfectly just and merciful. Adler pursues the point at length that there is a tremendous difference "between *believing God exists* and *believing in God*—confiding in him and having hope in him." Since I do not have a theological background, I have tried to encapsulate his point of view. The reader should study Adler for himself.

Accepting religious faith and truly believing in God involves a commitment to understand the obligations that come with it and therefore contains a profound responsibility. Too many people misuse a statement of faith, and are not honest with themselves. Their faith is a convenience, not a commitment to a life of moral responsibility, a life which is an example to others. Over 90 percent of people in this country profess a belief in God when polled, but how many of those 90 percent truly try to live up to the Ten Commandments? Five to ten percent is the answer I got when I surveyed a number of my psychiatrist friends, under the assumption that psychiatric patents are really telling the truth when in counseling. The 90 percent are simply giving an expected answer to polls on belief in God, not a deeply committed answer. Gallop & Lindsay in *Surveying the Religious Landscape*, published in 1999, note that while "93% of Americans have a copy of the Bible or other Scriptures in their household, yet only 42% of the nation can name even five of the Ten Commandments. Spirituality in America may be three thousand miles wide, but remains only three inches deep". These authors, going back over 50 years, quote Lincoln Barnett who commented on findings in a *Ladies' Home Journal* survey on religion and ethics conducted in 1947: "It is evident that a profound gulf lies between America's avowed ethical standards and the observable realities of national life. What may be more alarming is the gap between what Americans *think* they do and what they *do* do." Theologians representing Catholics, Protestants and Jews, reviewed the same survey. Dr Simon Greenberg offered the following reason for the lack of depth in religious belief: "While the mind that enters a university may be ready for adult fare in the secular field, all it gets in the religious field is infant food." (*Ladies' Home Journal*, November 1947). There is no escaping the thought that accepting faith requires recognizing and accepting the commitment that must go with it. Faith is commitment and commitment is faith. The best definition of this view of faith that I have found was developed by "Harvard professor Gordon Allport, who defined intrinsic faith as that which is internalized and practiced regardless of outside social pressure or personal consequences. Extrinsic faith, by contrast, is utilitarian, self-oriented, and concerned with obtaining status, personal security, or social goals. In short, intrinsic faith is for real, extrinsic faith is for show." (*Light & Death*, Michael Sabom, M.D.).

Good, Evil and the Garden of Eden

The Problem of Evil always crops up in a discussion of a proof of God. Obviously, an important question is: if an all-powerful God created us out of His goodness and benevolence why is there evil? Why didn't He create a world that is entirely good? This suggests the argument that since there is evil perhaps God does not exist. It is just another version of the illogical suggestion that since God is perfect, all of his creations should have perfect design, a point refuted in Chapter 7. I am comfortable with my answers to all aspects of the Problem of Evil. Accepting the premise that God created our universe and designed the laws of nature of that universe to allow the appearance of highly intelligent life, especially us, we must presume that an all-powerful supreme being made the very best universe He could for that purpose out of the type of energy He made available. It may be the only type of energy that allows the development of life. This assumes that the energy particles we have discovered, and will discover, are the only ones that can be employed in construction of a life-permitting universe. Scientists who propose strange forms of life in strange universes still must use the same energy particles in their suppositions. We can know no strange energy particles or strange universes and imagining them runs afoul of Occam's razor.

From the discussion in Chapter 2 we know that the universe is a highly dangerous and unfriendly place for life. The position of the Earth in our galaxy puts us in a most protected area, and the Earth itself and the setup of the solar system have special attributes that protect us from our own sun and the asteroids. The dangers in the universe are very threatening, but an all-powerful Creator allows those dangers. Why would God do that? Being all-powerful, why didn't God create the universe as a very benign and safe place for us? Perhaps this design is required and if He removed all the dangers He might not have been able to create us. Either such an arrangement must be required, although we may not understand why, or we really are in no danger under God's protection. There really are no other options and we cannot know the mind of God. The major impacts of asteroids on the earth, extensively discussed in Chapter 4, may supply an answer. Think of how the massive collisions affected evolution. There is a "growing indication that these destructive events *may be necessary* to promote evolutionary change. Most paleontologists believe that the Great Dying enabled the dinosaurs to thrive by opening niches previously occupied by other animals. Likewise, the demise of the dinosaurs allowed mammals to flourish. Whatever stimulated these mass extinctions, then, also made possible our own existence." ("Repeated Blows", Luann Becker, *Scientific American*, March 2002, my italics). Perhaps Schroeder, quoted in Chapter 4, who invoked God in the disappearance of the dinosaurs, reasonably answered the 'whatever stimulated' issue. Massive impacts may be destructive but not evil.

The same reasoning applies to the Earth itself. We experience floods, earthquakes, lightening-induced forest fires, and other disasters. Why didn't God make the Earth much more benign and safe for us? Must the Earth be constructed like it is, and if changed could it work to support and protect us? For example, the oceans must be large enough to moderate and control global temperatures. We must have large oceans to allow enough water to evaporate and bring enough rain to the land areas. The current division between land and ocean areas seems proper: as Ward and Brownlee summarized in their book, *Rare Earth*, in a section titled, "Buying time: The Persistence of Oceans and Moderate Temperature", (page 260), "it appears that Earth got it just right". Moderate temperatures over a very extended period allowed the appearance of life and the gradual evolution of us, and that period was 3.6 to 3.8 billion years! Because of these considerations, it looks like we can't get rid of the massive storms that bring the high winds, the rain, the lightening and the floods that occasionally occur, coincidently taking some lives. The laws of nature are fixed on Earth and for the universe: lightening is only an expression of some of the energy laws, as are tornadoes. The weather is naturally very variable following those same laws of nature, bringing droughts on a periodic basis, and creating deserts instead of arable land. In the same way earthquakes *must* happen; the continents float on the molten iron in the earth's core, movements of which create the magnetic field that protects us from massive doses of radiation, which bombards the earth. Moving continents bring earthquakes. I think it is a fortunate trade off. I'll take earthquakes over life-killing radiation. The Earth could possibly be more benign, but as with the universe, for His own reasons this is the planet He gave us. Along with those external dangers, we are also threatened by internal dangers, illness and disease. Why? All of these dangers fall under the category of the Problem of Evil. What we must accept is that it appears God allows life to be threatened by dangers. We don't live in the Garden of Eden, and God both allowed and demanded that Adam and Eve leave that protected place. Assuming God's benevolence in creating us, we must believe that He feels the dangers are not severe enough to destroy us. Remember we have been given consciousness and the intelligence to solve the problems that these dangers present.

Consider this line of reasoning: perhaps life is meant to be a challenge and the dangers are there to serve a purpose. It may well be that they are purposely kept, requiring us to learn to develop responsibility to care for others and ourselves. There is a reason I mention learning responsibility from danger. Viewing God as the Creator of the universe brings up the issue of God's benevolence, God's love, and God as our parent. In prayer we certainly say: "God, our Father." Let us consider God as our parent and think about the following: how do we develop into appropriately mature adults? An adult, by my definition, is a person who is willing to take responsibility for himself and others, and is willing to perform tasks that he would rather not be doing, but realizes must be done to solve whatever problems he faces. Confronting 'bad' things, struggling with evil, being tempted to sin are all challenges by which the psychologically growing individual, can become, by trial and error, a moral and trustworthy adult, the goal of our maturing process. That process is impossible in a Garden of Eden. In fact, I view a 'Garden of Eden' life as boring! Life is meant to be a challenge, and it is those challenges that make life more interesting and an adventure. As previously stated, for the physical dangers, consciousness, which I believe was given to us by God, provides us with the ability to discover the knowledge to combat them, to find solutions. These solutions, such as protecting the Earth from asteroids, require worldwide cooperation, teaching the earth's population to work together. Alternatively, if God were a totally protective parent, none of life's challenges would appear and we would not have the opportunity to be tested by those challenges and we would not grow.

In the moral and ethical issues of life that face us, it is the ways we solve challenges and problems that allow us to judge ourselves, and learn to grow. And we cannot learn to grow unless we analyze our own actions, our decisions, and our choices. Our actions are not pre-determined. They cannot be since we have been given free will and free choice, and exactly because we have been given consciousness. Consciousness provides all the joy and sadness of our emotions, while granting the ability to think and plan, and the ability to react to people and episodes in our lives, and finally to judge those reactions. We make the right decisions, the wrong decisions, and we make mistakes. We learn from all. We may mistakenly create 'bad' or even evil events by those decisions. Obviously free will allows some people to purposely create evil, and it is the responsibility of those people to be prepared to accept the consequences to them of that evil, the punishments society exacts. The evil created by people, obviously, is not God's fault.

Therefore, the dangers, the 'bad' events, and the presence of evil are all built-in challenges of life. And that should be no surprise. Opposites appear throughout the universe: the energy particles are either positive or negative; our emotions are two-sided, joy and sadness, love and hate, to give examples. It should not be surprising that there is good and evil, and it should be pleasing to note that civilized culture has progressively advanced in the direction of increased morality, driven, I think, by our religious instincts, as well as driven

226

by experienced-based reciprocal altruism, Wright's non-zero-sumness. Wright adds his opinion: "Once you have accepted that evil is, for whatever reason, built into the fabric of human experience, the basic trend lines don't look all that bad. This cultural development is closer to being evidence of divinity than its opposite would be." (*Non-Zero*, pg. 327, sentences reversed). Wright is another example of a scientifically oriented person studying what science is learning and becoming more theistic.

It is my belief that God has allowed these obstacles to a serene life, so that we can learn to grow and to evaluate ourselves all along the way. I am describing God as a 'tough love' parent, a parent who loves his children, but who does not make their life a cocoon of safety. He makes them accept the challenges and problems that are natural to life, and he insists they accept the responsibility for their choices and their actions. In this country it is easy to see the results of parents who have not followed that mode of parenting in the past 50 years: we have a population of many children and adults who are self-centered, self-indulgent, 'me-first' kind of people, who are not the responsibly moral and ethical adults necessary for a properly functioning society. I believe tough love is the most appropriate way to parent. If life is meant to be challenging and requires problem-solving, tough love is a most humane way of introducing children to the requirements of adult life, letting them stumble and struggle, but *always* offering love, support and help along the way. No parent can inject maturity into a child or impose maturity on him. That child must develop it through his own self-analysis and acceptance of responsibility of his actions and choices. Overprotective parents stifle that development.

I believe God is a tough-love parent who has allowed free will and free choice, and this is my answer to the Problem of Evil. I think it is a necessary part of life, tempting us, challenging us to sin or to grow. How can there be sin if there are no temptations? How do you prove to yourself your strength of moral character unless you must face problems and evil people? We are expected to judge ourselves and grow from that judgment. We are expected to judge others, and learn from what we see them do. Yet currently in this country we are told that we should not be 'judgmental' of others. It is not politically correct. The teaching of moral relativism started in the 1930's (Chapter 7) and what has happened to moral judgment in our current society is exemplified by a letter an ethics teacher wrote to the *Wall Street Journal* (Michael Levy, 11/15/99). "I teach an ethics class in a secular boarding school...and am constantly shocked at my students' inability to condemn obviously horrific behavior. My students defend slavery, female genital mutilation and other atrocities that are occurring in the world today with the argument: 'Well, it's just the way their culture works'." Levy's conclusion should be obvious: "If we continue to fear that moral instruction in any form in classrooms is simply a guise for religious indoctrination, we will surely continue to produce morally hollow graduates. As Adler wrote, 'When men no longer have confidence that right decisions in moral…matters can be rationally arrived at…the institutions of democracy are the walls of an empty house which will collapse under the pressure from without because of the vacuum within'."

As a means of justifying the self-centered moral decline in this country over the past generation, the idea has been developed "that a central message of Christianity is to forgive everyone who commits evil against anyone, no matter how great and cruel and whether or not the evildoer repents, [and] this has been accepted by much of Christendom." Why worry about your own moral actions if everyone will forgive you? Society's pressure disappears and the person can do what he wants to do. Dennis Prager's article in the *Wall Street Journal* fits my feelings exactly: "Though I am a Jew, I believe that a vibrant Christianity is essential if America's moral decline is to be reversed, and that despite theological differences, there is indeed a Judeo-Christian value system that has served as the bedrock of American civilization," and of all Western monotheistic countries (*WSJ*, 12/15/97). Prager, an author and talk show host in Los Angeles, quotes Luke 17:3-4 to clarify the true Christian moral tenet about forgiveness: "And if your brother sins against you, rebuke him; and if he repents, forgive him. And if seven times of the day he sins against you, and seven times of the day turns to you saying, I repent, you shall forgive him." The interpretation of those verses is obvious: "that forgiveness, even by God, is contingent on the sinner repenting, and that it can only be given to the sinner by the one against whom he sinned." Today's teaching that "judging evil is widely considered worse than doing evil," is patently wrong. It comes from the 1960s' 'do-your-own-thing' looseness of morality. It also comes from the post-modernism taught in our public schools and colleges, championing situational ethics and a relative moral value system, rather than the moral absolutes that have governed societal behavior until the middle of the Twentieth Century. Despite the obvious decline in morals over the past 50 years, according to Gallop "83 percent of adults in this country endorse absolute guidelines in determining good and evil in all situations." (*Surveying the Religious Landscape*). My own reaction to this poll is that people know what their answer should be, but don't practice their lives accordingly. Therefore, *do* study others and learn from their actions, their mistakes, and their sins. It is your choice whether you keep those observed lessons to yourself or speak out. I prefer speaking out.

One should begin to judge oneself throughout life before settling the question, does God judge us individually and is "God concerned with our conduct or cares what happens to us?" Pointing to an 18th century dispute between deists and orthodox theologians, whether "the Deity that both affirmed was one who cared about his creatures, was concerned with the disposition of their lives," Adler offers the philosopher's opinion that God being indifferent or concerned about each of us, "the odds are fifty-fifty either way". To want God to be concerned about each individual, about oneself, one must then turn to faith in a benevolent God who created us, believing in a God who promised eternal rewards and punishments. But I believe it is extremely adolescent and immature thinking to conduct one's life totally on the basis of looking to a divine parent for reward and punishment to guide us. "To acknowledge God's omnipotence and omniscience, as we must, is to acknowledge that he knows and understands us better than we understand ourselves, that nothing about us its hidden from him." (Adler). God will know how you truly lived your life, what drove you. There is a special purity in leading a morally responsible life for its own sake, not just for a reward. Living life out of fear of punishment is not responsible living. It is at the level of giving to charity and then asking for recognition. The reports of the Near to Death Experiencers describe a sense of a loving God, an anticipation of an eternal judgment guided by love. If you continually judge yourself honestly, you will be perfectly prepared for that eternal judgment.

Among all living things we alone anticipate our mortality; that realization drives us to find a deeper meaning in life, it makes our decisions more important, and makes us think deeply about what we want to accomplish in life. A meditation on death in the Jewish *Union Prayer Book* (edited by The Central Conference of American Rabbis) titled, "A Philosophy of Life and Death" stresses the point: "Judaism teaches us to understand death as part of the Divine pattern of the universe. Actually, we could not have our sensitivity without fragility. Mortality is the tax that we pay for the privilege of love, thought, creative work—the toll on the bridge of being from which clods of earth and snow-peaked mountain summits are exempt. Just because we are human, we are prisoners of the years. Yet that very prison is the room of discipline in which we, driven by the urgency of time, create." We are to try to live full, creative, productive lives and learn to face the challenges which make it so interesting. Unfortunately those challenges can be much too interesting.

Rabbi Harold Kushner in his book, *When Bad Things Happen To Good People*, (1981) attempted to answer the question implied in his title, why are some people so challenged? He has no answer, nor do I, but his assertions that God set up a universe with immutable natural laws, resulting in God not being in control of everything, I reject. "Can you accept the idea that some things happen for no reason, that there is randomness in the universe?" This sounds to me like the 'quantum theory' of theology. I agree with him that God does not send misfortunes to punish certain people on Earth, but I believe God purposely chose to allow free will to let us grow in life by our own endeavors. Free will allows people to be evil and create evil. God purposely designed a universe that would allow us to evolve. The universe is what it is. It is dangerous, but this universe is designed for us, and by God's plan it is the universe He wanted us to have. Further, there are those, who do not believe in God, second-guess God and assume He does not have complete control. They point to the lack of perfect design in some organs such as the eye. (Discussed in Chapter 7, I noted that skeptic Michael Shermer made much of this point.) Dembski makes a strong rebuttal: "The success of the suboptimality objection comes not from science at all but from shifting the terms of the discussion from science to theology. In place of 'How specifically can an existing structure be improved?' the question becomes 'What sort of God would create a structure like that?' Darwin, for instance, thought there was just 'too much misery in the world' to accept design: 'I cannot persuade myself that a beneficent and omnipotent God would have designedly created the Ichneumonidae with the express intention of their feeding within the living bodies of Caterpillars, or that a cat should play with mice…ants making slaves and the young cuckoo ejecting its foster brother.' The problem of suboptimal design is thus transformed into the problem of evil." (Web site: discovery.org article dated February 2, 2000). Evil devices can be designed, and are designed and used by evil people, because we have free will. As Dembski showed in Chapter 7, all that is required is intelligent design, not optimal design. "The existence of design is distinct from morality, aesthetics, goodness, optimality, or perfection of design." The design necessarily only needs to work adequately for the tasks at hand. As "beauty is altogether in the eye of the beholder," (Charles Eliot Norton) so is perfect design.

And let me ask you, did Darwin's objections, to 'evil events' in nature, quoted by Dembski, make sense to you, as a reason for questioning God's intentions? Darwin's own theory of natural selection requires competition between and among species, and competition within the challenges of the unrelenting demands of nature. Fine so far, but then Darwin forgets his own observations, that competition among living organisms involves a food chain. Staying alive depends upon an energy supply we call food. Animals have to dine on each other, while the dined-upon often are grazers on plant life, which then is also damaged if not destroyed. Darwin's next mistake is to anthropomorphize animals, to equate them with humans. Animals are not human and don't give a second thought to the feelings of their prey. Only we have consciousness and souls. Our species is the biologic pinnacle of creation. Genesis tells us that we have dominion over the Earth and its creatures. We raise animals to eat. Should that fact be used to deny the existence of God? I think not! Our obligation in the husbandry of animals is to be humane in their treatment during life and in death.

Which brings us to another 'bad' situation or form of evil to account for. Disease, illness and injury harm human beings. Why does God allow these assaults upon us? My answer is that we may be God's favored creatures, considering the degree of development we have been allowed, but we are subject to the same rules of evolution set up for the entire animal and plant kingdoms, as ordained by God. Bacteria, viruses, and fungi are all infectious living organisms that occupy a space on the chain of evolutionary development. They exist as challenges in the "survival of the fittest" mechanism, which does appear to be part of the evolutionary process. And God has not left us defenseless against this. We are challenged but with our intelligence, medical science is solving the problems presented by disease, and continues to learn how to repair injuries. Returning to Darwin's complaint that "there is too much misery in the world" in the 'natural selection' system, how else should that system work, if developing organisms are to be tested? Darwin is in conflict with himself: he appears to define his God in such a way, so as to disallow a God who would create the mechanisms within nature that lead to the theory of natural selection. I do not see any problem in believing in a benevolent and omnipotent God who chose to create the process of evolution in order to produce us. Adler reminds us that God is imperceptible and unknowable. What we are observing in this discussion are different definitions of God by Darwin and by me. There is a

231

Problem of Evil only for those who define God so as to create the Problem. And therefore, my definition of God allows me to state that for me there is no Problem of Evil.

Made in the Image of God

Genesis 1:26 tells us, "And God said: 'Let us make man in our image, after our likeness; and let them have dominion...over all the earth.'" The scientific material I have presented along with my own logic leads me to declare that God does not have arms and legs, yet I believe we are made in His image. Some people are startled when I make that declaration. They sort of imagine God having a physical form like us, without giving it much thought. It is important not to think of God in human terms, regarding His attributes, and also His physical being. We are made in His image, not He in ours. Adler makes a very strong point of warning us not to "anthropomorphize" God, for He cannot be thought of in human terms. As the Supreme Being He is a very different personage: we are finite, He is infinite; we are created, He is uncaused; our power is limited, He is omnipotent; our knowledge is limited, He is omniscient; we have material bodies, He is immaterial; and so forth. Yet just like us He can act voluntarily, exert His will, and we can conceive of Him living and knowing, in an analogical sense, as we do. But Adler warns: "when we say that God *lives*, that God *knows* and that God *wills* we must never forget that we cannot use the words "lives", "knows", and "wills" in the same sense we apply these words to human beings or anything else." Carrying this line of reason further, we can refer to God as a "person", based on the definition that persons are "living beings that have intellects capable of rational judgment and that have wills capable of free choice—in short, only human beings." Animals are living beings, but by this definition, not persons. Adler concludes: "The Divine being and human beings are analogically alike as persons—alike with all the differences between infinite and finite, immaterial and material, and so on. Nevertheless, this very thin analogical likeness permits us to understand what is meant when religious persons declare that, of all terrestrial beings, only human beings are made in the image of God, for nothing else on earth is a person."

I would carry this "made in the image of" one step further, and this step is implied by Adler in his definition of a person having an intellect capable of free choice. We are made in the image of God precisely in the construction and capacity of our mind, intellect and consciousness, a power of thought that exceeds many-fold the necessary capacity for survival on Earth. That gift of consciousness allows us to approach God in our religiosity, and to lead lives that are exceedingly rich compared to animal life. Animals cannot know God exists. Further, to me, this gift of consciousness implies an intellectual challenge from God, a direct challenge to study His works, to learn as much as we can of the intricacies and complexities of the universe and the miracle of life, which we do through scientific research. We are naturally very curious, constantly exploring and pushing back frontiers, whether they are frontiers of geography or of knowledge. Throughout this book I have tried to express a major precept of mine: scientific discoveries enhance religious belief. In this way the wonders of God becomes more open to us, and for me, fact and faith combine. I conceive of God as the intellect of the universe, the source of the energy that created the universe, and as such, God exists within and outside the universe; however, remembering Adler's rules of how to think about God, He is, at the same time, separate from and not a part of the universe He created. In Chapter 6 I referred to my philosophy professor in college, who noted that the universe is made solely of energy. The way he explained it, matter is energy on the 'outside' and the mind, intellect and consciousness are energy on the 'inside'. I, therefore, carry this reasoning to a final proposition: since God made us from the "stardust of the universe", our consciousness is part of the mind of God, who supplies and may actually be a universal consciousness. We are made in the image of God through our minds, because in a very small way our minds mimic God's mind and may be part of the mind of God.

Actually this pattern of thought about God being pure intellect goes back to the second century as stated by St. Irenaeus: "He is all mind, all spirit, all thought, all intelligence, all reason." (quoted in *Modern Physics and Ancient Faith*, Stephen M. Barr, page 225). Saint Thomas Aquinas in the Thirteenth Century (1225-1274) and the modern theologian Paul Tillich express the same concept: "God is 'Being-itself,' the spiritual basis of all reality. According to this way of thinking, God is infinite consciousness, wisdom and bliss, underlying and supporting the material cosmos. He is the spirit that is the deepest reality of a complex universe whose basic laws are not machine-like at all—think of the astonishingly indeterministic laws of quantum physics" described earlier in this book ("Houses of Worship, Giving Thanks Taking Credit," Dr. Keith Ward, regius professor of divinity University of Oxford, *Wall Street Journal*, 8/4/02).

Brother Wayne Teasdale, Ph.D. (see Chapter 5) puts it this way: "I believe that everything participates in a vast, universal system of consciousness, with other realms, reaching to the most ultimate, the Divine itself". To explain further he quoted "Meister Eckhart, the Christian mystic of the 13th century [who] understood the role of consciousness in its mediating function, when in the context of contemplative method he observed: 'The eye in which I see God is the same eye in which God sees me. My eye and God's eye are one eye and one seeing, one knowing and one loving'. Needless to say, this 'eye' isn't the ocular faculty, but is the mind, or self-awareness itself. That is the 'place' of encounter, the bridge that unites the Divine with the human". And Teasdale added: "The sea of Consciousness is where all things dwell and are revealed, the realm of Spirit...When we have a mystical experience, an aesthetic awakening, an interpersonal love eruption, we break out of our local, and often our regional awareness, and begin to ascend to other levels of consciousness beyond the horizon of the human, even to the ultimate realm of Divine Consciousness itself. This Divine Consciousness is a not a cold, analytical reason but has 'heart', is animated by unconditional compassion and love, an infinite kindness, mercy and sensitivity, a concern for all that is and can be." Brother Teasdale has reached this point of view through mysticism. "Mysticism is the awakening to the inner interdependence of everything, and their unity in the fontal Source, the Divine". (META-VIEWS.org 062, 8/10/00). I am not a mystic, and have not meditated nor practiced mysticism, but I can logically accept his reasoning. Our minds and our brains are but two integral parts of the same energy, the same energy that pervades the universe, all created by God.

I also have a theory, based on cosmology, of where heaven is. The theoretical mathematicians state that the original universe required ten or eleven dimensions, nine or ten physical plus time (*The Elegant Universe*). As the universe expanded from the Big Bang, six or seven of those dimensions got rolled up into very tiny forms. We in our three-dimensional state cannot appreciate them, but they are here with us, and I believe the energy of our souls goes to one or several of those dimensions. I mentioned this in Chapter 6. Therefore, I believe the departed are always with us. Obviously, I have no way of knowing if this is a correct view, but it illustrates how science and religion can work together to seek answers.

Only My Way is the Right Way

A friend of mine made the observation that probably more people have been killed in religious conflicts than from all other causes of unexpected death. I have no doubt he is correct. Once each of us has decided on a set of religious beliefs most of us are prepared to defend those beliefs unto death, and further to often create conflict with other beliefs by trying to impose our beliefs on them; the whole thing is beyond all reason. It is a tremendous conceit for any single religion to claim their beliefs are the only correct way for all people to worship God. It is only the 'correct way' for them. It is this emotional fervor, which leads me to believe that our religiosity is one of our strongest inherited traits at the behavioral level, equaled only by our sexuality. I cannot believe God approves of this murderous way we often solve religious conflict. And the shame of it is that very few of us seem to realize that no one has all the answers, or can even be sure of all the 'right' answers. What is really true is that we can study and reach beliefs that we feel are right for us individually. Note I use the word 'feel', because the final choices are based on faith and emotion. Reason only goes so far. I am describing what I have found that is right for me. I have no expectation that it must be right for you. There is no harm in your reading my point of view, and I certainly find no harm in being exposed to yours. One of us may well raise a concept that opens up whole avenues of inquiry and thought, broadening our philosophic and theological knowledge, our appreciation of the religious beliefs we have.

Even though God chose the Jewish Faith to be the first to bring His message to the world, He does not show favoritism to them. It is only reasonable to assume that all faiths must be equal in His view. I must vigorously encourage ecumenical solutions to religious bigotry and intolerance; we all must accept the rights of others to believe in God as they wish. I can express my view in another way: those of us in Western religions believe that our God created the universe and brought us into existence. The Eastern world does not believe in our God. I do not know why He has chosen not to reveal Himself to them, but I think His benevolence is extended to them in the East. Now turn this comment around and imagine that you are a Buddhist or a Hindu reading what I have just written. Look how self-serving my comments sound. The Eastern religions are completely satisfied with their beliefs. They have creation legends, levels of divinity and anticipation of afterlife, just as we do. For example, an Indian monk in 500 B.C., believing in a cyclical universe, through meditation equated a single day of Brahma to 4.32 billion years in human reckoning, inferring that to be the age of the universe in this cycle. That is not far off the mark from estimates in the Big Bang theory (B.J. Carr in *Modern Cosmology and Philosophy*, edited by John Leslie, 1998). Why should they think the Western way of religious thought is more correct than theirs? Fully half the world has a different way of expressing their religious thoughts than we do. I prefer to think that we are correct, but I cannot prove it, and therefore must be content to observe the differences without insisting that those who believe differently must change. On the other hand, there has been no harm in the past in presenting monotheism to primitive peoples, who practice pagan religious rites with multiple gods, specifically thinking of human sacrifices by the Incas, and of the headhunters of the world, as examples. These people and others have benefited from the moral teachings that accompany our religions.

Within this country interfaith workshops constantly run into the problem of the rigidity of thinking, "only our way", when trying to open up dialogue between religions. At the 16th National Workshop on Christian-Jewish Relations in Cincinnati in 1999, Jay Rock, a Presbyterian and a director of Interfaith Relations of the National Council of Churches commented on the problem: "Some people think salvation is only available through professing Jesus Christ. Some say salvation is totally in the hands of God. Others understand it in a more general way, saying that God is in process of saving the whole world, and if you're part of that process of healing, you're part of salvation." During the workshop, Rabbi James Rudin pointed out "gains in interfaith relations will require that 'Christians and Jews develop a theology that affirms pluralism'." (*Houston Chronicle*, 10/30/99). Expanding on the issue of salvation only for certain believers, Susan Lee wrote in her column, "Left Behind", about the "hard line that only evangelical Christians can be saved—no Jews, no Catholics (and of course no Muslims, Buddhists, pagans or atheists)." (*Wall Street Journal*, 7/14/00). A letter to the editor responded to this observation in very telling fashion: "the evangelical stricture described by Ms. Lee would deny any possibility of salvation to the vast majority of all people who have ever lived—which raises serious questions (ignored by most evangelicals) about the benevolence of the deity being worshipped." (*Wall Street Journal*, 7/25/00). It is very difficult to object to that observation. It is important for everyone to recognize that there may be several ways to enter heaven, through different religious practices, or just from living an exemplary moral life, even with little if any organized religious practice. The Catholic Church identifies the first way, through Catholic practices, as entering heaven through 'divine grace', and the latter approach as entering through 'natural grace'. Seems perfectly reasonable to me. All I ask from all of us is to be comfortable in your own beliefs, accept religious diversity and embrace pluralism. The enormous variety of religions will never disappear. Accept diversity of belief and a great deal of emotional heat will disappear from our society, and I believe God will be pleased.

My attitude about the reality of pluralism of religious belief comes from the teachings of my Jewish background. The Jewish People, now in their 58th century have never proselytized their beliefs. Yes, as the Chosen People they exhibited their beliefs to the world and introduced the Western world to monotheism, but they never tried to impose their religious tenets on others. In fact, prospective converts are questioned very closely regarding their reasons for desiring conversion to Judaism, and most conversions are the result of intermarriage. Someone who appears on his own asking for conversion must run a gauntlet of probing questions before starting lessons for conversion. And unlike Protestants who may simply switch from denomination to denomination, entering Judaism requires a series of rabbi-administered lessons over a period of time before one, in a recognized fashion, enters the faith. Generally Jews do not like to be proselytized. For this reason and others, Christian Faiths, following the teachings of their religion to preach to other religions salvation through Jesus, find few Jewish people who respond to them. We are confident of reaching heaven through the teachings in our Torah, the first five books of the Old Testament. For my part I do not resent these approaches; I appreciate their concern for my salvation and the fact that they are following their own teachings, as I follow mine. It just makes me wonder: should we expect or even think that God chooses sides between religions? Repeating myself, does He favor the one with which He has a covenant? I don't think so. And therefore, for emphasis, I repeat my plea: accept pluralism in religious belief, for it always will be present; I cannot imagine that God is disturbed by the multiple ways He is worshiped on this Earth.

For readers who do not have a religious affiliation and who seek a church that encourages independent thought, a church that does not have rigid tenets and dogma, there are such religious groups. The Unitarian Universalist Church is such an example: They assume everyone can reason. They do not tell people what to believe. They encourage each individual to develop a personal philosophy of life, to be tolerant of the religious ideas of others, to continue a search for the truth throughout life, and to understand that good works are the natural product of a good faith (*Houston Chronicle*, Religion Section, 2/5/00). This suggestion is offered for educational purposes only. As careful readers of this book must realize, I have no intention of proselytizing for this church, Judaism, or any other faith.

Science and Theology in Public Schools

The First Amendment to our Constitution in its very first section says:

"Congress shall make no law respecting establishment of religion, or prohibiting the free exercise thereof." Our Founders, having experienced the intolerance of the nationally mandated religions in Europe, were making sure there would be no state religion in this country. The importance of their intent is shown by the position of that statement at the very beginning of the Bill of Rights, which was placed in our Constitution to protect the individual from the government using its powers to encroach on his liberties. The courts have stretched that simple First Amendment totally out of shape. Religion has been completely wiped out of the public schools. I agree with some of the prohibitions: for example, with the religious diversity in schools now even representing Eastern beliefs, spoken prayer presents a problem, but silent devotion is a ready answer. Spoken prayer before school events has created a great deal of controversy, and the objections to those prayers represent a degree of hypocrisy especially when we note Congress opens with prayer. Even for Congress silent devotion may be the solution to maintain consistency. On the other hand, religion could reasonably by brought into the schools with courses in the history of religion and in comparative religion. With each major sect represented by clergy from that sect, this should bring better understanding between religions and hopefully increase tolerance. Teaching children about other religions and their beliefs, without challenging the children's beliefs, would enormously help to bring a better understanding of how we differ, and that 'difference' is not wrong. Further, the moral values present in all religions are really the same, and such courses might help raise the ethical standards of this country, which have slipped so badly. That suggestion does not represent trying to establish state religion, but there will be enormous opposition to comparative religion courses. People are very closed-minded about their own beliefs, as I have pointed out, and they will be literally frightened and angry that their children are being exposed to any other ideas. Unfortunate but true.

The greatest controversy is, of course, the teaching of the science of evolution in the schools. Scientists and Creationists are at the extremes of the discussion. I have shown that many scientists treat the Theory of Evolution almost as a religion in itself. Robert Shapiro's book, *Origins: A Skeptic's Guide to the Creation of Life on Earth* describes "just-so" statements by scientists. Shapiro, an evolution scientist himself, identifies and condemns scientists' flights of fancy, which are not at all supported by scientific evidence. In an opposite approach, Robert T. Pennock's, *The Tower of Babel; the Evidence against the New Creationism*, is a compendium of defenses against the Creationists, defending much of the flights of fancy Shapiro identified. No wonder the Creationists were on a tear, with the Kansas Board of Education, essentially attacking the teaching of evolution science in Kansas in August 1999. Ohio waged a similar battle in 2002. Both sides defend their point of view with a lack of rationality, and with all the emotionality that characterizes religious disputes.

Creationists use the Noachian Flood to claim that all of the scientific findings regarding evolution are suspect due to effects of the Flood. Yet Gerald Schroeder (Chapter 2), both a physicist and a biblical scholar, using Genesis as literally as the Creationists interpret it, showed clearly that the Biblical dating of the Bronze Age, before the Flood, exactly fits the scientific evidence. Therefore, he concludes, the Flood did not damage scientific evidence of the age of the universe or the earth. In my mind Schroeder, versed in both science and the bible, wins that debate. The Creationists recoil from the idea that we may have descended from monkeys, and fight the concept of evolution to avoid accepting that possibility. But they don't know absolute truth any more than I do. All they can do is point to *their* interpretation of Genesis, which is not the only interpretation that can be made by others. Think back to Chapter 5 on the growth of our brain and the marvelous mind that developed from it. We are infinitely superior to all the other primates, due to that brain. I don't care how we got here, but I am thrilled to be here, gifted with that magnificent intellect. It is my contention, as stated before, that God either pre-programmed DNA in the beginning or alternatively, guided our evolution; we may never know which possibility is true, unless scientists discover pre-programming in DNA. That event will be seemingly an absolute proof of God by science. No accident of nature could create such a circumstance. The key issue is that God gave us that brain, its consciousness and the soul that goes with it perhaps 150,000 years ago. In the ensuing centuries we learned how to use that brain, developing our aesthetic sense and religiosity in more recent times. The Creationists will object, saying it only took one day, according to Genesis. Schroeder and others have presented the possibility that God's day has a different length than a day in our terms. The method He used to create our appearance in this form and the actual time it took does not matter. Who are we to question His methods? Einstein has shown us that time is relative. The Bible allows various interpretations and appears to have some very hidden meanings. There has never been one accepted version of interpretation of the Bible, and never will be. What is needed is open debate and honesty in all the assertions made.

Scientists, at one extreme, approach their beliefs from science as if they were religious tenets, and at the other extreme Creationists will only accept the divine revelations of the Bible to explain the natural world. As in every facet of life, there is a middle ground. The National Academy of Sciences wants the definition of science to be, "the search for natural explanations." The Kansas Board of Education in 1999 changed that definition to "the search for *logical* explanations." (Gregg Easterbrook, "The New Fundamentalism", *Wall Street Journal*, 8/8/00). That definition by appealing for logical explanations brings us to the middle and allows the presentation of the new theory of "Intelligent Design", just as I have presented it in this book. Easterbrook, who is editor of BeliefNet.com, recommends teaching Intelligent Design in public schools from the following reasoning: "Unlike creationism, intelligent-design theory acknowledges that the universe is immensely old and that all living things are descended from earlier forms. But the theory goes on to contend that organic biology is so phenomenally complex that it is illogical to assume that life created itself. There must have been some force providing guidance...It is not a religious doctrine under the 1986 Supreme Court definition. Intelligent-design theory does not propound any specific faith or even say that the higher power is divine. It simply holds that there must be an unseen intellect imbedded in the cosmos." Obviously, I completely agree with his definition of intelligent design and its logical applicability to the study of evolution. And the logical step is to teach the theory in school along with Darwinism. "Present students with the arguments for and against natural and supernatural explanations of life and let them enter into this engaging, fertile debate." (Easterbrook). Unfortunately, both Easterbrook and I feel the country is not ready currently to allow this. The scientific community looks at intelligent design as religion in disguise and creationists feel it is a form of scientific attack on their biblical interpretations.

Until the debate is settled, including the issue of accepting intelligent design as a valid scientific theory, honesty is the key to how to teach science in the public schools. Students must be told that scientists in their experiments limit themselves and will only consider natural, materialistic theories derived from Reductionism, breaking everything down to underlying parts. Any consideration of the supernatural or metaphysical is prohibited. Students should be told that there is an alternate view, the possibility of design by a universal intelligence, and as philosopher of science, Del Ratzsch, concludes: "Whether design theories should prove to be ultimately scientifically successful or not, there is little to be said for a prohibitionism that forbids even the attempt to pursue whatever potential there might be." (*Nature, Design, and Science*). What should be presented to students are science texts that honestly show what the scientists really know: that evolution *appears* to have occurred during the 3.6 to 3.8 billion years of life on earth, but that only *modification* of existing species, responding to changes in nature, is proven so far. Further the scientists must admit that no one knows how life started, and none of their theories are close to figuring it out. The Young Earth Creationists will still insist that the universe and the earth are 10,000 years old or less. No matter. That is their right. The teachers should present what scientists believe, and have clearly proven, and tell their students to go home and discuss it with their parents, settling their religious interpretation at home, where such discussions always belong. This approach is the same appeal to rationality I have expressed throughout the book. In fact, the Congress passed a law in 2001 entitled, "No Child Left Behind Act of 2001," which instructs that "on controversial issues such as biologic evolution, 'the curriculum should help students to understand the range of scientific views that exist.'" This is interpreted to require "that the implementation of these scientific standards not be used to censor debate on controversial issues in science, including Darwin's theory of evolution." (*Discovery Institute News*, Press release, 3/20/2002).

Eventually intelligent-design theory may find its way into the schools. In 2002 the battle raged in Ohio. Fifty-two scientists, 39 professors in Ohio colleges and universities, signed a petition stating "that a science curriculum should help students understand why the subject of biologic evolution generates controversy; that where alternative scientific theories exist in any area of inquiry (such as…biologic evolution vs. intelligent design), students should be permitted to learn the evidence for and against them; that a scientific curriculum should encourage critical thinking and informed participation in public discussions about biologic origins." They opposed "the censorship of scientific views that may challenge current theories of origins." (*Discovery Institute*, 3/20/02). Currently only two states, Oklahoma and Alabama mandate that science textbooks "include information saying the theory of evolution is not a certainty."

That the future may allow my suggestion is shown in "a March, [2000] poll conducted by People for the American Way, [with] 83 percent of Americans believ[ing] evolution should be taught in the schools. But a majority of people also think creationism should also be taught." (*Houston Chronicle*, 8/20/00). Sixteen percent feel only creationism should be taught,

37 percent want only evolution taught. "In 1996 Pope John Paul reaffirmed the Catholic church's commitment to evolution, first stated in 1950, saying that his inspiration for doing so came from the Bible. Despite this, 40 percent of American Catholics in a 2001 Gallop poll said they believed that God created human life in the past 10,000 years. Indeed, fully 45 percent of all Americans subscribe to this creationist view." As measured by Lawrence Lerner of the Thomas B. Fordham Foundation, Washington, D.C., 18 states provide "unsatisfactory, useless or absent" teaching of evolution ("Down With Evolution", Rodger Doyle. *Scientific American*, pg. 30, March 2002). The battle will be fought through the state Boards of Education. Since they are elective positions, the American public will be able to vote its preferences, as they have recently tried to do in Kansas and Ohio.

Philosophic postscript

There is a pattern of thought, which I feel has undermined the modern human spirit in the Western world. To explain we must go back to a paragraph in Chapter 2, pg. 17. Quoting from that: Paul Davies in his book, *The Mind of God*, describes scientists, devoid of any sense of joy or elation from their discoveries, who feel "that science has robbed the universe of all mystery and purpose, and that the elaborate arrangement of the physical world is either a mindless accident or an inevitable consequence of mechanistic laws. 'The more the universe seems comprehensible, the more it also seems pointless', believes physicist Steven Weinberg. The biologist Jacques Monod echoes this dismal sentiment: 'the ancient covenant is in pieces: man at last knows that he is alone in the unfeeling immensity of the universe, out of which he has emerged only by chance. Neither his destiny nor his duty have been written down'." Weinberg has received a great deal of criticism about his statement, and his answer is to point out that the next and very last sentence in his book, *The First Three Minutes,* finishes with a "cheerful ending:" "But the one thing that does seem to help, one of the things that makes life worthwhile is doing scientific research." (*Origins. The Lives and Worlds of Modern cosmologists).* With sentiments such as these, no wonder profoundly religious people are suspicious of science.

These thoughts from Chapter 1 dovetail exactly with the tenets of existentialism. Existentialist thinkers are primarily atheistic or agnostic. They feel, as do the scientists, the universe is the result of contingency, the outcome of a series of chance events, without purpose or meaning. They reject the view most philosophers and theologians have held since Plato, that the highest ethical good is the same for everyone (*Encarta Encyclopedia,*

1999, Microsoft). Existentialists believe that since individuals have freedom of choice, and make those choices free of any external objective rational basis, all persons set their own morality entirely within themselves. If followed to an extreme, this type of individual freedom could lead to anarchy, tearing society apart. But on a more positive note existentialists caution that freedom of choice requires commitment and responsibility for one's actions, and accepting the risks attendant with those actions. Existentialists argue "that humanity finds itself in an incomprehensible, indifferent world. Human beings can never hope to understand why they are here; [they are] aware of the certainty of death and the ultimate meaninglessness of one's life." Jean-Paul Sartre, the 20th Century French philosopher, concludes: "human beings require a rational basis for their lives but are unable to achieve one, and thus human life is a 'futile passion'." (*Encarta Encyclopedia*). In brief, if we are here totally by chance and accident, is there any meaning to our existence?

There is a positive way to answer the question. Viktor E. Frankl insists we must find meaning and have meaning in our lives (*Man's Search For Meaning*, 1984, an enlarged version of *From Death-Camp to Existentialism*). He was the famous Viennese Jewish psychiatrist who was forced to spend over three years in Hitler's concentration camps, and survived primarily because he discovered meaning in the life he suffered in the camps. He comments on what meaninglessness has meant to society: "Every age has its own collective neurosis…The existential vacuum which is the mass neurosis of the present time can be described as a private and personal form of nihilism; for nihilism can be defined as the contention that being has no meaning…There is a danger inherent in the teaching that man's 'nothingbutness,' the theory that man is nothing but the result of biological, psychological and sociological conditions, or the product of heredity and environment. Such a view of man makes a neurotic believe what he is prone to believe anyway, namely, that he is the pawn and victim of outer influences or inner circumstances…The drug scene is one aspect of a more general mass phenomenon, namely the feeling of meaninglessness resulting from a frustration of our existential needs which in turn become a universal phenomenon in our industrial societies." Existential needs are our desire to understand why we are here and what it means. Frankl offers a way to understand: "The meaning of life differs from man to man, from day to day and from hour to hour. What matters…is the specific meaning of a person's life at a given moment…one should not search for an abstract meaning of life. Everyone has his own specific vocation or mission in life to carry out a concrete assignment which demands fulfillment. Therein he cannot be replaced, nor can his life be repeated. Thus, everyone's task is as unique as is his specific opportunity to implement it…In a word, each man is questioned by life; and he can only answer to life by *answering for* his own life; to life he can only respond by being responsible. Responsibleness [is] the very essence of human experience."

From an existentialist standpoint Frankl's view of a meaningful life is perfectly reasonable. I have no argument with it and I support it. We must search for the meaning in our lives. But it is incomplete and there is a richer way, which adds to the meaning he describes. This book shows that finding or strengthening faith in God lies in the discoveries of science that lead to the conclusion that we are not here by chance or by accident. The existentialist conclusion is wrong, and in fact dangerous to society in general if Frankl's contention is correct that it is the source of the drug culture. Existentialism denies a general moral code: each individual is free to do as he wishes. No. We are here because of God's purpose to have us here, and we do have an overarching moral code to guide us. How much richer life is, how much more meaningful life is in light of that knowledge. Too many people are lost in meaninglessness. Frankl's approach, with the inclusion of religious faith, provides an answer that I think is ideal.

Let me close by repeating once again: no one can tell you how to think, how to have faith. I have written this book to challenge your mind, not your faith. I have tried to present ideas that may be new to you. I have raised some thoughts about God, religion, the afterlife and heaven with which I am comfortable, and with which you may agree or disagree. That is your privilege. I hope I have been stimulating and perhaps expanded the horizons of your mind.

Index

absolute morals, 212, 228, 236, 238, 242

absolute void, 187

abstract ideas as unique to humans, 129, 130

abstraction, God as, 219

acceleration of universe expansion, 49, 52

accidental evolution. *See* chance in evolution

adaptation and microevolution, 89, 99–100, 102

Adler, Mortimer J., 31, 67, 180–83, 222, 228, 229

aesthetic sensibility as unique to humans, 106, 131

afterlife, 10, 18, 170–71, 222, 234. *See also* near-death experiences (NDEs); out-of-body experiences (OBEs)

age of universe/Earth, 25, 28–29, 45, 50–52. *See also* Big Bang theory

agnosticism and science, 19. *See also* chance in evolution

agricultural revolution, 125

altruism and religion, 210, 227

amino acids, role in life's beginning, 73–84. *See also* DNA

Ankerberg, John, 24, 25–28, 29

anthropic principle, 188–91

anti-matter/matter reactions, 47, 54

Ark, Noah's, 27–28

Armstrong, Karen, 106, 212, 219, 220

art as unique to *homo sapiens,* 106, 131

artificial intelligence and consciousness, 136

Aspect, Alain, 169–70

asteroid impacts and evolution, 103–6

astronomy
and challenges to medieval faith, 13–14
intuitive math and new discoveries, 141–42
See also cosmology

atheism and science, 19, 42–43, 119. *See also* chance in evolution

At Home in the Universe (Kauffman), 82

Atwater, P. M. H., 150, 160–61, 213

Australopithecus, 122–23

authority, spiritual, as sourced in individual, 221

autocatalytic sets, 82–83, 85

background microwave radiation, universal, 50–52, 142

bacteria and life's beginning, 73, 88–89, 91, 195

Bad Genes or Bad Luck? (Raup), 90

ballistic movements and human development, 127, 129–30

Barnett, Lincoln, 223

Barrett, Sir William, 161

Bartel, David, 79–80

Bayes's theorem, 209

Behe, Michael, 33, 34, 35, 36–40, 190, 205

Being-itself, God as, 233

belief, religious
as based on reason, 10
Darwin's challenge to, 14
vs. faith, 183, 216, 221–23
individuality of, 217
level among scientists, 42–43
need for openness to new wisdom, 20

belief, religious (continued)
scientific contributions to, 8, 10–12, 17, 42
See also creationism
Belief in God in an Age of Science (Polkinghorne), 17
Best Evidence (Schmiker), 161
Beyond IBM (McKeown), 171
Beyond Science (Polkinghorne), 190
Beyond the Light (Atwater), 160
Bible
and Big Bang theory, 9–10, 25
as incomplete source of God knowledge, 20
interpretive issues for, 23–35, 197–98, 219–21, 239
lack of mandate for organized religion, 11–12
support for scientific truths in, 9–10, 21–23, 27, 30–31
See also creationism
Big Bang theory
biblical references to, 9–10, 25
creation as prior to, 183–84
overview of, 45–55
problems of origin, 61–67
religious references to, 21, 67–69
Big Crunch theory, 49, 63–64, 184
biology. *See* evolution
black holes, 48, 65
Blackmore, Susan
background, 150
biases in skeptical argument, 153–57, 163–64, 165, 166, 168
on Kubler-Ross, 158–59
personal OBE experience, 145–46
Black Sea and universal flood stories, 27
blind people and NDEs/OBEs, 158–59
blood clotting and irreducible complexity, 36–40

blue-tit case of universal consciousness, 174–75
Borde, Arvine, 184
Borel, Emile, 78
Boulter, Michael, 203
bounded vs. unbounded universe, 62–63, 184, 195–96
Bracht, John, 103
Bradley, Walter, 77
brain development, human
and consciousness, 135–39
and convergence theory, 96
and drive to complexity, 93
extra capacity as built-in, 125, 134–35, 142
intuitive knowing, 139–42
as more than size issue, 106–7
religion as hardwired in, 131–33, 210–12
and social development, 125–31
uniqueness of, 95–96, 122–25, 239
brine shrimp evolution, 107, 109–10
Bronze Age, 30–31
Brownlee, Donald, 57–58, 225
bubble theory of space structure, 65
Buddhism, 68, 164

Calvin, William H., 71, 103, 122, 129, 134, 135
Cambrian explosion of species, 92, 93, 95, 97–99, 107–10
carbon-14 dating, 94
carbon dioxide-rock cycle, 56
carbon element, importance for life, 59
cataclysmic extinctions, 103–6
catalytic RNA idea, 78–80, 82–83, 85
Catholic Church, 13–14, 19–20, 28, 236, 242
CBI (Cosmic Background Imager), 51
chance in evolution
critique of Dawkins' mechanism, 112–14

critique of Gould's thesis, 88–93
and drive to complexity, 40, 70–87,
    93–103, 119–21
and first cause argument for God,
    183
and gradualism vs. sudden
    evolutionary change, 103–6
and human brain development,
    106–7
mathematical problems with, 114–
    19, 196
and mutation role in evolution,
    111–12
and probability of universe
    existence, 54
and regulatory genes, 100–102,
    107–11, 120
See also DNA
chaos theory, 84
chaotic inflation, 65–66
character building experience, evil/
    danger as, 226, 227
children, NDEs of, 152, 160–61
Children of the Millennium (Atwater),
    160–61
Christianity
    Catholic Church, 13–14, 19–20,
        28, 236, 242
    Golden Rule, 218
    and Judaism, 237
    and judgment issue, 228
    See also creationism
civilization, religion as necessary to,
    212–13, 226–27
Clark, Kimberly, 153–54
CMB (cosmic microwave
    background), 50–52, 142
COBE (Cosmic Background
    Explorer), 50
commitment to faith, current lack of,
    223
compassion, 178–79, 234

complexity
    in human development, 106–7,
        123, 124
    inherent drive to, 70–87, 90–103,
        119–21, 138, 202–6
    and intelligent design argument,
        195, 199
    irreducible, 36–41, 85
consciousness
    as argument for God, 206–15
    of evolution, 99–102, 119
    and human brain development,
        135–39
    and humans as image of God, 232–
        33
    as interactive dimension, 173
    and NDEs/OBEs, 162–63
    as quantum entity, 189
    survival beyond life, 172
    uniqueness of human, 60
    universal, 173–79, 233–34
    of universe, 16
constrained optimization in design,
    194
contingent evolution, 70–71. *See also*
    chance in evolution
convergence principle, 96–98
cooperation and human survival, 126–
    27, 132, 210–11
Copernicus, Nicolaus, 13
Cosmic Background Explorer
    (COBE), 50
Cosmic Background Imager (CBI), 51
cosmic microwave background
    (CMB), 50–52, 142
cosmological constant, 54
cosmology
    and explanatory limitations of
        science, 47, 53, 61–67
    interdisciplinary approach, 68
    reductionist contribution to, 52–53
    See also Big Bang theory

Craig, William Lane, 184
creationism, 11, 23–35, 197–98, 238–
42
Creation Versus Evolution
(Muncaster), 24
creator
and evolution in human arrival on
Earth, 10
God as creator of time, 185
and reason for life, 84, 209
scientific avoidance of pre-Big
Bang issue, 61–67
See also creationism; God;
intelligent design
Cretaceous plant explosion, 99
Cro-Magnon man, 106, 131
cumulative selection, 113–14
cyclical universe, 63–64

D'Aquili, Eugene, 132–33, 165, 167
dark energy, 49
dark matter, 48–49
Darwin, Charles
challenge to religious beliefs, 14
on drive to complexity, 91–92
on intelligent design, 72, 230–31
on natural selection, 90
open-mindedness of, 35–36, 118
Darwinism
and argument for God, 197–206
author's initial encounter with, 9
and Darwin's religious faith, 19
flaws in, 114–21, 124–25
and information theory, 103
vs. intelligent design, 187–88
mechanistic view of, 112–13
protectionism in, 33, 34
scientific challenges to, 35–41
See also chance in evolution;
gradual Darwinism
Darwin's Black Box (Behe), 33
Darwin's finches, 200–201

Darwin's Leap of Faith (Ankerberg
and Weldon), 24, 25
DASI (degree angular scale
interferometer), 51
dating of fossils, 94
Davis, Kenneth C., 14
Davies, Paul
on consciousness, 137–38, 208
on deism, 198
God as creator of time, 185
God as present in scientific
discovery, 20
on multiple universes theory, 183
need for science/religion
cooperation, 18
and scientific sense of
meaninglessness, 17
universe as tailored for life, 60–61
Da Vinci, Leonardo, 14
Dawkins, Richard, 112–14
dead people as only contacts in NDEs,
151, 167, 168
Dead Sea Scrolls, 21–22
death, prospect of, and impetus to live
good life, 229–30. *See also*
near-death experiences (NDEs)
Deathbed Visions (Barrett), 161
deism, 197, 198
delirium tremens, 166–67
Dembski, William, 15, 78, 119, 192–
96, 230
density of universe, 49–51
Denton, Michael, 39, 76
Descartes, Rene, 136
design, argument for God from. *See*
intelligent design
Devlin, Mark, 184
Did Darwin Get It Right? (Johnston), 28
dimensions, multiple. *See* multiple
dimensions
dinosaur era, 103–4
diversification of living creatures, 95.

See also complexity
divine vs. natural grace, 236
DNA (deoxyribonucleic acid)
    chance vs. design, 25, 72–84, 112–
        13, 198–200
    and complexity argument, 119–20
    and embryonic development, 110–12
    limitations of knowledge on, 89–90
    mutation effects, 105, 204
    and regulatory genes, 107–11
    as source of organizing principle,
        99, 101–2, 121, 204–5
Draper, John William, 31
dreams, 166, 176
dualism, scientific attachment to, 136
dying and NDEs, 164–65

Earth
    and age of universe, 25, 28–29, 45,
        50–52
    position in universe, 13
    protected nature of, 187
    specificity of conditions for life,
        55–61
    See also life, evolution of
Easterbrook, Gregg, 27, 240
Eastern vs. Western religious
        concepts, 20–21, 68, 144–45,
        163–64, 235
ecumenism, 236
Eddington, Arthur, 140–41
Ediacarans, 94, 95
education, science and religion in, 32,
        237–42
Einstein, Albert, 53, 139–40, 189
Eldredge, Niles, 92
electromagnetism, 46, 47, 54, 162–63, 169
electron/proton relationships, 47, 54
The Elegant Universe (Greene), 62
elements, chemical, 47–48, 52, 59
emergent property, consciousness as,
        136–37

emotionalism
    in creationist/scientist debate, 31,
        41–42
    and religious intolerance, 211, 218,
        234–37, 239
emotions and consciousness, 207
The Emperor's New Mind (Penrose),
        53–54
energy/matter relationships, 46–51,
        54, 178, 185. See also four
        forces theories
environmental change
    DNA adaptations, 89
    and extinctions, 103–6
    genetic response to, 100–102
    and luck vs. genes in extinction, 90
    See also microevolution; rapid
        evolution
enzymes for DNA/RNA activities, 78–
        79, 81, 82
eukaryotes, 89, 94–95
evidentialism, 209
evil, problem of, 214, 223–32
evolution
    Catholic support for, 19
    and creation, 10, 11
    vs. creationism, 23–35
    end of, 91, 134
    God's role in, 197–206
    and intelligent design argument,
        191–96
    lack of scientific consensus on, 33–
        34, 35–41, 98–99, 116–17
    in public school curriculum, 32,
        238–42
    religion as development of, 210–11
    See also brain development;
        Darwinism; life, evolution of
    exaptations in human
        development, 130–31, 133,
        204–5

exclusivity of religious truth, 218,
234–37, 238
existence of God
consciousness argument, 206–15
from Darwinism's flaws, 197–206
vs. faith in, 183, 216, 221–23
first cause argument, 182, 183–87,
215
intelligent design argument, 187–
97
introduction to arguments for, 180–
83
mathematical proof attempts, 18
proof vs. persuasion of, 12
The Existence of God (Swinburne),
209
existentialism, 242–44
expansion of universe
and conditions for life, 59
fine-tuning for present
configuration, 54
inflationary model, 45, 48–52, 62, 66
and problem of creation, 184
See also Big Bang theory
experimental verification of theory,
140–41
explanatory limitations of science
and consciousness, 209–10
and cosmology, 47, 53, 61–67
and reductionism, 53
and time problem with evolution, 78
extinctions, mass, 89, 90, 103–6
extraterrestrial intelligence, 86
extrinsic vs. intrinsic faith, 223

faith
as based on rational belief, 10
and moral responsibility, 222–23,
225–26, 244
vs. reason, 181, 221–23, 235
scientific challenges to, 13–14
See also creationism; religion

feedback, biological, 77, 79
Ferguson, Kitty, 12, 221
Finding Darwin's God (Miller), 29
fine-tuned universe. *See* intelligent
design
first cause argument for God, 182,
183–87, 215
flat geometry of space, 49–50, 52, 54
flood stories, 26–28, 30–31, 239
fossil record, 26, 94, 118, 200
Foster, David, 76
four forces theories
electromagnetism, 46, 47, 54, 162–
63, 169
overview, 45
strong nuclear force, 46–47, 55
unification of, 53
weak nuclear force, 46–47, 54
See also gravity
Frankl, Viktor E., 243–44
free will
and existentialism, 243
and humans as image of God, 232
and problem of evil, 226, 227, 230
and religion as moral leash, 213
functional design, 191–94, 224–25,
230–31

galaxies, 47–48, 52
Galileo, 13
Gamow, George, 50
Genesis and the Big Bang
(Schroeder), 9–10, 30–31
genetic role in evolution
common codes and differing
morphologies, 90, 96
intelligence as gene source, 103
preprogrammed instructions, 70–
87, 107–10, 112–13, 116, 121
regulatory genes, 100–102, 107–
11, 120
See also DNA

geology of Earth and conditions for life, 56
Giant Panda's thumb and functional design, 191–92
Gisin, Nicholas, 170
global flood stories, 26–28, 30–31, 239
goal-directed nature of evolution, 93–103, 119–21, 138, 202–6
God
    as active player vs. absentee landlord, 39, 197–98, 229, 230
    cosmological inferences for, 67, 138–39, 187
    as creator, 10, 193
    evolutionary inferences for, 119–21
    as intellectual abstraction, 219
    nature and properties of, 222, 231–34
    numbers of believers, 7–8
    in private lives of scientists, 34
    and problem of evil, 223–32
    proof vs. persuasion of existence, 12
    and religious tolerance, 235, 236, 237
    and scientific humanism, 14–20
    as separate from creation, 181–82
    See also existence of God
Godel's Theorem, 15
"God module" in human brain, 131–32, 167–68
God of the Gaps concept, 14–15
Golden Rule, 218
Goldsmith Donald W., 49
Gonzalez, Guillermo, 57
good, argument for God from, 209–10, 212
Gordon, Bruce, 66
Gould, Stephen Jay
    on complexity and passive evolution, 88–93

evolution by chance thesis, 70–72
    and intelligent design argument, 191–92
    Morris's refutation of, 96–98
    punctuated equilibrium theory, 107–8, 117, 200
grace, divine vs. natural, 236
gradual Darwinism
    and gaps in fossil record, 35, 200–201
    and inherent complexity, 205–6
    initial challenge to, 36–40
    vs. punctuated equilibrium, 92–93, 108, 115–16, 117–18, 200
    vs. sudden evolutionary change, 103–6, 124
Grand Unified Theory of forces, 53
gravity
    fine-tuning of, 54, 55
    limitations of understanding, 52–53
    quantum, 53, 62, 67
    and relativity of time, 140
    role of, 46–49
Greene, Brian, 62, 64–65
Greyson, Bruce, 154
Gross, Paul R., 124–25
group mind idea, 173–79
guppies and rapid adaptation, 100
Guth, Alan H.
    on anthropic principle, 188
    creation from nothing, 61, 62–64
    inflationary universe theory, 45, 47, 50, 142
    space as false vacuum, 186
    on time/space and Big Bang, 184

Haisch, Bernard, 164, 171, 172
Haldane, J. B. S., 114–15
hallucinations vs. NDEs/OBEs, 165–67
handedness, nucleotide and amino acid, 74, 77, 78, 79

Hawking, Stephen, 62, 63, 184
Hazen, Robert M., 79–80
heaven, quantum location of, 234
Hemingway, Ernest, 145
hemoglobin
    no evolutionary pattern, 39
    odds against spontaneous formation
        of, 76
Higgs boson, 52–53
Hillel, Rabbi, 218
Hinduism and Big Bang theory, 68
homeobox genes, 108
Homo habilis, 122–23
Homo sapiens, complexity of brain
    development, 106–7. *See also*
    humans
Hoover, James R., 171
Hot Big Bang Inflationary Model, 51
How to Think About God (Adler), 31,
    180
How We Believe (Shermer), 16
Hox genes, 108–9
Hoyle, Sir Fred, 34, 59, 76, 141–42
humanism and scientific development,
    14–20
humans
    chance and evolution of, 70–72
    complexities of evolution, 120–21
    cosmic purpose of, 10
    embryonic development, 110–12,
        120
    evolution vs. creationism on, 24–25
    exaptations in, 130–31, 133, 204–5
    as image of God, 232–34
    religion as natural to, 106, 127,
        131–33, 167–68
    religious self-centredness of, 13–14
    social development of, 125–31
    unique characteristics of, 60, 106,
        128–31, 134–35
    See also brain development
human species consciousness, 175–79

humility vs. arrogance and organized
    religion, 217–18
hundredth monkey phenomenon, 173–74
hunter-gatherer societies, 125–28
hydrothermal vents and life's
    beginning, 79

IANDS (International Association for
    Near-Death Studies), 146
Ice Ages and human brain
    development, 122
image of God, humans as, 232–34
imaginary time, 62, 184
imagination, human capacity for, 130,
    134–35, 137
independent thinking and organized
    religion, 216–21
individuality of religious belief, 217
inerrancy of Scripture issue, 220–21
inflationary universe, 45, 48–52, 62,
    65–66, 142. *See also* expansion
    of universe
The Inflationary Universe (Guth), 45
information theory and evolution,
    102–3, 120, 202, 205
inheritance, Darwin's failure to
    understand, 35. *See also* genetic
    role in evolution
intellect, God as, 233
intellectual honesty in creationists and
    scientists, 29–30
intelligence
    chance as source of evolution to,
        70
    extraterrestrial, 86
    as God's protective gift, 214–15
    as source of genetic information,
        103
    uniqueness of human, 60, 129,
        134–35
    See also brain development;
        consciousness

intelligent design
as argument for God, 187–97, 199
Behe vs. Pennock, 34, 35
intelligent design (continued)
and consciousness, 137, 208
in evolution, 119
functional design, 191–94, 224–25,
230–31
and innate religious sensibility,
168–69
and intuitive knowing, 139–42
and irreducible complexity, 36–41
and NDEs/OBEs, 143–44
need for scientists to accept, 43
and preprogrammed genetics, 70–
87, 107–10, 112–13, 116, 121
and problem of evil, 223–24
in public school curriculum, 240–41
and structure of universe, 60–61
Intelligent Design (Dembski), 194
interfaith relations, 236
internal drives of organisms and
evolutionary change, 99–102
International Association for Near-
Death Studies (IANDS), 146
intraspecies rapid evolution, 100–102.
See also microevolution
intrinsic vs. extrinsic faith, 223
intuitive knowing, 68, 139–42, 168,
170–71
inventiveness, human, 128
irreducible complexity, 36–41, 205–6

Jahn, R. J., 176
Johanson, Donald, 24, 133–34
John Paul II, Pope, 19–20
Johnston, George Sim, 28, 36, 55, 66,
118
Judaism, 67–69, 164, 173, 218, 237
judgment, moral importance of
cultivating, 227–29
junk DNA, 101–2, 121

Kabbalah, 68, 164, 173
Kafatos, Menas, 17, 173
Kauffman, Stuart, 34, 82–83, 84–85,
114
Kepler, Johannes, 13
King James version, 22, 23
knowledge
intuitive, 68, 139–42, 168, 170–71
as source of spirituality, 16
as supreme good, 209
Kovac, John, 51
Kubler-Ross, Elisabeth, 149–50, 158–59
Kuhn, Thomas, 33
Kushner, Harold, 230

Lancet report on OBEs, 161–62, 165,
168–69
language
and biblical interpretation, 21–22,
219
and human social development,
126–27, 128–31
Lapin, Rabbi Daniel, 93
laws of nature
evidence for authorship of, 68–69
origin of, 66
and problem of evil, 225
and universal design for life
generation, 188
Lederman, Leon, 17
Leibniz, Gottfried Wilhelm, 185
Leitch, Eric, 51
Leslie, John, 64, 182
Le Verrier, Urbain-Jean-Joseph, 141
Levy, David, 58, 228
life, evolution of
bacteria as beginning, 73, 88–89,
91, 195
and chance vs. design/
preprogramming, 70–87
Darwinism's inability to address, 41

life, evolution of (continued)
  Earth's special conditions for, 55–61
  as probable from design of
    universe, 187–88
  See also DNA
life after death, 10, 18, 170–71, 222,
    234.   *See also* near-death
    experiences (NDEs); out-of-
    body experiences (OBEs)
Life After Life (Moody), 159
Life at Death (Ring), 155
Lifetide (Watson), 173
Light and Death (Sabom), 157
Linde, Andrei, 62, 63, 65–66, 188
literalism, biblical, 23–35, 197–98,
    220–21
Locke, John, 209
Lommel, Pim van, 161–63
loop quantum gravity (LQG), 53, 67
love and compassion, 178–79, 234

macroevolution, flaws in, 115–19. *See*
    also species, changes in
magnetic field, Earth's, and conditions
    for life, 57
Magueijo, Joao, 67
Maimonides, 21
Malin, Shimon, 186
Malone, Michael S., 96
Marshack, Alexander, 106
mass extinctions, 103–6
master genes, 108–10, 112
materialism of science, 34, 42. *See*
    also reductionism
mathematics
  aesthetics of, 62, 141
  and attempts to prove God's
    existence, 18
  God-given nature of, 138–39
  intuitive, 141–42
  and odds for major evolutionary
    spikes, 107

as outrunning scientific validation,
    66–67
problems with timing of evolution,
    114–19
as unique human trait, 106
matter/energy relationships, 46–51,
    54, 178, 185. *See also* Big
    Bang theory
Mattick, John S., 102
Mayr, Ernst, 115
McCrone, John, 122, 131, 207
McDougall, William, 174
McGinnis, William, 108–9
McKeown, Katie, 171
meaning of life, basic human need for,
    17, 242–44
measurement, creative quantum, 186
mechanistic view of Darwinism, 112–
    13
meditation, 132–33, 144, 163–64
Mediterranean Sea and flood stories,
    27
mediums, 171–72
Meerloo, Joost, 176–77
membrane theory, 62, 64, 185, 187
Mendel, Gregor, 35
metaphysical naturalism, 66–67, 181
metaphysics, inapplicability of
    scientific method to, 17–18.
    See also religion
meteorites as seeds of life, 85–86
microevolution
  Darwinism's advantage in, 115,
    116, 124, 197
  and intraspecies adaptation, 89,
    99–100, 102
Miller, Christopher, 51
Miller, Kenneth R., 28–29, 30, 38–39,
    200
Miller, Stanley L., 73–74
mind, human. *See* brain development;
    consciousness; intelligence

mind/body relationship and NDEs/
    OBEs, 162
The Mind of God (Davies), 17
Mindsight (Ring), 155
mineral scaffolds and life's beginning,
    79, 80
Mobley, Louis, 171
Monod, Jacques, 17, 242
monotheism
    and Eastern vs. Western religious
        sensibilities, 20
    gifts to paganism, 236
    importance of ethics/morals to,
        104, 212
    and importance of God's existence,
        7
    mysticism in, 164
    See also God; religion
Monroe, Robert, 171
Moody, Raymond A., Jr., 149, 159,
    166
moral codes
    and challenge of evil, 226–29
    and consciousness, 135
    and existentialism, 242–44
    as learned concepts, 126, 211–12
    and monotheism vs. paganism, 236
    religion as necessary to, 210
    and responsibility of faith, 222–23
moral relativism, 227–29, 243
Moreland, James, 63
Morowitz, Harold J., 77
morphogenic fields, 177, 199
Morris, Conway, 33, 92–93, 94–98,
    107–8, 114, 116–17
Morris, H. M., 29
Morris, Richard, 35–36, 116
mortality and impetus to live good
    life, 229–30
motion, continuous universal, 48
Mullan, Dermott, 77
multiple dimensions

and Big Bang theory, 62–66
and heaven, 234
and OBEs, 170
as psychic phenomena sources,
    171–72, 173
and universal consciousness, 177–
    78
multiple universes and avoidance of
    first cause, 64–66, 182, 183,
    188
Muncaster, Ralph O., 24–25
mutations
    and challenges to Darwinism, 40,
        114–15
    effect on DNA, 204
    oxygen's potential role in, 107
    and passive vs. driven evolution,
        201–2
    radiation effects on, 105
    role in evolution, 100, 109, 111–12
mysticism
    and Big Bang theory, 68
    and consciousness as compassion,
        178–79, 234
    and consciousness of God, 213–14
    and electromagnetic energy, 169
    and experience as evidence, 178
    internal vs. external sources for,
        132–33
    meditation, 132–33, 144, 163–64
    and universal consciousness, 173
mythology in Darwinian evolution
    science, 83–84

Nadeau, Robert, 17, 173
Nahmanides, 21, 67–69
natural processes
    biblical support for, 21–23
    as fundamental to science, 15
    and God as natural feature of
        universe, 18
    metaphysical naturalism, 66, 181

natural processes (continued)
  as neutral toward religion, 34
  for psychic phenomena, 171–79
  and science's contribution to
    knowledge, 7
natural selection
  vs. cataclysmic events, 105–6
  and consciousness, 136–37
  Darwinian attachment to, 117
  Darwin's view of, 90
  and functional design, 192, 193
  and intraspecies changes, 92–93
  and mechanistic view of evolution,
    113
  and natural disasters for humans,
    231
  reactionary nature of, 103
  and religious hardwiring in brain,
    132
  scientific debate on, 33, 35–41
  and self-organization, 83
  and survival of best practices, 125
natural theology, 66–67, 181
natural vs. divine grace, 236
Nature Loves to Hide (Malin), 186
Neanderthals, 24, 106, 123
near-death experiences (NDEs)
  case studies, 151–52, 155–59,
    160–61
  and consciousness of God, 213–14
  vs. hallucinations, 165–68
  history of investigation into, 149–
    51
  overview, 10, 143–47
  skeptical vs. open-minded views of,
    162–65
  source possibilities, 168–71
near-Earth asteroids, 105
Neo-Darwinism, 102, 198
neurological developments,
    suddenness of, 95–96. *See also*
    brain development

Newberg, Andrew, 132–33, 167
Newton, Isaac, 19
nihilism, 243
Noah and flood story, 26–28, 30–31,
  239
non-DNA genetic information, 111
non-locality of quantum particles,
  169–70, 189
The Non-Local Universe (Nadeau and
  Kafatos), 17–18
non-sensory perception, 162
non-zero-sum games and social
  cooperation, 126–27
Non-Zero (Wright), 126–27
nothing, creating something from, 61,
  62–64, 186–87

Occam's Razor, 12, 64, 182, 183, 189
Olber's paradox, 59
Old Earth creationism, 24–25, 197
Onkelos, 21
opportunities for growth, life's
  challenges as, 226
optimal vs. intelligent design, 192–94,
  230–31
organic molecules, 74, 79
organized religion and independent
  thinking, 216–21
organizing principle in evolution
  in Cambrian explosion, 98–99
  DNA as source of, 99, 101–2, 121,
    204–5
  and holistic approach to creation, 114
  logical need for, 190
  preprogrammed genetic
    instructions, 70–87, 107–10,
    112–13, 121
  See also complexity; intelligent
    design
Orgel, Leslie, 72
Origin of Species (Darwin), 14
Origins (Shapiro), 199

out-of-body experiences (OBEs)
  case studies, 152–55, 157–60,
    161–62
  vs. hallucinations, 165–68
  overview, 143–47
  skeptical vs. open-minded views of,
    162–65
  source possibilities, 168–71
Overman, Dean L., 47, 102, 103
ozone layer and mutation role in
  evolution, 107

paganism, 211, 236
paradigms, scientific, 33–34
parallel solutions in evolution, 96
parent, God as, 225–26, 227
particle physics
  and cosmological unity, 172
  and non-locality, 169–70, 189
  and support for Big Bang, 52
  See also quantum theory
parts vs. whole. See whole as greater
  than sum of parts
passive vs. driven evolution, 88–103,
    113, 201–4
pax-6 gene, 90, 107–8
Pennock, Robert T., 31–33, 34, 36,
    37–38, 40, 113–14
Penrose, Roger, 53–54, 78, 136–37,
    138–39, 188, 208
Penzias, Arno, 50
perfect vs. functional design, 191–94,
    230–31
Persinger, Michael, 169
Petroski, Henry, 194
physics, theoretical. See cosmology;
  quantum theory
The Physics of Immortality (Tipler),
    18, 143
Pikaia, 95
planning, human capacity for, 127–28,
    129, 135

plants and evolution, 56, 99
Plato, 145
pluralism, religious, 236–37
polarization of cosmic background
  radiation, 51
Polkinghorne, John, 17, 18, 60, 68,
    190–91, 208
Pollack, Andrew, 194
Popper, Karl, 118
postmodernism and moral relativism,
    228
Prager, Dennis, 228
prayer, 177, 222, 238
prebiologic molecules, 74, 79
preprogrammed genetic instructions,
    70–87, 107–10, 112–13, 116,
    121
preservative vs. creative cause, God
  as, 182
primates
  and consciousness issue, 206
  human brains vs., 122, 128–29, 239
prime mover unmoved argument for
  God, 183–87, 215
probability bound, 195–96
protein molecules and life's
  beginnings, 72, 73–84
  See also DNA
proton/electron relationships, 47, 54
psychic phenomena, 144, 147–49,
    171–79. See also near-death
    experiences (NDEs); out-of-
    body experiences (OBEs)
public schools, science and religion in,
    32, 237–42
punctuated equilibrium theory
  and catastrophic extinctions, 103–6
  vs. Darwinist gradualism, 92–93,
    102, 115–16, 117–18, 200
  genetic support for, 108
  and human brain development, 124
Puthoff, Hal, 172

quantum froth, 61
quantum gravity, 53, 62, 67
quantum potentialities and first cause
    argument, 186–87
quantum theory
    and hidden universe reality, 189
    intuitive math and new discoveries,
        142
    and OBEs, 169–70
    overview, 52–53
    and psychic phenomena, 172–73
    and relativity, 62
    See also multiple dimensions
quantum uncertainty/fluctuation, 61–62
quantum vacuum energy, 172
quintessence, 49

rapid evolution
    and flaws in Darwinism, 103–6,
        117, 124
    and human development, 95–96,
        106–7, 122
    and intraspecies adaptation, 100–
        102
    and master genes, 108, 109–10,
        112
    and oxygen levels in atmosphere,
        98–99, 107
    See also punctuated equilibrium
        theory
Rare Earth (Ward and Brownlee), 57–
    58
Rashi, 21
rationalism
    and belief in God's existence, 183,
        216, 221–23
    vs. faith, 181, 221–23, 235
Ratzsch, Del, 35, 240–41
Raup, David, 90, 104–5, 108, 203
Raymo, Chet, 15–16, 19, 218–19
reality, God as basis of, 233

reason. *See* rationalism
reductionism
    as basis for secular humanism, 15
    and chance in human evolution, 71
    vs. consciousness, 136
    contribution to cosmology, 52–53
    in Dawkins' mechanistic view, 114
    demise of, 43
    explanatory power of, 194–95
    and public school science
        curriculum, 240
    scientific emotional stake in, 42
    vs. whole as greater than sum of
        parts, 53, 83
regulatory genes, 100–102, 107–11, 120
relativity, theories of, 53, 62, 139–41
religion
    author's background, 8–10
    call for tolerance, 221–42
    Eastern vs. Western concepts, 20–
        21, 68, 144–45, 163–64, 235
    emotionalism and intolerance, 42,
        211, 218, 234–37, 239
    historical overview vs. science, 13–14
    importance for civilization, 212–
        13, 226–27
    and independent thinking, 216–21
    as natural to humans, 106, 127,
        131–33, 167–69, 210–12
    number of believers in God, 7–8
    as partner with science, 20, 43–44,
        216, 234
    prayer, 177, 222, 238
    psychological need for, 18–19
    in public schools, 32, 237–42
    references to Big Bang, 21, 67–69
    scientific method as inapplicable
        to, 17–18
    souls and quantum theory, 163–64,
        170, 234
    See also belief, religious; God;
        mysticism

reproduction, 81, 89, 202
responsibility and faith, 222–23, 225–26, 244
Reznick, David, 100
Richards, Paul, 50–51
Ring, Kenneth, 154, 155–56, 157
The River That Flows Uphill (Calvin), 122
RNA, 75, 78–84, 85, 120
Rock, Jay, 236
Rodonaia, George, 160
Rommer, Barbara R., 213–14
rubidium-strontium decay, 94
Rudd, Pauline, 43
Rudin, Rabbi James, 236

Sabom, Michael, 150, 156–57
Sagan, Carl, 73
salvation, universalization of, 234–37
Sartre, Jean-Paul, 243
Schmiker, Michael, 154, 161
Schoonmaker, Fred, 154
Schroeder, Gerald
    on biblical exegesis sources, 219–20
    cataclysmic evolutionary opportunities, 104
    on Genesis and Big Bang, 9–10, 21
    interdisciplinary approach to cosmology, 68
    odds on human development through evolution, 107, 112–13
    refutation of Noah's flood literalism, 30–31
    religious faith of, 17
Schwartz, Gary, 172
Schwartz, Jeffrey H., 102, 108, 117
science
    biblical support for, 9–10, 21–23, 27, 30–31
    Catholic support for, 19–20
    contribution to belief, 8, 10–12, 17, 42

explanatory limitations of, 47, 53, 61–67, 78, 209–10
    as gift from God, 233
    historical overview vs. religion, 13–14
    and humanist development, 14–20
    lack of consensus in, 33–34, 35–41, 98–99, 116–17, 138
    as partner to religion, 18, 20, 43–44, 216, 234
    vs. religion in public schools, 32, 237–42
    as replacement for faith, 14–15
    scientific method, 30, 34, 154–55, 172
    subjectivity in, 23, 41–42
    verification of biblical history, 27, 31
    See also cosmology; evolution; quantum theory
The Science of God (Schroeder), 10, 21
scientific method, 30, 34, 154–55
scientism, 8, 15–16
Search for Extraterrestrial Intelligence (SETI), 86
self-consciousness, 135, 207
self-organization of organisms, 82–83, 98, 138. *See also* organizing principle in evolution
self-replicating RNA, 78–79, 81
sexual reproduction, 89, 202
Shanks, Hershel, 21–22
Shapiro, Robert, 77, 82, 83–84, 199–200
Sheldrake, Rupert, 138, 174–75, 177–78, 199
Shermer, Michael, 12, 16, 40, 191–92, 219
Shreeve, James, 24
shrimp evolution, 107, 109–10
silent devotion vs. public prayer, 238

Simpson, Sarah, 73
situational ethics, 228
Smolin, Lee, 65
social development of humans, 125–
    31
souls and quantum theory, 163–64,
    170, 234
space
    bounded vs. unbounded, 62–63,
        184, 195–96
    bubble structure, 65
    flat geometry of, 49–50, 52, 54
    as not empty, 185, 186
    See also Big Bang theory
species, changes in
    and cataclysmic environmental
        changes, 105
    and Darwinism's flaws, 92, 114–
        15, 124, 201, 203–4
    master genes and suddenness of,
        108, 109–10
    mutations as problematic for, 111–12
specified complexity, 195
speed of light, 189
Spetner, Lee, 81, 99–100, 102
spin network architecture, 53
spirituality. *See* mysticism; religion
stars
    availability to Adam and age of
        universe, 28–29
    and darkness of night sky, 58–59
    formation of, 47–48
    precise universal conditions for, 54
    and sun's contribution to life, 55, 57
Stenger, Vic, 195–96
stromatolites, 73
strong nuclear force, 46–47, 55
The Structure of Scientific Revolutions
    (Kuhn), 33
subjectivity
    and functional vs. perfect design,
        230–31

in science, 23, 41–42
of truth, 11–12, 20–21, 218–19
successful species and end of
    evolution, 91, 134
Sudden Origins (Schwartz), 108, 117
supernovas, 48, 49, 105
superstring theory
    and grand unified theory, 53
    lack of experimental verification,
        67
    membrane theory, 64
    and multiple dimensions, 62
    and OBEs, 170
    and quantum potentialities, 187
survival of the fittest, flaws in
    concept, 119
Swinburne, Richard, 208–10
symbolic thought, human capacity for,
    130, 134–35, 207

Talbot, Michael, 152–53, 165
Talmud, creation and Big Bang, 21
Tart, Charles T., 8
Tattersall, Ian, 130–31, 133
Teasdale, Wayne Robert, 136, 178,
    233–34
teleological arguments, 183–87, 202–
    3
telepathy author's experiences, 147–
    49
temperature, Earth's, and conditions
    for life, 56–57
tenure system and scientific resistance
    to change, 33–34
testing of Darwinism, difficulties of,
    118–19
Thaxton, Charles, 77
The Crucible of Creation (Morris), 33
theism and God as activist, 197, 198
*The Mystery and Meaning of the Dead
    Sea Scrolls* (Shanks), 21–22
theology. *See* religion

The Standard Model of the universe, 45. *See also* Big Bang theory; quantum theory

Tibetan book of the dead, 152

Tillich, Paul, 233

time
Big Bang theory of creation, 45, 183–84
direction of, 62–63
God as creator of, 185
human vs. other animals' perceptions, 127–28, 129, 135
imaginary, 62, 184
problems with timing of evolution, 72–84, 111, 112–13, 114–19, 196
relativity of, 139–40

Tipler, Frank J., 18, 19, 143

tit-for-tat as early moral code, 126

tolerance, religious, 221–42

Torah, 21, 220

The Tower of Babel (Pennock), 31–33

transcendence, 15, 162, 164, 168–69

transitional evolutionary forms, lack of, 115–16

translation of Bible, 21–23

truth
biblical support for scientific, 9–10, 21–23, 27, 30–31
exclusivity of religious, 218, 234–37, 238
and mathematical elegance, 62
subjectivity of, 11–12, 20–21, 218–19

Turner, Michael, 50

Turney, Jon, 67

Tuval-Cain, 30

Tyndale, William, 22

unbounded vs. bounded universe, 62–63, 184, 195–96

Unitarian Universalism, 237

unity of cosmos, 172, 173, 234

universal consciousness, 173–79, 233–34

universal flood traditions, 26–28, 30–31, 239

universe
age of, 25, 28–29, 45, 50–52
bounded vs. unbounded, 62–63, 184, 195–96
density of, 49–51
multiple universes theory, 64–66, 182, 183, 188
as not God, 181–82
See also Big Bang theory; quantum theory

Universes (Leslie), 64

unknowable, God as, 181

unobservable entities problem, 182, 183, 189, 196–97

uranium-thorium decay, 94

Urey, Harold C., 73–74

Utts, Jessica, 171

Valenkin, Alexander, 184

vertebrate animals, sudden development of, 95–96, 98

Viney, Geoff, 158

Vulgate Bible, 22

Ward, Peter D., 57–58, 225

water on Earth and conditions for life, 56–57, 58

Watson, Lyall, 173

weak nuclear force, 46–47, 54

Weinberg, Steven, 17, 242

Weldon, John, 24, 25–28, 29

Western vs. Eastern religious concepts, 20–21, 68, 144–45, 163–64, 235

When Bad Things Happen to Good People (Kushner), 230

Whitcomb, J. C., 29

White, Andrew Dickson, 31
whole as greater than sum of parts
    and consciousness, 135–36, 173
    and intelligent design argument,
      199
    and organizing principles in nature,
      85, 114
    and phenomena beyond science, 15
    vs. reductionism, 53, 83
Wickramasinghe, Chandra, 76
Wilkinson Microwave Anisotrophy
      Probe (WMAP), 51–52
Wilson, Edward O., 19, 23, 24, 71,
      132, 210–11
Wilson, Robert, 50
WMAP (Wilkinson Microwave
      Anisotrophy Probe), 51–52
Wolfram, Stephen, 96–97
worldwide flood stories, 26–28, 30–
      31, 239
Wright, Robert, 126–27, 192, 211,
      227

Yockley, Hubert, 76

Printed in the United States
21874LVS00004B/91-99